GLEIM®
CIA Review
Part 1
Internal Audit Basics

2016 EDITION

by

Irvin N. Gleim, Ph.D., CPA, CIA, CMA, CFM

Gleim Publications, Inc.
P.O. Box 12848
University Station
Gainesville, Florida 32604
(800) 874-5346
(352) 375-0772
Fax: (352) 375-6940
Internet: www.gleim.com
Email: admin@gleim.com

> For updates to the first printing of the 2016 edition of *CIA Review: Part 1*
>
> **Go To:** www.gleim.com/updates
>
> **Or:** Email update@gleim.com with **CIA 1 2016** in the subject line. You will receive our current update as a reply.
>
> Updates are available until the next edition is published.

ISSN: 2332-0451

ISBN: 978-1-58194-608-6 *CIA Review: Part 1*
ISBN: 978-1-58194-609-3 *CIA Review: Part 2*
ISBN: 978-1-58194-610-9 *CIA Review: Part 3*
ISBN: 978-1-58194-626-0 *How to Pass the CIA Exam: A System for Success*

This edition is copyright © 2015 by Gleim Publications, Inc. Portions of this manuscript are taken from previous editions copyright © 1981-2014 by Gleim Publications, Inc.

First Printing: May 2015

ALL RIGHTS RESERVED. No part of this material may be reproduced in any form whatsoever without express written permission from Gleim Publications, Inc. Reward is offered for information exposing violators. Contact copyright@gleim.com.

ACKNOWLEDGMENTS FOR PART 1

The author is grateful for permission to reproduce the following materials copyrighted by The Institute of Internal Auditors: Certified Internal Auditor Examination Questions and Suggested Solutions (copyright © 1980-2015), excerpts from *Sawyer's Internal Auditing* (5th and 6th editions), parts of the 2013 *Certification Candidate Handbook*, The IIA Code of Ethics, *International Standards for the Professional Practice of Internal Auditing*, Practice Advisories, and parts of Practice Guides.

CIA® is a Registered Trademark of The Institute of Internal Auditors, Inc. All rights reserved.

> **Environmental Statement** -- This book is printed on recyclable, environmentally friendly groundwood paper, sourced from certified sustainable forests and produced either TCF (totally chlorine-free) or ECF (elementally chlorine-free).

The publications and online services of Gleim Publications and Gleim Internet are designed to provide accurate and authoritative information with regard to the subject matter covered. They are sold with the understanding that Gleim Publications and Gleim Internet, and their respective licensors, are not engaged in rendering legal, accounting, tax, or other professional advice or services. If legal advice or other expert assistance is required, the services of a competent professional person should be sought.

You assume all responsibilities and obligations with respect to the selection of the particular publication or online services to achieve your intended results. You assume all responsibilities and obligations with respect to any decisions or advice made or given as a result of the use or application of your selected publication or online services or any content retrieved therefrom, including those to any third party, for the content, accuracy, and review of such results.

ABOUT THE AUTHOR

Irvin N. Gleim is Professor Emeritus in the Fisher School of Accounting at the University of Florida and is a member of the American Accounting Association, Academy of Legal Studies in Business, American Institute of Certified Public Accountants, Association of Government Accountants, Florida Institute of Certified Public Accountants, The Institute of Internal Auditors, and the Institute of Management Accountants. He has had articles published in the *Journal of Accountancy*, *The Accounting Review*, and *The American Business Law Journal* and is author/coauthor of numerous accounting books, aviation books, and CPE courses.

REVIEWERS AND CONTRIBUTORS

Garrett W. Gleim, B.S., CPA (not in public practice), received a Bachelor of Science degree from The Wharton School at the University of Pennsylvania. Mr. Gleim coordinated the production staff, reviewed the manuscript, and provided production assistance throughout the project.

Grady M. Irwin, J.D., is a graduate of the University of Florida College of Law, and he has taught in the University of Florida College of Business. Mr. Irwin provided substantial editorial assistance throughout the project.

Lawrence Lipp, J.D., CPA (Registered), is a graduate from the Levin College of Law and the Fisher School of Accounting at the University of Florida. Mr. Lipp provided substantial editorial assistance throughout the project.

Dr. Steven A. Solieri, CPA, CMA, CIA, CISA, CITP, CFF, CRISC, is an Assistant Professor at Queens College in Flushing, New York, and is a Founding Member in the Firm of Solieri & Solieri, CPAs, PLLC, New Hyde Park, NY, where he currently practices. Dr. Solieri earned his Ph.D. from Binghamton University and holds four Masters from the University of Michigan, Pace University, Kettering University, and Binghamton University. Dr. Solieri helped develop the instructor materials to be used in conjunction with this text.

A PERSONAL THANKS

This manual would not have been possible without the extraordinary effort and dedication of Jacob Brunny, Julie Cutlip, Kelsey Olson, Jake Pettifor, Teresa Soard, Justin Stephenson, Joanne Strong, and Elmer Tucker, who typed the entire manuscript and all revisions and drafted and laid out the diagrams and illustrations in this book.

The authors also appreciate the production and editorial assistance of Jessica Felkins, James Harvin, Kristen Hennen, Jeanette Kerstein, Katie Larson, Diana León, Cary Marcous, Shane Rapp, Drew Sheppard, and Martha Willis.

The authors also appreciate the critical reading assistance of Brett Babir, Ellen Buhl, Paul Davis, Jack Hahne, Nathan Kaplan, Melissa Leonard, Yating Li, Monica Metz, Tyler Rankin, Sunny Shang, Justin Shifrin, Daniel Sinclair, Tingwei Su, Nanan Toure, and Diana Weng.

Finally, we appreciate the encouragement, support, and tolerance of our families throughout this project.

Returns of books purchased from bookstores and other resellers should be made to the respective bookstore or reseller. For more information regarding the Gleim Return Policy, please contact our offices at (800) 874-5346 or visit www.gleim.com/returnpolicy.

TABLE OF CONTENTS

	Page
Detailed Table of Contents	vi
Preface	viii
Preparing For and Taking the CIA Exam	1
Study Unit 1. Mandatory Guidance	9
Study Unit 2. Independence, Objectivity, and Due Care	29
Study Unit 3. Control Frameworks and Fraud	55
Study Unit 4. Control: Types and Techniques	81
Study Unit 5. Data Gathering and Data Analysis	113
Study Unit 6. Conducting the Engagement: Sampling	135
Study Unit 7. Procedures, Analysis, Conclusions, and Documentation	159
Appendix A: The IIA Glossary	183
Appendix B: The IIA CIA Exam Syllabus and Cross-References	187
Appendix C: The IIA Standards and Practice Advisories Discussed in Part 1	189
Appendix D: The IIA Examination Bibliography	191
Appendix E: Glossary of Accounting Terms U.S. to British vs. British to U.S.	193
Index	195

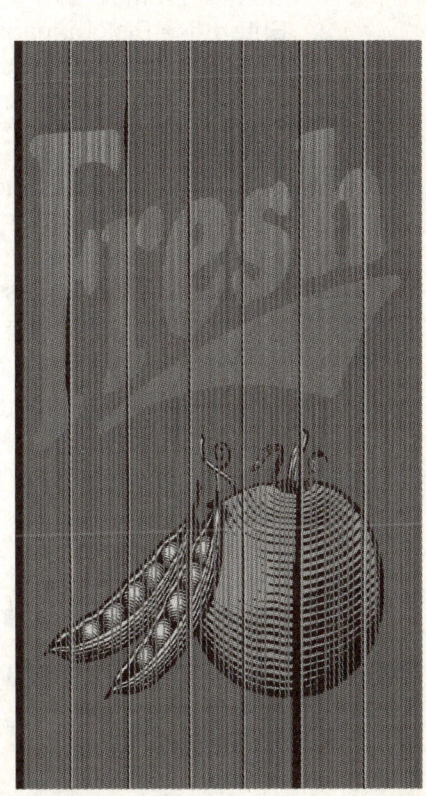

GLEIM® Updates

Keeping your CIA Review materials FRESH

gleim.com/CIAUpdate

Updates are available until the next edition is published

DETAILED TABLE OF CONTENTS

                                                                                      Page

Study Unit 1. Mandatory Guidance
- 1.1. Applicable Standards 9
- 1.2. Codes of Ethical Conduct for Professionals 14
- 1.3. Internal Audit Ethics -- Introduction and Principles 14
- 1.4. Internal Audit Ethics -- Integrity 16
- 1.5. Internal Audit Ethics -- Objectivity 16
- 1.6. Internal Audit Ethics -- Confidentiality 17
- 1.7. Internal Audit Ethics -- Competency 18
- 1.8. Internal Audit Charter 18

Study Unit 2. Independence, Objectivity, and Due Care
- 2.1. Independence of the Internal Audit Activity 30
- 2.2. Objectivity of Internal Auditors 32
- 2.3. Impairment to Independence and Objectivity 34
- 2.4. Auditor Proficiency 37
- 2.5. Internal Audit Resources 38
- 2.6. Due Professional Care and Continuing Professional Development 40
- 2.7. Quality Assurance and Improvement Program 42
- 2.8. Reporting on Quality Assurance 43
- 2.9. Internal and External Assessments 44

Study Unit 3. Control Frameworks and Fraud
- 3.1. Control Frameworks 55
- 3.2. Enterprise Risk Management 65
- 3.3. Risk Management Processes 68
- 3.4. Fraud -- Nature, Prevention, and Detection 70
- 3.5. Fraud -- Indicators 72

Study Unit 4. Control: Types and Techniques
- 4.1. Overview of Control 82
- 4.2. Classifying Controls 82
- 4.3. Flowcharts and Process Mapping 86
- 4.4. Accounting Cycles and Associated Controls 90
- 4.5. Management Controls 101

Study Unit 5. Data Gathering and Data Analysis
- 5.1. The Four Qualities of Information 113
- 5.2. Sources and Nature of Information 115
- 5.3. Establishing Engagement Objectives 117
- 5.4. Questionnaires 120
- 5.5. Interviewing 121
- 5.6. Other Data-Gathering Techniques 125

Study Unit 6. Conducting the Engagement: Sampling
- 6.1. Statistical Concepts 135
- 6.2. Sampling Concepts 138
- 6.3. Attribute Sampling 141
- 6.4. Variables Sampling 143
- 6.5. Process Control Techniques 146

	Page
Study Unit 7. Procedures, Analysis, Conclusions, and Documentation	
7.1. Analytical Review Techniques	159
7.2. Benchmarking	162
7.3. Performing Audit Procedures	164
7.4. Drawing Conclusions	165
7.5. Working Papers -- Functions and Preparation	168
7.6. Working Papers -- Control and Retention	170
7.7. Computerized Audit Tools and Techniques	172

PREFACE

The purpose of this book is to help **you** prepare to pass Part 1 of the CIA exam. Our overriding consideration is to provide an inexpensive, effective, and easy-to-use study program. This book

1. Explains how to optimize your grade by focusing on Part 1 of the CIA exam.
2. Defines the subject matter tested on Part 1 of the CIA exam.
3. Outlines all of the subject matter tested on Part 1 in 7 easy-to-use-and-complete study units, including all relevant authoritative pronouncements.
4. Presents multiple-choice questions from past CIA examinations to prepare you for questions in future CIA exams. Our answer explanations are presented to the immediate right of each question for your convenience. Use a piece of paper to cover our explanations as you study the questions.
5. Suggests exam-taking and question-answering techniques to help you maximize your exam score.

The outline format, the spacing, and the question-and-answer formats in this book are designed to facilitate readability, learning, understanding, and success on the CIA exam. Our most successful candidates use the Gleim CIA Review System*, which includes books, Test Prep, Audio Review, Gleim Online, Exam Rehearsals, and access to a Personal Counselor. Students who prefer to study in a group setting may attend Gleim Professor-Led Reviews, which combine the Gleim Review System with the coordination and feedback of a professor. (Check our website for live courses we recommend.)

To maximize the efficiency and effectiveness of your CIA review program, augment your studying with *How to Pass the CIA Exam: A System for Success*. This booklet has been carefully written and organized to provide important information to assist you in passing the CIA examination.

Thank you for your interest in our materials. We deeply appreciate the thousands of letters and suggestions we have received from CIA, CMA, CPA, and EA candidates and accounting students and faculty during the past 5 decades.

If you use Gleim materials, we want YOUR feedback immediately after the exam and as soon as you have received your grades. The CIA exam is NONDISCLOSED, and you must maintain the confidentiality and agree not to divulge the nature or content of any CIA question or answer under any circumstances. We ask only for information about our materials, i.e., the topics that need to be added, expanded, etc.

Please go to www.gleim.com/feedbackCIA1 to share your suggestions on how we can improve this edition.

Good Luck on the Exam,

Irvin N. Gleim

May 2015

*Visit www.gleim.com or call (800) 874-5346 to order.

PREPARING FOR AND TAKING THE CIA EXAM

Read How to Pass the CIA Exam: A System for Success	1
Overview of the CIA Examination	1
Subject Matter for Part 1	2
Nondisclosed Exam	2
The IIA's Requirements for CIA Designations	2
Eligibility Period	3
Maintaining Your CIA Designation	3
How to Use the Gleim Review System	3
Gleim Knowledge Transfer Outlines	4
Time-Budgeting and Question-Answering Techniques for the Exam	5
Learning from Your Mistakes	7
How to Be in Control while Taking the Exam	7
If You Have Questions about Gleim Materials	8
Feedback	8

READ *HOW TO PASS THE CIA EXAM: A SYSTEM FOR SUCCESS*

1. Scan the Gleim *How to Pass the CIA Exam: A System for Success* booklet and note where to revisit later in your studying process to obtain a deeper understanding of the CIA exam.

    a. *How to Pass the CIA Exam: A System for Success* has six study units:

    Study Unit 1: The CIA Examination: An Overview and Preparation Introduction
    Study Unit 2: CIA Exam Syllabus
    Study Unit 3: Content Preparation, Test Administration, and Performance Grading
    Study Unit 4: Multiple-Choice Questions
    Study Unit 5: Preparing to Pass the CIA Exam
    Study Unit 6: How to Take the CIA Exam

2. *How to Pass the CIA Exam: A System for Success* is available as an e-book at www.gleim.com/PassCIA.

OVERVIEW OF THE CIA EXAMINATION

The total exam is 6.5 hours of testing (including 5 minutes per part for a survey). It is divided into three parts, as follows:

CIA Exam (3-Part)			
Part	Title	Exam Length	Number of Questions
1	Internal Audit Basics	2.5 hrs	125 multiple-choice
2	Internal Audit Practice	2 hrs	100 multiple-choice
3	Internal Audit Knowledge Elements	2 hrs	100 multiple-choice

All CIA questions are multiple-choice. The exam is offered continually throughout the year. The CIA exam is computerized to facilitate easier testing. Pearson VUE, the testing company that The IIA contracts to proctor the exams, has hundreds of testing centers worldwide. The Gleim CIA Test Prep, Gleim Online, and Gleim CIA Exam Rehearsals provide exact exam emulations of the Pearson VUE computer screens and procedures to prepare you to PASS.

SUBJECT MATTER FOR PART 1

Below, we have provided The IIA's abbreviated CIA Exam Syllabus for Part 1. The percentage coverage of each topic is indicated to its right. The IIA provides a range of % coverage, but for simplicity Gleim provides the average of that range. We adjust the content of our materials to any changes in The IIA's CIA Exam Syllabus.

Part 1: Internal Audit Basics
I. Mandatory Guidance	40%
II. Internal Control/Risk	30%
III. Conducting Internal Audit Engagements – Audit Tools and Techniques	30%

Appendix B contains the CIA Exam Syllabus in its entirety as well as cross-references to the subunits in our text where topics are covered. Remember that we have studied and restudied the syllabus in developing our *CIA Review* materials. Accordingly, you do not need to spend time with Appendix B. Rather, it should give you confidence that Gleim *CIA Review* is the best review source available to help you PASS the CIA exam.

NONDISCLOSED EXAM

As part of The IIA's nondisclosure policy and to prove each candidate's willingness to adhere to this policy, a confidentiality and nondisclosure statement must be accepted by each candidate before each part is taken. This statement is reproduced here to remind all CIA candidates about The IIA's strict policy of nondisclosure, which Gleim consistently supports and upholds.

> *This exam is confidential and is protected by law. It is made available to you, the examinee, solely for the purpose of becoming certified. You are expressly prohibited from disclosing, publishing, reproducing, or transmitting this exam, in whole or in part, in any form or by any means, verbal or written, electronic or mechanical, for any purpose, without the prior written permission of The Institute of Internal Auditors (IIA).*
>
> *In the event of any actual or anticipated breach by you of the above, you acknowledge that The IIA will incur significant and irreparable damage for each such breach that The IIA has no adequate remedy at law for such breach. You further acknowledge that such breach may result in your certification being revoked, disqualification as a candidate for future certification, and suspension or revocation of membership privileges at The IIA's discretion.*
>
> *If you do not accept the exam non-disclosure agreement, your exam will be terminated. If this occurs, your registration will be voided, you will forfeit your exam registration fee, and you will be required to register and pay for that exam again in order to sit for it in the future.*

THE IIA'S REQUIREMENTS FOR CIA DESIGNATIONS

The CIA designation is granted only by The IIA. Candidates must complete the following steps to become a CIA®:

1. Complete the appropriate certification application form online and register for the part(s) you are going to take. The *How to Pass the CIA Exam: A System for Success* booklet contains concise instructions on the application and registration process and a useful worksheet to help you keep track of your process and organize what you need for exam day. Detailed instructions and screenshots for every step of the application and registration program can also be found at www.gleim.com/accounting/cia/steps.
2. Pass all three parts of the CIA exam within 4 years of application approval.
3. Fulfill or expect to fulfill the education and experience requirements (see *How to Pass the CIA Exam: A System for Success*).
4. Provide a character reference proving you are of good moral character.
5. Comply with The IIA's Code of Ethics.

ELIGIBILITY PERIOD

Credits for parts passed can be retained as long as the requirements are fulfilled. However, candidates must complete the program certification process within 4 years of application approval. If a candidate has not completed the certification process within 4 years, all fees and exam parts will be forfeited.

Candidates who have not successfully completed their exam(s), or who have been accepted into the program but have not taken their exam(s), have the opportunity to extend their program eligibility by 12 months. To take advantage of The IIA's one-time Certification Candidate Program Extension, candidates must pay a set fee per applicant.

MAINTAINING YOUR CIA DESIGNATION

After certification, CIAs are required to maintain and update their knowledge and skills. Practicing CIAs must complete and report 40 hours of Continuing Professional Education (CPE) every year. The reporting deadline is December 31. Complete your CPE Reporting Form through the online Certification Candidate Management System. Nonmembers must submit a US $100 processing fee with their report. Contact Gleim for all of your CPE needs at www.gleim.com/cpe.

HOW TO USE THE GLEIM REVIEW SYSTEM

To ensure that you are using your time effectively, we have formulated a three-step process that includes all components (book, CIA Test Prep, Audio Reviews, and Gleim Online) together and should be applied to each study unit.

Step 1: Diagnostic

a. Multiple-Choice Quiz #1 (20 minutes, plus 10 minutes for review) – In Gleim Online, complete Multiple-Choice Quiz #1 in 20 minutes. This is a diagnostic quiz, so it is expected that your scores will be lower.

   1) Immediately following the quiz, review the questions you flagged and/or answered incorrectly. For each question, analyze and understand why you flagged it or answered it incorrectly. This step is essential to identifying your weak areas. "Learning from Your Mistakes" on page 7 has tips on how to determine why you missed the questions you missed.

Step 2: Comprehension

a. Audiovisual Presentation (30 minutes) – This Gleim Online presentation provides an overview of the study unit. The Gleim CIA Audio Review can be substituted for audiovisual presentations.

b. True/False Quiz (45 minutes) – Complete the True/False quiz in Gleim Online and receive immediate feedback.

c. Knowledge Transfer Outline (60-80 minutes) – Study the Knowledge Transfer Outline, particularly the troublesome areas identified from your Multiple-Choice Quiz #1 in Step 1. The Knowledge Transfer Outlines can be studied either online or in the book.

d. Multiple-Choice Quiz #2 (20 minutes, plus 10 minutes for review) – Complete Multiple-Choice Quiz #2 in Gleim Online.

   1) Immediately following the quiz, review the questions you flagged and/or answered incorrectly. This step is an essential learning activity. "Learning from Your Mistakes" on page 7 has tips on how to determine why you missed the questions you missed.

Step 3: Application

a. CIA Test Prep (40 minutes, plus 20 minutes for review) -- Complete two 20-question quizzes using the Practice Exam feature. Spend 20 minutes taking each quiz and then spend about 10 minutes reviewing each quiz as needed.

Final Review

1. CIA Exam Rehearsal (2.5 hours/150 minutes) -- Take the Exam Rehearsal at the beginning of your final review stage. It contains 125 multiple-choice questions, just like the CIA exam. This will help you identify where you should focus during the remainder of your final review.

2. CIA Test Prep (10-20 hours) -- Use Test Prep to focus on your weak areas identified from your Exam Rehearsal. Also, be sure to do a cumulative review to refresh yourself with topics you learned at the beginning of your studies. View your performance chart to make sure you are scoring 75% or higher.

The times mentioned above are recommendations based on prior candidate feedback and how long you will have to answer questions on the actual exam. Each candidate's time spent in any area will vary depending on proficiency and familiarity with the subject matter.

GLEIM KNOWLEDGE TRANSFER OUTLINES

This edition of the Gleim *CIA Review* books has the following features to make studying easier:

1. **Guidance Designations:** In an effort to help CIA candidates better grasp The IIA authoritative literature, we have come up with visual indicators that clearly identify each type of guidance. If the following information does not make sense to you now, please come back and reread this section of the Introduction after you have read pages 9-11 in Study Unit 1. This is where we explain the hierarchy of The IIA authoritative literature.

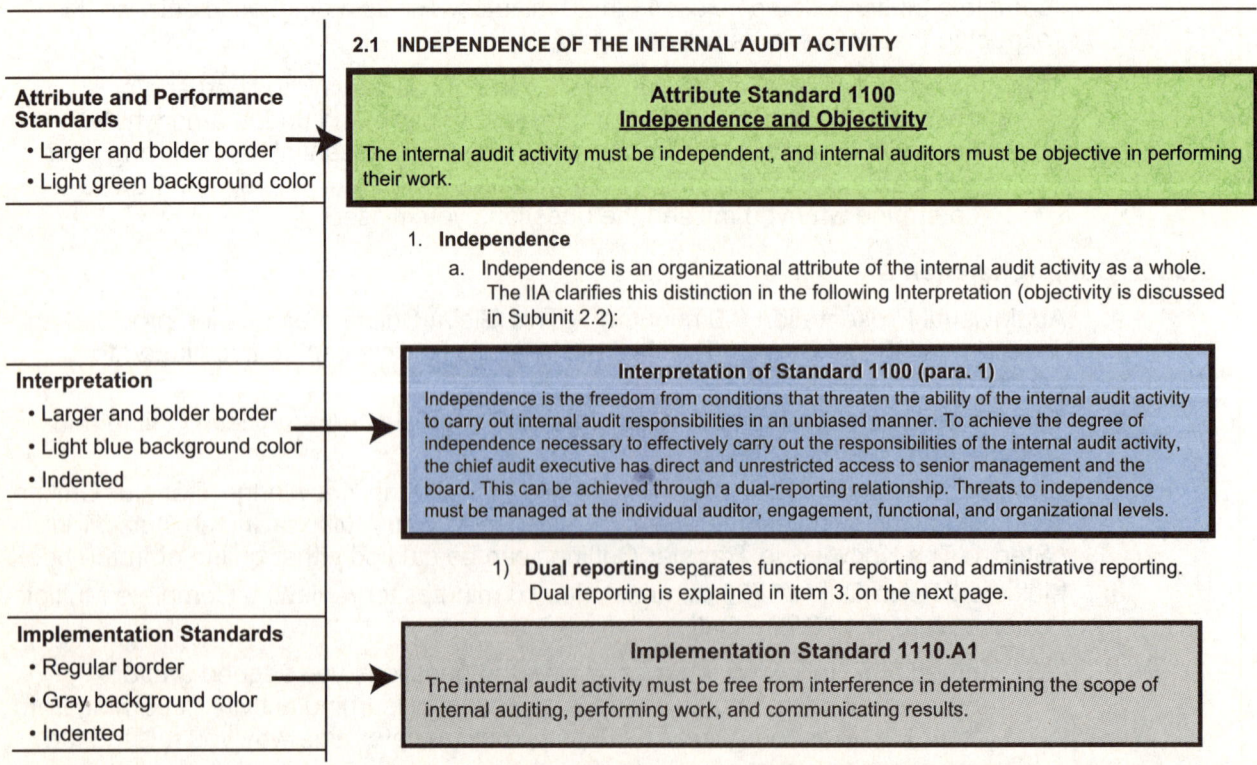

2. **Examples:** We use illustrative examples, set off in shaded, bordered boxes, to make the concepts more relatable.

> **EXAMPLE**
>
> Assume a sample is taken from a population of 500. According to standard acceptance sampling tables, if the sample consists of 25 items and not one is defective, the probability is 93% that the population deviation rate is less than 10%. If 60 items are examined and no defects are found, the probability is 99% that the deviation rate is less than 10%. If two defects in 60 units are observed, the probability is 96% that the deviation rate is less than 10%.

3. **Gleim Success Tips:** These tips supplement the core exam material by suggesting how certain topics might be presented on the exam or how you should prepare for an issue.

The practice of internal auditing is governed by professional standards. Thus, how an internal auditor performs an engagement is as important as the final product. Part 1 of the CIA exam contains numerous questions regarding (1) the procedures to be applied in a given situation and (2) the proper documentation. Working papers must be formatted and cross-referenced so that a reviewer can understand how the engagement was conducted and whether the evidence gathered supports the results reported.

4. **Memory Aids:** We offer mnemonic devices to help you remember important concepts.

    The following memory aid is for the functions that should be kept separate for proper segregation of duties:

A	Authorization
R	Recordkeeping
C	Custody

TIME-BUDGETING AND QUESTION-ANSWERING TECHNIQUES FOR THE EXAM

The following suggestions are to assist you in maximizing your score on Part 1 of the CIA exam. Remember, knowing how to take the exam and how to answer individual questions is as important as studying/reviewing the subject matter tested on the exam.

1. **Budget your time.**

    a. We make this point with emphasis. Just as you would fill up your gas tank prior to reaching empty, so too should you finish your exam before time expires.

    b. You have 150 minutes to answer 125 questions. We suggest you attempt to answer one question per minute, which would result in completing 125 questions in 125 minutes to give you 25 minutes to review questions that you have flagged.

    c. Use the wipeboard provided by Pearson VUE for your Gleim Time Management System at the exam. List the question numbers for every 20 questions (i.e., 1, 21, 41, etc.) in a column on the left side of the wipeboard. The right side of the wipeboard will have your start time at the top and allows you to fill in the time you have remaining at each question checkpoint. Stay consistent with 1 minute per question.

2. **Answer the items in consecutive order.**

    a. Do **not** agonize over any one item. Stay within your time budget.

    b. Note any items you are unsure of by clicking the "Flag for Review" button in the upper-right corner of your screen, and return to them later if time allows. Plan on going back to all the questions you flagged.

    c. Never leave a question unanswered. Make your best guess in the time allowed. Your score is based on the number of correct responses out of the total scored questions, and you will not be penalized for guessing incorrectly.

3. **For each multiple-choice question,**
    a. **Try to ignore the answer choices.** Do not allow the answer choices to affect your reading of the question.
        1) If four answer choices are presented, three of them are incorrect. These incorrect answers are called **distractors** for good reason. Often, distractors are written to appear correct at first glance until further analysis.
        2) In computational items, distractors are carefully calculated such that they are the result of making common mistakes. Be careful and double-check your computations if time permits.
    b. **Read the question carefully** to determine the precise requirement.
        1) Focusing on what is required enables you to ignore extraneous information and to proceed directly to determining the correct answer.
            a) Be especially careful to note when the requirement is an **exception**; e.g., "Which of the following is **not** an indication of fraud?"
    c. **Determine the correct answer** before looking at the answer choices.
        1) However, some multiple-choice questions are structured so that the answer cannot be determined from the stem alone. See the stem in b.1)a) above.
    d. **Then, read the answer choices carefully.**
        1) Even if the first answer appears to be the correct choice, do not skip the remaining answer choices. Questions often ask for the "best" of the choices provided. Thus, each choice requires your consideration.
        2) Treat each answer choice as a true/false question as you analyze it.
    e. **Click on the best answer.**
        1) If you are uncertain, you have a 25% chance of answering the question correctly by blindly guessing. Improve your odds with educated guessing.
        2) For many of the multiple-choice questions, two answer choices can be eliminated with minimal effort, thereby increasing your educated guess to a 50-50 proposition.
4. After you have answered all 125 questions, return to the questions that you flagged. Also, verify that all questions have been answered.
5. **If you don't know the answer:**
    a. Again, guess but make it an educated guess, which means select the best possible answer. First, rule out answers that you think are incorrect. Second, speculate on what The IIA is looking for and/or the rationale behind the question. Third, select the best answer, or guess between equally appealing answers. Your first guess is usually the most intuitive. If you cannot make an educated guess, read the stem and each answer and pick the most intuitive answer. It's just a guess!
    b. Make sure you accomplish this step within your predetermined time budget per checkpoint.

LEARNING FROM YOUR MISTAKES

Learning from questions you answer incorrectly is very important. Each question you answer incorrectly is an **opportunity** to avoid missing actual test questions on your CIA exam. Thus, you should carefully study the answer explanations provided until you understand why the original answer you chose is wrong, as well as why the correct answer indicated is correct. This study technique is clearly the difference between passing and failing for many CIA candidates.

Also, you **must** determine why you answered questions incorrectly and learn how to avoid the same error in the future. Reasons for missing questions include

1. Misreading the requirement (stem)
2. Not understanding what is required
3. Making a math error
4. Applying the wrong rule or concept
5. Being distracted by one or more of the answers
6. Incorrectly eliminating answers from consideration
7. Not having any knowledge of the topic tested
8. Employing bad intuition when guessing

It is also important to verify that you answered correctly for the right reasons. Otherwise, if the material is tested on the CIA exam in a different manner, you may not answer it correctly.

HOW TO BE IN CONTROL WHILE TAKING THE EXAM

You have to be in control to be successful during exam preparation and execution. Control can also contribute greatly to your personal and other professional goals. Control is a process whereby you

1. Develop expectations, standards, budgets, and plans
2. Undertake activity, production, study, and learning
3. Measure the activity, production, output, and knowledge
4. Compare actual activity with expected and budgeted activity
5. Modify the activity, behavior, or study to better achieve the desired outcome
6. Revise expectations and standards in light of actual experience
7. Continue the process or restart the process in the future

Exercising control will ultimately develop the confidence you need to outperform most other CIA candidates and PASS the CIA exam! Obtain our *How to Pass the CIA Exam: A System for Success* booklet for a more detailed discussion of control and other exam tactics.

IF YOU HAVE QUESTIONS ABOUT GLEIM MATERIALS

Content-specific questions about our materials will be answered most rapidly if they are sent to us via the methods described below. Our team of accounting experts will give your correspondence thorough consideration and a prompt response.

There are two methods for submitting an inquiry to our accounting experts:

1. The preferred method is to utilize the "Submit Question Feedback" link that appears beneath the answer explanations of all questions in a Review Session. Use this method if you have an inquiry about a question in Gleim Online, CIA Test Prep, Exam Rehearsals, or Diagnostic Quizzes.

2. For inquiries regarding your Gleim Review book or Test Prep Software Download, please visit www.gleim.com/questions and submit your inquiry using the on-screen form.

In order for us to deliver your response directly to your Personal Classroom, you will need to log in to your Gleim account to submit your inquiry.

Questions regarding the information in this introduction (study suggestions, studying plans, exam specifics) should be emailed to personalcounselor@gleim.com.

Questions concerning orders, prices, shipments, or payments should be sent via email to customerservice@gleim.com and will be promptly handled by our competent and courteous customer service staff.

For technical support, you may use our automated technical support service at www.gleim.com/support, email us at support@gleim.com, or call us at (800) 874-5346.

FEEDBACK

Please fill out our online feedback form (www.gleim.com/feedbackCIA1) IMMEDIATELY after you take the CIA exam so we can adapt to changes in the exam. Our approach has been approved by The IIA.

Have something to say?

Tell Gleim what's on your mind!

gleim.com/FeedbackCIA1

STUDY UNIT ONE
MANDATORY GUIDANCE

(12 pages of outline)

1.1	Applicable Standards	9
1.2	Codes of Ethical Conduct for Professionals	14
1.3	Internal Audit Ethics -- Introduction and Principles	14
1.4	Internal Audit Ethics -- Integrity	16
1.5	Internal Audit Ethics -- Objectivity	16
1.6	Internal Audit Ethics -- Confidentiality	17
1.7	Internal Audit Ethics -- Competency	18
1.8	Internal Audit Charter	18

This study unit is the first of two covering **Section I: Mandatory Guidance** from The IIA's CIA Exam Syllabus. This section makes up 35% to 45% of Part 1 of the CIA exam and is tested at the **proficiency level**. The relevant portion of the syllabus is highlighted below. (The complete syllabus is in Appendix B.)

I. **MANDATORY GUIDANCE (35%–45%)**

A. Definition of Internal Auditing
  1. Define purpose, authority, and responsibility of the internal audit activity

B. Code of Ethics
  1. Abide by and promote compliance with The IIA Code of Ethics

C. International Standards
  1. Comply with The IIA's Attribute Standards
     a. Determine if the purpose, authority, and responsibility of the internal audit activity are documented in the audit charter, approved by the Board, and communicated to the engagement clients
     b. Demonstrate an understanding of the purpose, authority, and responsibility of the internal audit activity

  2. Maintain independence and objectivity
  3. Determine if the required knowledge, skills, and competencies are available
  4. Develop and/or procure necessary knowledge, skills, and competencies collectively required by the internal audit activity
  5. Exercise due professional care
  6. Promote continuing professional development
  7. Promote quality assurance and improvement of the internal audit activity

---

1.1 APPLICABLE STANDARDS

1. **Mandatory Guidance**

    a. The Institute of Internal Auditors' (The IIA's) International Professional Practices Framework (IPPF) contains both mandatory guidance and strongly recommended guidance.

        1) The IIA considers adherence to the mandatory guidance essential for the professional practice of internal auditing.

b. The mandatory guidance consists of three parts: the Definition of Internal Auditing, the Code of Ethics, and the *Standards*.

    1) The Definition of Internal Auditing is a concise statement of the role of the internal audit activity in the organization.

Definition of Internal Auditing

Internal auditing is an independent, objective assurance and consulting activity designed to add value and improve an organization's operations. It helps an organization accomplish its objectives by bringing a systematic, disciplined approach to evaluate and improve the effectiveness of risk management, control, and governance processes.

---

    2) The detailed text of the Code of Ethics can be found in Subunits 1.2 through 1.7.

    3) The *Standards* (known formally as the *International Standards for the Professional Practice of Internal Auditing*) serve the following four purposes described by The IIA:

Purpose of the *Standards*

1. Delineate basic principles that represent the practice of internal auditing.
2. Provide a framework for performing and promoting a broad range of value-added internal auditing.
3. Establish the basis for the evaluation of internal audit performance.
4. Foster improved organizational processes and operations.

---

c. The *Standards* are vital to the practice of internal auditing, but CIA candidates need not memorize them. However, the principles they establish should be thoroughly understood and appropriately applied.

    1) **Attribute Standards**, numbered in the 1000s, govern the responsibilities, attitudes, and actions of the organization's internal audit activity and the people who serve as internal auditors. They are displayed in green boxes throughout this text.

    2) **Performance Standards**, numbered in the 2000s, govern the nature of internal auditing and provide quality criteria for evaluating the internal audit function's performance. Performance Standards also are displayed in green boxes.

        a) **Interpretations** are provided by The IIA to clarify terms and concepts referred to in Attribute or Performance Standards. Interpretations are in light blue.

    3) **Implementation Standards** expand upon the individual Attribute or Performance Standards that apply to all internal audit engagements.

        a) Each Implementation Standard describes the requirements of either an assurance or a consulting engagement.

        b) Implementation Standards are displayed in grey boxes.

2. **Strongly Recommended Guidance**

    a. The pronouncements that constitute strongly recommended guidance have been developed by The IIA through a formal approval process. They describe practices for effective implementation of the Definition of Internal Auditing, Code of Ethics, and *Standards*.

        1) The three strongly recommended elements of the IPPF are (a) Position Papers, (b) Practice Advisories, and (c) Practice Guides.

3. **Graphical Depiction of the Hierarchy of IIA *Standards*: The IIA's International Professional Practices Framework**

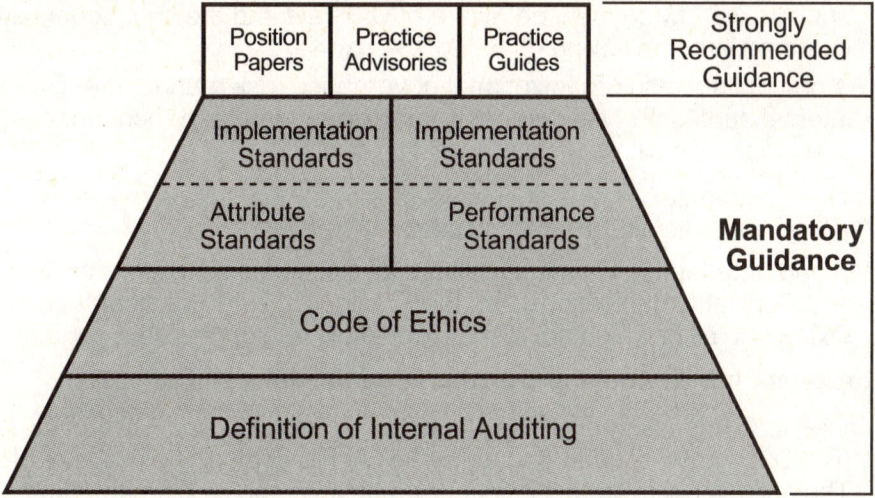

Figure 1-1

 The IPPF contains a few broad definitions and a tremendous amount of detailed guidance. As a whole, this framework provides an invaluable aid to those engaged in the everyday practice of internal auditing. Only certain key provisions, however, are crucial for passing the CIA exam. The purpose of the Gleim *CIA Review* is to furnish you with only those parts of the IPPF that are pertinent to the areas most likely to be tested. Your chances of success will increase if you thoroughly absorb and understand how to implement and follow the Standards, Interpretations, and Practice Advisory excerpts presented in these outlines.

4. **Purpose, Authority, and Responsibility of the Internal Audit Activity**

   a. **Purpose**

      1) As defined in The IIA Glossary, the purpose of the internal audit activity is to provide "independent, objective assurance and consulting services designed to add value and improve an organization's operations. The internal audit activity helps an organization accomplish its objectives by bringing a systematic, disciplined approach to evaluate and improve the effectiveness of governance, risk management and control processes."

   b. **Authority**

      1) The support of management and the board is crucial when inevitable conflicts arise between the internal audit activity and the department or function under review. Thus, the internal audit activity should be empowered to require auditees to grant access to all records, personnel, and physical properties relevant to the performance of every engagement.

         a) A formal charter for the internal audit activity that defines the internal audit activity's purpose, authority, and responsibility must be adopted, and it should contain a grant of sufficient authority. Final approval of the charter resides with the board.

   c. **Responsibility**

      1) The internal audit activity's responsibility is to provide the organization with assurance and consulting services that will add value and improve the organization's operations. Specifically, the internal audit activity must evaluate and improve the effectiveness of the organization's governance, risk management, and control processes.

5. **Compliance with Federal Laws**

    a. Many non-U.S. companies issue stock or track stock on U.S. exchanges. Internal auditors worldwide must be aware of U.S. law and the consequences of a public corporation not following it.

    b. As part of its role in organizational governance, risk management, and control, the internal audit activity is responsible for evaluating (and recommending improvements to) compliance with relevant federal laws.

    1) Common examples of such laws are (a) regulations regarding the discharge of pollutants and (b) workplace safety rules.

    c. As part of federal law, an internal auditor should be aware of the Racketeer Influenced and Corrupt Organizations Act, the Foreign Corrupt Practices Act, and the Sarbanes-Oxley Act, all of which are discussed below and on the next page.

6. **The Racketeer Influenced and Corrupt Organizations Act of 1970**

    a. In 1970, Congress passed the Racketeer Influenced and Corrupt Organizations (RICO, commonly pronounced *ree*-ko) Act to combat the problem of organized crime. The act's goals were to eliminate organized crime by concentrating on the transfer of illegal monies.

    1) RICO has both civil and criminal provisions. The criminal portion provides for fines and prison sentences, and the civil portion provides for the awarding of treble damages and attorney's fees to the successful plaintiff.

    b. RICO specifically makes the following activities unlawful:

    1) Conspiring to commit any of the offenses in items 2)-4)
    2) Using income derived from a pattern of racketeering activity to acquire an interest in an enterprise
    3) Acquiring or maintaining an interest in an enterprise through a pattern of racketeering activity
    4) Conducting the affairs of an enterprise through a pattern of racketeering activity

    c. Despite the intent of the RICO act to be deployed against the Mafia and other organized crime groups, it has had unforeseen consequences.

    1) RICO has been used against Wall Street insider traders, Major League Baseball, anti-abortion protesters, and public accounting firms—none of which was intended by Congress when the law was originally passed.
    2) Probably the most significant of these cases in terms of business ethics was that of investment bank Drexel Burnham Lambert and its former employee Michael Milken. Both the firm and Milken individually were threatened with indictment by U.S. Attorney Rudolph Giuliani under RICO in the late 1980s for trading on inside information.

7. **The Foreign Corrupt Practices Act of 1977**

    a. The Foreign Corrupt Practices Act (FCPA) was enacted in 1977 in response to the flood of bribes handed out by U.S. companies to foreign government officials, a phenomenon that came to light during the Watergate investigations of 1973-74.

    b. The FCPA contains two sets of provisions:

    1) All public companies must devise and maintain a system of internal accounting control, regardless of whether they have foreign operations.
    2) Public companies may not make corrupt payments to any foreign official, foreign political party or official thereof, or candidate for political office in a foreign country.

    c. As under RICO, individuals found in violation of the FCPA are subject to both a fine and imprisonment. A corporation may be assessed a fine as well.

8. **The Sarbanes-Oxley Act of 2002**
    a. The Sarbanes-Oxley Act of 2002 (SOX) was a response to the numerous financial reporting scandals of late 2001 and early 2002.
    b. SOX imposes specific governance practices on issuers of publicly traded securities.
        1) Each member of the issuer's audit committee must be an independent member of the board of directors.
        2) At least one member of the audit committee must be a financial expert.
        3) The audit committee must be directly responsible for appointing, compensating, and overseeing the work of the independent auditor.
        4) The independent auditor must report directly to the audit committee, not to management.
    c. SOX also imposes specific reporting requirements, among them a provision that the issuer's CEO and CFO must certify to the effectiveness of the system of internal control.
    d. Criminal penalties were provided for those who conceal or destroy accounting or other records in an attempt to obstruct an investigation.

9. **Compliance with Control Frameworks**
    a. Control frameworks do not carry the force of law, but they are extremely useful tools for ensuring the organization addresses all aspects of a comprehensive system of internal control. The following five frameworks–developed in different nations–are tested on the CIA exam.
        1) The **COSO Framework**, known formally as *Internal Control -- Integrated Framework*, is the most prominent control framework in the United States.
            a) Published in 1992, and most recently modified in 2013, the COSO Framework was issued by the Committee of Sponsoring Organizations (COSO) of the Treadway Commission (named for James C. Treadway, its first chairman).
        2) **CoCo** (a nickname based on its original title, *Criteria of Control*) is known formally as *Guidance on Control*. It was published in 1995 by the Canadian Institute of Chartered Accountants (CICA).
        3) The **Turnbull Report**, known formally as *Internal Control: Guidance for Directors on the Combined Code*, is named for Nigel Turnbull, chair of the committee that drafted the report.
            a) It was originally published in 1999 by the Financial Reporting Council (FRC) of the UK and re-released as *Internal Control: Revised Guide for Directors on the Combined Code* in 2005.
        4) **COBIT**, known formally as *Control Objectives for Information and Related Technology*, is the best-known framework specifically for IT controls. Version 5 of this document was published in 2012 by the Information Systems Audit and Control Associations (ISACA).
        5) **eSAC** is an alternative control model for IT. Known formally as *Electronic Systems Assurance and Control*, it is a publication of The Institute of Internal Auditors Research Foundation.

Stop and review! You have completed the outline for this subunit. Study multiple-choice questions 1 through 3 on page 20.

1.2 CODES OF ETHICAL CONDUCT FOR PROFESSIONALS

1. **Reasons for Codes of Ethical Conduct**
   a. The primary purpose of a code of ethical conduct for a professional organization is to promote an ethical culture among professionals who serve others.
   b. Additional functions of a code of ethical conduct for a professional organization include
      1) Communicating acceptable values to all members,
      2) Establishing objective standards against which individuals can measure their own performance, and
      3) Communicating the organization's values to outsiders.

2. **Aspects of Codes of Ethical Conduct**
   a. The mere existence of a code of ethical conduct does not ensure that its principles are followed or that those outside the organization will believe that it is trustworthy. A measure of the cohesion and professionalism of an organization is the degree of voluntary compliance with its adopted code.
      1) A code of ethical conduct worded so as to reduce the likelihood of members being sued for substandard work would not earn the confidence of the public.
   b. A code of ethical conduct can help establish minimum standards of competence, but it is impossible to require equality of competence by all members of a profession.
   c. To be effective, the code must provide for disciplinary action for violators.

3. **Typical Components of a Code of Ethical Conduct**
   a. A code of ethical conduct for professionals should contain at least the following:
      1) **Integrity.** A refusal to compromise professional values for personal gain. Another facet of integrity is performance of professional duties in accordance with relevant laws.
      2) **Objectivity.** A commitment to providing stakeholders with unbiased information. Another facet of objectivity is a commitment to independence from conflicts of economic or professional interest.
      3) **Confidentiality.** A refusal to use organizational information for private gain.
      4) **Competency.** A commitment to acquiring and maintaining an appropriate level of knowledge and skill.
   b. These four elements are the core principles of The IIA's Code of Ethics.

Stop and review! You have completed the outline for this subunit. Study multiple-choice questions 4 through 6 on page 21.

1.3 INTERNAL AUDIT ETHICS -- INTRODUCTION AND PRINCIPLES

1. **Introduction**
   a. The IIA incorporates the Definition of Internal Auditing into the Introduction to the Code of Ethics and specifies the reasons for establishing the Code.

Introduction to The IIA's Code of Ethics

The purpose of The Institute's Code of Ethics is to promote an ethical culture in the profession of internal auditing.

Internal auditing is an independent, objective assurance and consulting activity designed to add value and improve an organization's operations. It helps an organization accomplish its objectives by bringing a systematic, disciplined approach to evaluate and improve the effectiveness of risk management, control, and governance processes.

-- Continued on next page --

> -- *Continued from previous page* --
>
> A code of ethics is necessary and appropriate for the profession of internal auditing, founded as it is on the trust placed in its objective assurance about governance, risk management, and control.
>
> The Institute's Code of Ethics extends beyond the Definition of Internal Auditing to include two essential components:
>
> 1. Principles that are relevant to the profession and practice of internal auditing.
> 2. Rules of Conduct that describe behavior norms expected of internal auditors. These rules are an aid to interpreting the Principles into practical applications and are intended to guide the ethical conduct of internal auditors.
>
> "Internal auditors" refers to Institute members, recipients of or candidates for IIA professional certifications, and those who perform internal audit services within the Definition of Internal Auditing.

2. **Applicability**
    a. The provisions of the Code are applied broadly to all organizations and persons who perform internal audit services, not just CIAs and members of The IIA.

> **Applicability and Enforcement of the Code of Ethics**
>
> This Code of Ethics applies to both entities and individuals that perform internal audit services.
>
> For IIA members and recipients of or candidates for IIA professional certifications, breaches of the Code of Ethics will be evaluated and administered according to The Institute's Bylaws and Administrative Directives. The fact that a particular conduct is not mentioned in the Rules of Conduct does not prevent it from being unacceptable or discreditable, and therefore, the member, certification holder, or candidate can be liable for disciplinary action.

    b. Violations of rules of ethics should be reported to The IIA's Board of Directors.
3. **Core Principles**
    a. The Rules of Conduct in the Code are grouped around the same four principles described on the previous page: integrity, objectivity, confidentiality, and competency.
        1) The integrity of internal auditors establishes trust and thus provides the basis for reliance on their judgment.
        2) Internal auditors exhibit the highest level of professional objectivity in gathering, evaluating, and communicating information about the activity or process being examined. Internal auditors make a balanced assessment of all the relevant circumstances and are not unduly influenced by their own interests or by others in forming judgments.
        3) Internal auditors respect the value and ownership of information they receive and do not disclose information without appropriate authority unless there is a legal or professional obligation to do so.
        4) Internal auditors apply the knowledge, skills, and experience needed in the performance of internal audit services.

Stop and review! You have completed the outline for this subunit. Study multiple-choice questions 7 and 8 on page 22.

1.4 INTERNAL AUDIT ETHICS -- INTEGRITY

1. **Rules of Conduct – Integrity**

> ### Rules of Conduct – Integrity
> Internal auditors:
> 1.1. Shall perform their work with honesty, diligence, and responsibility.
> 1.2. Shall observe the law and make disclosures expected by the law and the profession.
> 1.3. Shall not knowingly be a party to any illegal activity, or engage in acts that are discreditable to the profession of internal auditing or to the organization.
> 1.4. Shall respect and contribute to the legitimate and ethical objectives of the organization.

> **EXAMPLE**
> An internal auditor is working for a cosmetics manufacturer that may be inappropriately testing cosmetics on animals. If, out of loyalty to the employer, no information about the testing is gathered, the auditor violated the Rules of Conduct by
> 1. Knowingly becoming a party to an illegal act,
> 2. Engaging in an act discreditable to the profession,
> 3. Failing to make disclosures expected by the law, and
> 4. Not performing the work diligently.

Stop and review! You have completed the outline for this subunit. Study multiple-choice questions 9 and 10 beginning on page 22.

1.5 INTERNAL AUDIT ETHICS -- OBJECTIVITY

1. **Rules of Conduct – Objectivity**

> ### Rules of Conduct – Objectivity
> Internal auditors:
> 2.1. Shall not participate in any activity or relationship that may impair or be presumed to impair their unbiased assessment. This participation includes those activities or relationships that may be in conflict with the interests of the organization.
> 2.2. Shall not accept anything that may impair or be presumed to impair their professional judgment.
> 2.3. Shall disclose all material facts known to them that, if not disclosed, may distort the reporting of activities under review.

2. **Conflict of Interest Policy**
   a. A conflict of interest policy should
      1) Prohibit the transfer of benefits between an employee and those with whom the organization deals
      2) Prohibit the use of organizational information for private gain

> **EXAMPLE**
>
> At the end of the year, an internal auditing team made observations and recommendations that an organization can use to improve operating efficiency. To express gratitude, the division manager presented the internal audit team with a gift of moderate value. The internal audit team meets to discuss whether to accept the gift. The following reasons for accepting or not accepting the gift were discussed:
>
> One auditor said, "we *should* accept the gift because its value is insignificant."
>
> Another auditor said, "we *should not* accept the gift until after we submit our final engagement communication."
>
> A third auditor said, "we *should not* accept the gift."
>
> The lead auditor considered the opinions of the other auditors and the intent of the Rules of Conduct. The lead auditor then decided that acceptance of the gift would be inappropriate because of the presumed impairment of the internal auditor's professional judgment.

Stop and review! You have completed the outline for this subunit. Study multiple-choice questions 11 through 16 beginning on page 23.

1.6 INTERNAL AUDIT ETHICS -- CONFIDENTIALITY

1. **Rules of Conduct – Confidentiality**

> **Rules of Conduct – Confidentiality**
>
> Internal auditors:
>
> 3.1. Shall be prudent in the use and protection of information acquired in the course of their duties.
>
> 3.2. Shall not use information for any personal gain or in any manner that would be contrary to the law or detrimental to the legitimate and ethical objectives of the organization.

> **EXAMPLE**
>
> Which of the following violate(s) The IIA's Code of Ethics?
>
> - Investigating a lead sales person's expense reports based on rumors of overstatement.
>   - Investigating potential instances of fraud is within the internal auditor's normal responsibilities. It is not a violation.
> - Purchasing stock in a target organization after reading reports that it may be acquired.
>   - Rule of Conduct 3.2 states, "Internal auditors shall not use information for any personal gain." The stock purchase is a violation.
> - Disclosing confidential information in response to a court order.
>   - The principle of confidentiality permits the disclosure of confidential information given a legal or professional obligation to do so. This disclosure is not a violation.

Stop and review! You have completed the outline for this subunit. Study multiple-choice questions 17 and 18 on page 25.

1.7 INTERNAL AUDIT ETHICS -- COMPETENCY

1. **Rules of Conduct – Competency**

> **Rules of Conduct – Competency**
>
> Internal auditors:
>
> 4.1. Shall engage only in those services for which they have the necessary knowledge, skills, and experience.
>
> 4.2. Shall perform internal audit services in accordance with the *International Standards for the Professional Practice of Internal Auditing (Standards)*.
>
> 4.3. Shall continually improve their proficiency and the effectiveness and quality of their services.

> **EXAMPLE**
>
> Which of the following violate(s) The IIA's Code of Ethics?
>
> - After obtaining evidence that an employee is embezzling funds, the internal auditor interrogates the suspect. The organization has a security department.
>   - Internal auditors generally lack the knowledge, skills, or experience regarding interrogation of suspects possessed by security specialists. The lack of proficiency most likely is a violation.
> - An internal auditor has been assigned to perform an engagement in the warehousing department next year. The auditor currently has no expertise in this area but accepted the assignment and plans to take continuing professional education courses in warehousing.
>   - The internal auditor plans to acquire the required knowledge and skills prior to the start of this engagement. The internal auditor most likely did not violate the Code of Ethics.

Stop and review! You have completed the outline for this subunit. Study multiple-choice questions 19 through 21 beginning on page 26.

1.8 INTERNAL AUDIT CHARTER

> **Attribute Standard 1000**
> **Purpose, Authority, and Responsibility**
>
> The purpose, authority, and responsibility of the internal audit activity must be formally defined in an internal audit charter, consistent with the Definition of Internal Auditing, the Code of Ethics, and the *Standards*. The chief audit executive must periodically review the internal audit charter and present it to senior management and the board for approval.

1. **Internal Audit Charter**

    a. According to The IIA Glossary, the internal audit charter is a formal document that defines the internal audit activity's purpose, authority, and responsibility. The internal audit charter establishes the internal audit activity's position within the organization; authorizes access to records, personnel, and physical properties relevant to the performance of engagements, and defines the scope of internal audit activities.

b. The importance of a formal, written internal audit charter cannot be overstated. The IIA provides the following Interpretation to emphasize this point:

> **Interpretation of Standard 1000**
>
> The internal audit charter is a formal document that defines the internal audit activity's purpose, authority, and responsibility. The internal audit charter establishes the internal audit activity's position within the organization, including the nature of the chief audit executive's functional reporting relationship with the board; authorizes access to records, personnel, and physical properties relevant to the performance of engagements; and defines the scope of internal audit activities. Final approval of the internal audit charter resides with the board.

    1) An auditee must not be able to place a scope limitation on the internal audit activity by refusing to make relevant records, personnel, and physical properties available to the internal auditors.

c. Engagement clients must be informed of the internal audit activity's purpose, authority, and responsibility. This will prevent misunderstandings about access to records and personnel.

d. Further guidance can be found in Practice Advisory 1000-1, *Internal Audit Charter*.

    1) "Providing a formal, written internal audit charter is critical in managing the internal audit activity. The internal audit charter provides a recognized statement for review and acceptance by management and for approval, as documented in the minutes, by the board. It also facilitates a periodic assessment of the adequacy of the internal audit activity's purpose, authority, and responsibility, which establishes the role of the internal audit activity. If a question should arise, the internal audit charter provides a formal, written agreement with management and the board about the organization's internal audit activity" (para. 1).

    2) "The chief audit executive (CAE) is responsible for periodically assessing whether the internal audit activity's purpose, authority, and responsibility, as defined in the internal audit charter, continue to be adequate to enable the activity to accomplish its objectives. The CAE is also responsible for communicating the result of this assessment to senior management and the board" (para. 2).

e. As described in the following Standard, the charter itself must refer to the mandatory guidance portion of the IPPF:

> **Attribute Standard 1010**
> **Recognition of the Definition of Internal Auditing, the Code of Ethics, and the *Standards* in the Internal Audit Charter**
>
> The mandatory nature of the Definition of Internal Auditing, the Code of Ethics, and the *Standards* must be recognized in the internal audit charter. The chief audit executive should discuss the Definition of Internal Auditing, the Code of Ethics, and the *Standards* with senior management and the board.

f. CIA candidates who prefer to study using specific examples should download The IIA's model internal audit charter from the following source: global.theiia.org/standards-guidance/Public%20Documents/ModelCharter.pdf.

2. **Key Definitions from the Glossary**

   a. The complete IIA Glossary is in Appendix A. The definitions do not need to be memorized, but they are useful to exam candidates and practitioners.

      1) **Chief audit executive (CAE)** describes a person in a senior position responsible for effectively managing the internal audit activity in accordance with the internal audit charter and the Definition of Internal Auditing, the Code of Ethics, and the *Standards*.

         a) The CAE, or others reporting to the CAE, will have appropriate professional certifications and qualifications.

         b) The specific job title of the CAE may vary across organizations.

      2) A **board** is an organization's governing body, such as a board of directors; supervisory board; head of an agency or legislative body; board of governors or trustees of a not-for-profit organization; or any other designated body of the organization, including the audit committee, to whom the chief audit executive may functionally report.

Stop and review! You have completed the outline for this subunit. Study multiple-choice questions 22 through 25 beginning on page 27.

QUESTIONS

1.1 Applicable Standards

1. Which Standards expand upon the other categories of Standards?

A. Performance Standards.
B. Attribute Standards.
C. Implementation Standards.
D. All of the choices are correct.

Answer (C) is correct.
REQUIRED: The Standards that expand upon other Standards.
DISCUSSION: Implementation Standards expand upon the Attribute and Performance Standards. They provide requirements applicable to specific engagements.
Answer (A) is incorrect. Performance Standards apply to all internal audit services. Answer (B) is incorrect. Attribute Standards apply to all internal audit services. Answer (D) is incorrect. Only Implementation Standards expand upon the standards in other categories.

2. The purpose of the internal audit activity can be best described as

A. Adding value to the organization.
B. Providing additional assurance regarding fair presentation of financial statements.
C. Expressing an opinion on the adequate design and functioning of the system of internal control.
D. Assuring the absence of any fraud that would materially affect the financial statements.

Answer (A) is correct.
REQUIRED: The best description of the internal audit activity.
DISCUSSION: Internal auditing is an independent, objective assurance and consulting activity designed to add value and improve an organization's operations (Definition of Internal Auditing).

3. The *Standards* consist of three types of Standards. Which Standards apply to the characteristics of providers of internal auditing services?

A. Implementation Standards.
B. Performance Standards.
C. Attribute Standards.
D. Independence Standards.

Answer (C) is correct.
REQUIRED: The Standards describing the traits of entities and individuals providing internal auditing services.
DISCUSSION: Attribute Standards concern the characteristics of organizations and parties providing internal auditing services.
Answer (A) is incorrect. Implementation Standards apply to specific types of engagements. Answer (B) is incorrect. Performance Standards describe the nature of internal auditing and provide quality criteria for evaluation of internal audit performance. Answer (D) is incorrect. The IPPF does not contain Independence Standards.

1.2 Codes of Ethical Conduct for Professionals

4. A formal code of ethics should do all of the following **except**

- A. Effectively communicate acceptable values to all members.
- B. Communicate the organization's value system to outsiders.
- C. Reflect only legal standards of conduct for individuals and the organization.
- D. Provide a method of policing and disciplining members of the organization for violations.

Answer (C) is correct.
REQUIRED: The item not a function of a code of ethics.
DISCUSSION: An ethical organization aspires to a higher standard of behavior than mere legality.
Answer (A) is incorrect. A code of ethics should effectively communicate acceptable values to all organization members. Answer (B) is incorrect. A code of ethics should communicate the organization's value system to those outside the organization. Answer (D) is incorrect. A code of ethics should indeed provide a method of policing and disciplining members for violations.

5. A typical code of ethical conduct for financial managers or management accountants in an organization requires all of the following **except**

- A. Integrity and a refusal to compromise professional values for the sake of personal goals.
- B. Independence from conflicts of economic interest.
- C. Independence from conflicts of professional interest.
- D. Subjectivity in presenting information, preparing reports, and making analyses.

Answer (D) is correct.
REQUIRED: The item not a requirement of a code of ethical conduct for financial managers.
DISCUSSION: The code of ethical conduct for financial managers or management accountants in an organization should require objectivity in presenting information, preparing reports, and making analyses.
Answer (A) is incorrect. A typical code of ethical conduct for financial managers or management accountants in an organization requires integrity and a refusal to compromise professional values for the sake of personal goals. Answer (B) is incorrect. A typical code of ethical conduct for financial managers or management accountants requires independence from conflicts of economic interest. Answer (C) is incorrect. A typical code of ethical conduct for financial managers or management accountants requires independence from conflicts of professional interest.

6. Objectivity is an ethical requirement for all persons engaged in the professional practice of internal auditing. One aspect of objectivity requires

- A. Performance of professional duties in accordance with relevant laws.
- B. Avoidance of conflict of interest.
- C. Refraining from using confidential information for unethical or illegal advantage.
- D. Maintenance of an appropriate level of professional expertise.

Answer (B) is correct.
REQUIRED: The aspect of the objectivity requirement.
DISCUSSION: Commitment to independence from conflicts of economic or professional interest is an aspect of objectivity.
Answer (A) is incorrect. Observing the law is a component of integrity. Answer (C) is incorrect. Not using confidential information for unethical or illegal advantage is an aspect of confidentiality. Answer (D) is incorrect. Maintenance of an appropriate level of professional expertise is an aspect of competency.

1.3 Internal Audit Ethics -- Introduction and Principles

7. In complying with The IIA's Code of Ethics, an internal auditor should

- A. Use individual judgment in the application of the principles set forth in the Code.
- B. Respect and contribute to the objectives of the organization even if it is engaged in illegal activities.
- C. Go beyond the limitation of personal technical skills to advance the interest of the organization.
- D. Primarily apply the competency principle in establishing trust.

Answer (A) is correct.
REQUIRED: The action complying with The IIA's Code of Ethics.
DISCUSSION: The IIA's Code of Ethics includes principles that internal auditors are expected to apply and uphold. They are interpreted by the Rules of Conduct, behavior norms expected of internal auditors. That a particular conduct is not mentioned in the Rules of Conduct does not prevent it from being unacceptable or discreditable. Consequently, a reasonable inference is that individual judgment is necessary in the application of the principles and the Rules of Conduct.
Answer (B) is incorrect. An internal auditor "shall not knowingly be a party to any illegal activity." Furthermore, an internal auditor is bound to respect and contribute only to the legitimate and ethical objectives of the organization. Answer (C) is incorrect. Internal auditors "shall engage only in those services for which they have the necessary knowledge, skills, and experience." Answer (D) is incorrect. Applying and upholding the integrity principle is the means by which an internal auditor establishes trust as a basis for reliance on his or her judgment.

8. An internal auditor who encounters an ethical dilemma **not** explicitly addressed by The IIA's Code of Ethics should always

- A. Seek counsel from an independent attorney to determine the personal consequences of potential actions.
- B. Take action consistent with the principles embodied in The IIA's Code of Ethics.
- C. Seek the counsel of the audit committee before deciding on an action.
- D. Act consistently with the employing organization's code of ethics even if such action would not be consistent with The IIA's Code of Ethics.

Answer (B) is correct.
REQUIRED: The proper action that always should be taken by an internal auditor who encounters an ethical dilemma not explicitly addressed by The IIA's Code of Ethics.
DISCUSSION: The IIA's Code of Ethics is based on principles relevant to the profession and practice of internal auditing that internal auditors are expected to apply and uphold: integrity, objectivity, confidentiality, and competency. Furthermore, the Code states that particular conduct may be unacceptable or discreditable even if it is not mentioned in the Rules of Conduct.
Answer (A) is incorrect. The auditor must act consistently with the spirit of The IIA's Code of Ethics. It is not practical to seek the advice of legal counsel for all ethical decisions. Moreover, unethical behavior may not be illegal. Answer (C) is incorrect. It is not feasible to seek the audit committee's advice for all potential dilemmas. Furthermore, the advice might not be consistent with the profession's standards. Answer (D) is incorrect. If the organization's standards are not consistent with, or as high as, the profession's standards, the internal auditor should abide by the latter.

1.4 Internal Audit Ethics -- Integrity

9. Which situation is most likely a violation of The IIA's Code of Ethics?

- A. Reporting apparent violations of antitrust statutes by officers to government regulators.
- B. Cooperating with the government's criminal investigation of the organization.
- C. Reporting apparent violations of antitrust statutes by officers to the board of directors.
- D. Immediately reporting a violent crime observed at work to local law enforcement agencies.

Answer (A) is correct.
REQUIRED: The violation of the The IIA's Code of Ethics.
DISCUSSION: An internal auditor must (1) not knowingly be a party to any illegal activity (Rule of Conduct 1.3); (2) disclose all material facts known to him or her that, if not disclosed, might distort the reporting of activities under review (Rule of Conduct 2.3); and (3) respect and contribute to the legitimate and ethical objectives of the organization (Rule of Conduct 1.4). Thus, when apparent violations of antitrust statutes by officers come to the internal auditor's attention, (s)he should report to the board of directors rather than directly to the government regulators. An internal auditor also must observe the law and make any disclosures required by the law or by the profession (Rule of Conduct 1.2).
Answer (B) is incorrect. Everyone has a legal obligation to cooperate with a criminal investigation. An internal auditor must observe the law and make any disclosures required by the law or by the profession (Rule of Conduct 1.2). Answer (C) is incorrect. An internal auditor should report apparent improprieties to the board. Answer (D) is incorrect. Everyone has a legal and moral obligation to report violent crimes immediately.

10. The IIA's Code of Ethics requires internal auditors to perform their work with

A. Honesty, diligence, and responsibility.
B. Timeliness, sobriety, and clarity.
C. Knowledge, skills, and competencies.
D. Punctuality, objectivity, and responsibility.

Answer (A) is correct.
REQUIRED: The qualities internal auditors should exhibit in the performance of their work.
DISCUSSION: Rule of Conduct 1.1 under the integrity principle states, "Internal auditors shall perform their work with honesty, diligence, and responsibility."
Answer (B) is incorrect. Timeliness, sobriety, and clarity are not mentioned in the Code. Answer (C) is incorrect. Knowledge, skills, and competencies are mentioned in the *Standards*. Answer (D) is incorrect. Punctuality is not mentioned in the Code.

1.5 Internal Audit Ethics -- Objectivity

11. Which of the following concurrent occupations could appear to subvert the ethical behavior of an internal auditor?

A. Internal auditor and a well-known charitable organization's local in-house chairperson.
B. Internal auditor and part-time business insurance broker.
C. Internal auditor and adjunct faculty member of a local business college that educates potential employees.
D. Internal auditor and landlord of multiple housing that publicly advertises for tenants in a local community newspaper listing monthly rental fees.

Answer (B) is correct.
REQUIRED: The concurrent occupations that could create an ethical issue.
DISCUSSION: Rule of Conduct 2.1 under the objectivity principle states, "Internal auditors shall not participate in any activity or relationship that may impair or be presumed to impair their unbiased assessment. This participation includes those activities or relationships that may be in conflict with the interests of the organization." As a business insurance broker, the internal auditor may lose his or her objectivity because (s)he might benefit from a change in the employer's insurance coverage.
Answer (A) is incorrect. The activities of a charity are unlikely to be contrary to the interests of the organization. Answer (C) is incorrect. Teaching is compatible with internal auditing. Answer (D) is incorrect. Whereas dealing in commercial properties might involve a conflict, renting residential units most likely does not.

12. An internal auditor discovered some material inefficiencies in a purchasing function. The purchasing manager is the internal auditor's next-door neighbor and best friend. In accordance with The IIA's Code of Ethics, the internal auditor should

A. Objectively include the facts of the case in the engagement communications.
B. Not report the incident because of loyalty to the friend.
C. Include the facts of the case in a special communication submitted only to the friend.
D. Not report the friend unless the activity is illegal.

Answer (A) is correct.
REQUIRED: The proper internal auditor action given a conflict between professional duty and friendship.
DISCUSSION: Rule of Conduct 2.3 under the objectivity principle states, "Internal auditors shall disclose all material facts known to them that, if not disclosed, may distort the reporting of activities under review."

13. Which of the following activities of an internal auditor is most likely to be acceptable under The IIA's Code of Ethics?

A. Late arrivals and early departures from work because this practice is common in the organization.
B. Frequent luncheons and other socializing with major suppliers of the organization without the consent of senior management.
C. Conducting an unrelated business outside of office hours.
D. Acceptance of a material gift from a supplier.

Answer (C) is correct.
REQUIRED: The acceptable activity under The IIA's Code of Ethics.
DISCUSSION: Nothing in The IIA's Code of Ethics prohibits operating an unrelated business outside of regular office hours. The activity is not, in itself, (1) a conflict of interest, (2) a use of information for personal gain, or (3) an impairment of the internal auditor's unbiased assessment.
Answer (A) is incorrect. Internal auditors should exercise diligence in performing their duties. Answer (B) is incorrect. Rule of Conduct 2.1 under the objectivity principle states, "Internal auditors shall not participate in any activity or relationship that may impair or be presumed to impair their unbiased assessment. This participation includes those activities or relationships that may be in conflict with the interests of the organization." Answer (D) is incorrect. Rule of Conduct 2.2 under the objectivity principle states, "Internal auditors shall not accept anything that may impair or be presumed to impair their professional judgment."

14. In their reporting, internal auditors are required by The IIA's Code of Ethics to

A. Present sufficient factual information without revealing confidential matters that could be detrimental to the organization.
B. Disclose all material information obtained by the auditor as of the date of the final engagement communication.
C. Obtain factual information within the established time and budget parameters.
D. Disclose material facts known to the internal auditor that could distort the final engagement communication if not revealed.

Answer (D) is correct.
REQUIRED: The reporting responsibility under The IIA's Code of Ethics.
DISCUSSION: Rule of Conduct 2.3 under the objectivity principle states, "Internal auditors shall disclose all material facts known to them that, if not disclosed, may distort the reporting of activities under review."
Answer (A) is incorrect. The Code requires only that internal auditors be prudent in the use and protection of information. Answer (B) is incorrect. The Code does not address disclosure this specifically. Answer (C) is incorrect. Time and budget parameters are not addressed in the Code.

15. In their communication of results, internal auditors are required by The IIA's Code of Ethics to

A. Obtain factual information within the established time and budget parameters.
B. Reveal material facts that could distort communications if not revealed.
C. Present sufficient factual information without revealing confidential information that could be detrimental to the organization.
D. Disclose all material information obtained as of the date of the final engagement communication.

Answer (B) is correct.
REQUIRED: The requirement for internal auditors in their communication of results.
DISCUSSION: Internal auditors should disclose all material facts known to them that, if not disclosed, may distort the reporting of activities under review (Rule of Conduct 2.3).
Answer (A) is incorrect. Obtaining information pertains to performing the engagement, not communicating results. Answer (C) is incorrect. The Code of Ethics does not prohibit communicating confidential information to appropriate parties within the organization, e.g., senior management and the board. Answer (D) is incorrect. Disclosures by the internal auditors are not limited to information obtained as of the date of the final engagement communication.

16. Which of the following situations is a violation of The IIA's Code of Ethics?

A. An internal auditor, with the knowledge and consent of management, accepted a token gift from a customer of the organization that was not presumed to impair and did not impair judgment.
B. Knowing that management was aware of the situation, an internal auditor purposely left a description of an unlawful practice out of the final engagement communication.
C. An internal auditor shared techniques with internal auditors from another organization.
D. Based upon knowledge of the probable success of the employer's business, an internal auditor invested in a mutual fund that specialized in the same industry.

Answer (B) is correct.
REQUIRED: The violation of the Code of Ethics.
DISCUSSION: Rule of Conduct 2.3 under the objectivity principle states, "Internal auditors shall disclose all material facts known to them that, if not disclosed, may distort the reporting of activities under review." Moreover, Rule of Conduct 1.3 under the integrity principle states, "Internal auditors shall not knowingly be a party to any illegal activity, or engage in acts that are discreditable to the profession of internal auditing or to the organization."
Answer (A) is incorrect. Acceptance of anything from a customer is prohibited but only if it would impair or be presumed to impair professional judgment. Answer (C) is incorrect. Rule of Conduct 4.3 under the competency principle states, "Internal auditors shall continually improve their proficiency and the effectiveness and quality of their services." Answer (D) is incorrect. Although an internal auditor is prohibited from using confidential information for personal gain, and an investment in the organization's stock would be questionable, an investment in a mutual fund is acceptable.

1.6 Internal Audit Ethics -- Confidentiality

17. Which of the following actions taken by a chief audit executive (CAE) could be considered professionally ethical under The IIA's Code of Ethics?

A. The CAE decides to delay an engagement at a branch so that his nephew, the branch manager, will have time to "clean things up."

B. To save organizational resources, the CAE cancels all staff training for the next 2 years on the basis that all staff are too new to benefit from training.

C. To save organizational resources, the CAE limits procedures at foreign branches to confirmations from branch managers that no major personnel changes have occurred.

D. The CAE refuses to provide information about organizational operations to his father, who is a part owner.

Answer (D) is correct.
REQUIRED: The action considered ethical under The IIA's Code of Ethics.
DISCUSSION: Rule of Conduct 3.1 under the confidentiality principle states, "Internal auditors shall be prudent in the use and protection of information acquired in the course of their duties." Additionally, Rule of Conduct 3.2 states, "Internal auditors shall not use information for any personal gain or in any manner that would be contrary to the law or detrimental to the legitimate and ethical objectives of the organization." Thus, such use of information by the CAE might be illegal under insider trading rules.
Answer (A) is incorrect. According to Rule of Conduct 1.1, "Internal auditors shall perform their work with honesty, diligence, and responsibility." Answer (B) is incorrect. According to Rule of Conduct 4.3, "Internal auditors shall continually improve their proficiency and the effectiveness and quality of their services." Answer (C) is incorrect. According to Rule of Conduct 4.2, "Internal auditors shall perform internal audit services in accordance with the *International Standards for the Professional Practice of Internal Auditing (Standards)*." The *Standards* require supporting information to be sufficient, reliable, relevant, and useful.

18. An internal auditor is performing services in a division in which the chief financial officer is a close personal friend, and the internal auditor learns that the friend is to be replaced after a series of critical labor negotiations. The internal auditor relays this information to the friend. Has a violation of The IIA's Code of Ethics occurred?

A. No. The use of the confidential information resulted in no personal gain to the internal auditor.

B. No. The internal auditor was just being honest with his or her friend.

C. Yes. The internal auditor had a conflict of interest with the organization.

D. Yes. The internal auditor was not prudent in the use of information acquired in the course of his or her duties.

Answer (D) is correct.
REQUIRED: The basis for the violation, if any, of The IIA's Code of Ethics.
DISCUSSION: Rule of Conduct 3.1 under the confidentiality principle states, "Internal auditors shall be prudent in the use and protection of information acquired in the course of their duties." Rule of Conduct 3.2 states, "Internal auditors shall not use information for any personal gain or in any manner that would be contrary to the law or detrimental to the legitimate and ethical objectives of the organization." In this case, the decision whether to notify the financial officer of his or her replacement was properly the organization's. Accordingly, the internal auditor was bound not to tell his or her friend.
Answer (A) is incorrect. The Rules of Conduct specifically prohibit using information in a manner that would be detrimental to the legitimate and ethical objectives of the organization. Answer (B) is incorrect. The Rules of Conduct specifically prohibit using information in a manner that would be detrimental to the legitimate and ethical objectives of the organization. Answer (C) is incorrect. The facts do not suggest that a conflict of interest existed. However, such a conflict would be present, for example, if the internal auditor used confidential information to seize a business opportunity that rightfully belonged to the organization.

1.7 Internal Audit Ethics -- Competency

19. Internal auditors who fail to maintain their proficiency through continuing education could be found to be in violation of

A. The *International Standards for the Professional Practice of Internal Auditing*.

B. The IIA's Code of Ethics.

C. Both the *International Standards for the Professional Practice of Internal Auditing* and The IIA's Code of Ethics.

D. None of the answers are correct.

Answer (C) is correct.
REQUIRED: The effect of failing to meet continuing education requirements.
DISCUSSION: Rule of Conduct 4.3 under the competency principle states, "Internal auditors shall continually improve their proficiency and the effectiveness and quality of their services." Furthermore, Attr. Std. 1230 states, "Internal auditors must enhance their knowledge, skills, and other competencies through continuing professional development." Hence, both The IIA's Code of Ethics and the *Standards* are violated by failing to earn continuing education credits.
Answer (A) is incorrect. The IIA's Code of Ethics also is violated. Rule of Conduct 4.3 under the competency principle states, "Internal auditors shall continually improve their proficiency and the effectiveness and quality of their services." Answer (B) is incorrect. The *Standards* also are violated because they require auditors to enhance their knowledge, skills, and other competencies through continuing professional development. Answer (D) is incorrect. Both the Code and the *Standards* would be violated.

20. Which of the following most likely constitutes a violation of The IIA's Code of Ethics?

A. Auditor A has accepted an assignment to perform an engagement at the electronics manufacturing division. Auditor A has recently joined the internal audit activity. But Auditor A was senior auditor for the external audit of that division and has audited many electronics organizations during the past 2 years.

B. Auditor B has been assigned to perform an engagement at the warehousing function 6 months from now. Auditor B has no expertise in that area but accepted the assignment anyway. Auditor B has signed up for continuing professional education courses in warehousing that will be completed before the assignment begins.

C. Auditor C is content as an internal auditor and has come to look at it as a regular 9-to-5 job. Auditor C has not engaged in continuing professional education or other activities to improve effectiveness during the last 3 years. However, Auditor C feels performance of quality work is the same as before.

D. Auditor D discovered an internal financial fraud during the year. The books were adjusted to properly reflect the loss associated with the fraud. Auditor D discussed the fraud with the external auditor when the external auditor reviewed working papers detailing the incident.

Answer (C) is correct.
REQUIRED: The violation of The IIA's Code of Ethics.
DISCUSSION: Rule of Conduct 4.3 under the competency principle states, "Internal auditors shall continually improve their proficiency and the effectiveness and quality of their services."
Answer (A) is incorrect. No professional conflict of interest exists per se, especially given that the internal auditor was previously in public accounting. However, the internal auditor should be aware of potential conflicts. Answer (B) is incorrect. An internal auditor must possess the necessary knowledge, skills, and competencies at the time an engagement is conducted, not the time it is accepted. Answer (D) is incorrect. The information was disclosed as part of the normal process of cooperation between the internal and external auditor. Because the books were adjusted, the external auditor was expected to inquire as to the nature of the adjustment.

21. Why does The IIA's Code of Ethics in Rule of Conduct 4.2 require that due professional care be used in obtaining information to support an engagement opinion?

A. Sufficient, reliable, relevant, and useful information lends credibility to the opinion.
B. To preclude any conflict of interest.
C. To require honesty in performing work.
D. If internal auditors were permitted to communicate engagement results without obtaining sufficient information, they would be in a position to accept fees or gifts from engagement clients.

Answer (A) is correct.
REQUIRED: The reason for requiring that due care be used in obtaining information.
DISCUSSION: Engagements must be performed with proficiency and due professional care (Attr. Std. 1200), and the engagement results must be communicated (Perf. Std. 2400). Engagement results include observations, conclusions, opinions, recommendations, and action plans (PA 2410-1). If internal auditors expressed opinions or otherwise communicated engagement results without substantive investigation and compliance with the *Standards*, such communications would be meaningless. The *Standards* are therefore incorporated by reference into The IIA's Code of Ethics by Rule of Conduct 4.2. Thus, internal auditors must identify sufficient, reliable, relevant, and useful information to achieve the engagement's objectives (Perf. Std. 2310).
Answer (B) is incorrect. A separate ethics rule prohibits conflicts of interest. Rule of Conduct 2.1 states, "Internal auditors shall not participate in any activity or relationship that may impair or be presumed to impair their unbiased assessment. This participation includes those activities or relationships that may be in conflict with the interests of the organization." Answer (C) is incorrect. Rule of Conduct 1.1 requires honesty, diligence, and responsibility in the performance of work. Answer (D) is incorrect. Rule of Conduct 2.2 prohibits accepting anything that may impair or be presumed to impair the professional judgment of an internal auditor.

1.8 Internal Audit Charter

22. The authority of the internal audit activity is limited to that granted by

A. The board and the controller.
B. Senior management and the *Standards*.
C. Management and the board.
D. The board and the chief financial officer.

Answer (C) is correct.
REQUIRED: The source of authority of the internal audit activity.
DISCUSSION: The purpose, authority, and responsibility of the internal audit activity must be formally defined in a charter. The CAE must periodically review and present the charter to senior management and the board for approval (Attr. Std. 1000).
Answer (A) is incorrect. The controller is not the only member of management. Answer (B) is incorrect. The *Standards* cannot provide actual authority to an internal audit activity. Answer (D) is incorrect. Management and the board, not a particular manager, give the internal audit activity its authority.

23. The chief audit executive (CAE) is best defined as the

A. Inspector general.
B. Person responsible for the internal audit function.
C. Outside provider of internal audit services.
D. Person responsible for overseeing the contract with the outside provider of internal audit services.

Answer (B) is correct.
REQUIRED: The best definition of the CAE.
DISCUSSION: The CAE is a person in a senior position responsible for effectively managing the internal audit activity in accordance with the internal audit charter and the Definition of Internal Auditing, the Code of Ethics, and the *Standards* (The IIA Glossary).
Answer (A) is incorrect. The specific job title of the chief audit executive may vary across organizations (The IIA Glossary). Answer (C) is incorrect. The internal audit activity may be insourced. Answer (D) is incorrect. The term "chief audit executive" is defined broadly because (1) the internal audit activity may be insourced or outsourced and (2) many different titles are used in practice.

24. The chief audit executive meets with the members of the internal audit activity at scheduled staff meetings. Which of the following is the most appropriate function of such a staff meeting?

A. Developing the engagement work schedule.
B. Revising travel, promotion, and compensation policies.
C. Explaining administrative policies and obtaining suggestions from the staff.
D. Developing long-range training programs that will meet the staff's needs.

Answer (C) is correct.
REQUIRED: The most appropriate activity at an audit staff meeting.
DISCUSSION: One reason for staff meetings is to explain routine administrative matters, to teach new techniques, and even to let off steam. For example, staff members should be able to raise questions about ineffective procedures, promotions, salaries, or other problems.
Answer (A) is incorrect. Management of the internal audit activity should develop engagement work schedules. Answer (B) is incorrect. Management of the internal audit activity should revise travel, promotion, and compensation policies. Answer (D) is incorrect. Developing long-range training programs that will meet the staff's needs should be done by management of the internal audit activity.

25. Which one of the following must be included in the internal audit charter?

A. Internal audit objectivity.
B. Internal audit responsibility.
C. Chief audit executive's compensation plan.
D. Number of full-time internal audit employees deemed to be the necessary minimum.

Answer (B) is correct.
REQUIRED: The item required to be included in the internal audit charter.
DISCUSSION: The purpose, authority, and responsibility of the internal audit activity must be formally defined in an internal audit charter.
Answer (A) is incorrect. Objectivity is an attribute of individual auditors and is not included in the internal audit charter. Answer (C) is incorrect. The CAE's compensation plan is not an appropriate matter to include in the internal audit charter. Answer (D) is incorrect. The staffing of the internal audit activity is determined by the CAE and the board; it is not an appropriate matter to include in the internal audit charter.

Practice even more exam-emulating questions in **Gleim CIA Test Prep**!

STUDY UNIT TWO
INDEPENDENCE, OBJECTIVITY, AND DUE CARE

(18 pages of outline)

2.1	Independence of the Internal Audit Activity	30
2.2	Objectivity of Internal Auditors	32
2.3	Impairment to Independence and Objectivity	34
2.4	Auditor Proficiency	37
2.5	Internal Audit Resources	38
2.6	Due Professional Care and Continuing Professional Development	40
2.7	Quality Assurance and Improvement Program	42
2.8	Reporting on Quality Assurance	43
2.9	Internal and External Assessments	44

This study unit is the second of two covering **Section I: Mandatory Guidance** from The IIA's CIA Exam Syllabus. This section makes up 35% to 45% of Part 1 of the CIA exam and is tested at the **proficiency level**. The relevant portion of the syllabus is highlighted below. (The complete syllabus is in Appendix B.)

I. **MANDATORY GUIDANCE (35%–45%)**
   A. **Definition of Internal Auditing**
      1. Define purpose, authority, and responsibility of the internal audit activity
   B. **Code of Ethics**
      1. Abide by and promote compliance with The IIA Code of Ethics
   C. **International Standards**
      1. Comply with The IIA's Attribute Standards
      2. Maintain independence and objectivity
         a. Foster independence
            1) Understand organizational independence
            2) Recognize the importance of organizational independence
            3) Determine if the internal audit activity is properly aligned to achieve organizational independence
         b. Foster objectivity
            1) Establish policies to promote objectivity
            2) Assess individual objectivity
            3) Maintain individual objectivity
            4) Recognize and mitigate impairments to independence and objectivity
      3. Determine if the required knowledge, skills, and competencies are available
         a. Understand the knowledge, skills, and competencies that an internal auditor needs to possess
         b. Identify the knowledge, skills, and competencies required to fulfill the responsibilities of the internal audit activity
      4. Develop and/or procure necessary knowledge, skills, and competencies collectively required by the internal audit activity
      5. Exercise due professional care
      6. Promote continuing professional development
         a. Develop and implement a plan for continuing professional development for internal audit staff
         b. Enhance individual competency through continuing professional development
      7. Promote quality assurance and improvement of the internal audit activity
         a. Monitor the effectiveness of the quality assurance and improvement program
         b. Report the results of the quality assurance and improvement program to the board or other governing body
         c. Conduct quality assurance procedures and recommend improvements to the performance of the internal audit activity

2.1 INDEPENDENCE OF THE INTERNAL AUDIT ACTIVITY

> **Attribute Standard 1100**
> **Independence and Objectivity**
>
> The internal audit activity must be independent, and internal auditors must be objective in performing their work.

1. **Independence**
   a. Independence is an organizational attribute of the internal audit activity as a whole. The IIA clarifies this distinction in the following Interpretation (objectivity is discussed in Subunit 2.2):

   > **Interpretation of Standard 1100 (para. 1)**
   >
   > Independence is the freedom from conditions that threaten the ability of the internal audit activity to carry out internal audit responsibilities in an unbiased manner. To achieve the degree of independence necessary to effectively carry out the responsibilities of the internal audit activity, the chief audit executive has direct and unrestricted access to senior management and the board. This can be achieved through a dual-reporting relationship. Threats to independence must be managed at the individual auditor, engagement, functional, and organizational levels.

   1) **Dual reporting** separates functional reporting and administrative reporting. Dual reporting is explained in item 3. on the next page.

2. **Achieving Independence through Reporting to the Board**
   a. In this Standard, the reporting level that assures independence is identified in general terms:

   > **Attribute Standard 1110**
   > **Organizational Independence**
   >
   > The chief audit executive must report to a level within the organization that allows the internal audit activity to fulfill its responsibilities. The chief audit executive must confirm to the board, at least annually, the organizational independence of the internal audit activity.

   b. The related Interpretation specifies a particular reporting relationship that effectively achieves independence:

   > **Interpretation of Standard 1110**
   >
   > Organizational independence is effectively achieved when the chief audit executive reports functionally to the board. Examples of functional reporting to the board involve the board:
   >
   > - Approving the internal audit charter;
   > - Approving the risk based internal audit plan;
   > - Approving the internal audit budget and resource plan;
   > - Receiving communications from the chief audit executive on the internal audit activity's performance relative to its plan and other matters;
   > - Approving decisions regarding the appointment and removal of the chief audit executive;
   > - Approving the remuneration of the chief audit executive; and
   > - Making appropriate inquiries of management and the chief audit executive to determine whether there are inappropriate scope or resource limitations.

   1) The components of functional reporting are described in item 3.a.3) on the next page.

3. **Facilitating Independence through Dual Reporting**
    a. The dual-reporting relationship mentioned in the Interpretation of Standard 1100 is described in Practice Advisory 1110-1, *Organizational Independence*:
        1) "Support from senior management and the board assists the internal audit activity in gaining the cooperation of engagement clients and performing their work free from interference" (para. 1).
        2) "The chief audit executive (CAE), reporting functionally to the board and administratively to the organization's chief executive officer, facilitates organizational independence. At a minimum the CAE needs to report to an individual in the organization with sufficient authority to promote independence and to ensure broad audit coverage, adequate consideration of engagement communications, and appropriate action on engagement recommendations" (para. 2).
        3) "**Functional reporting** to the board typically involves the board:
            - Approving the internal audit activity's overall charter.
            - Approving the internal audit risk assessment and related audit plan.
            - Receiving communications from the CAE on the results of the internal audit activities or other matters that the CAE determines are necessary, including private meetings with the CAE without management present, as well as annual confirmation of the internal audit activity's organizational independence.
            - Approving all decisions regarding the performance evaluation, appointment, or removal of the CAE.
            - Approving the annual compensation and salary adjustment of the CAE.
            - Making appropriate inquiries of management and the CAE to determine whether there is audit scope or budgetary limitations that impede the ability of the internal audit activity to execute its responsibilities" (para. 3).

        NOTE: This list is similar to the examples of functional reporting given in the Interpretation of Standard 1110. The board must approve these items for functional reporting to be done correctly.

        4) "**Administrative reporting** is the reporting relationship within the organization's management structure that facilitates the day-to-day operations of the internal audit activity. Administrative reporting typically includes:
            - Budgeting and management accounting.
            - Human resource administration, including personnel evaluations and compensation.
            - Internal communications and information flows.
            - Administration of the internal audit activity's policies and procedures" (para. 4).
    b. Graphical depiction of dual reporting:

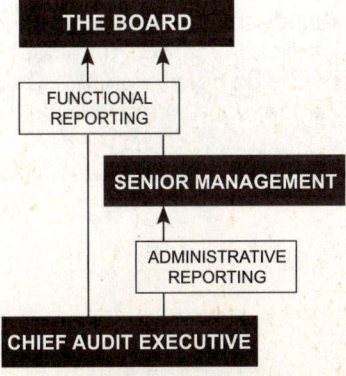

Figure 2-1

        c.   The following Implementation Standard clarifies how internal audit's independence is applied as a practical matter:

> **Implementation Standard 1110.A1**
>
> The internal audit activity must be free from interference in determining the scope of internal auditing, performing work, and communicating results.

4. **Board Interaction**

    a. As the following Standard makes clear, limits may not be placed on the CAE's access to the board:

> **Attribute Standard 1111**
> **Direct Interaction with the Board**
>
> The chief audit executive must communicate and interact directly with the board.

    b. The nature and purpose of the CAE's direct communication with the board are described in Practice Advisory 1111-1, *Board Interaction*:

    1) "Direct communication occurs when the chief audit executive (CAE) regularly attends and participates in board meetings that relate to the board's oversight responsibilities for auditing, financial reporting, organizational governance, and control. The CAE's attendance and participation at these meetings provide an opportunity to be apprised of strategic business and operational developments, and to raise high-level risk, systems, procedures, or control issues at an early stage. Meeting attendance also provides an opportunity to exchange information concerning the internal audit activity's plans and activities and to keep each other informed on any other matters of mutual interest" (para. 1).

    2) "Such communication and interaction also occurs when the CAE meets privately with the board, at least annually" (para. 2).

Stop and review! You have completed the outline for this subunit. Study multiple-choice questions 1 through 3 beginning on page 46.

2.2 OBJECTIVITY OF INTERNAL AUDITORS

1. **Objectivity**

    a. Internal auditors must be objective in performing their work.

    1) Objectivity is an attribute of individual internal auditors. The IIA defines and clarifies this distinction in the following Interpretation:

> **Interpretation of Standard 1100 (para. 2)**
>
> Objectivity is an unbiased mental attitude that allows internal auditors to perform engagements in such a manner that they believe in their work product and that no quality compromises are made. Objectivity requires that internal auditors do not subordinate their judgment on audit matters to others. Threats to objectivity must be managed at the individual auditor, engagement, functional, and organizational levels.

b. The importance of objectivity as an attribute of individual internal auditors is embodied in the following Standard:

Attribute Standard 1120
Individual Objectivity

Internal auditors must have an impartial, unbiased attitude and avoid any conflict of interest.

---

2. **Conflict of Interest**

   a. The IIA Glossary defines conflict of interest as any relationship that is, or appears to be, not in the best interest of the organization. A conflict of interest would prejudice an individual's ability to perform his or her duties and responsibilities objectively.

   b. The importance of identifying potential conflicts of interest of individual internal auditors is clarified in the following Interpretation:

Interpretation of Standard 1120

Conflict of interest is a situation in which an internal auditor, who is in a position of trust, has a competing professional or personal interest. Such competing interests can make it difficult to fulfill his or her duties impartially. A conflict of interest exists even if no unethical or improper act results. A conflict of interest can create an appearance of impropriety that can undermine confidence in the internal auditor, the internal audit activity, and the profession. A conflict of interest could impair an individual's ability to perform his or her duties and responsibilities objectively.

---

3. **Aspects of Objectivity**

   a. The IIA discusses the means of achieving, and threats to, objectivity in specific cases in Practice Advisory 1120-1, *Individual Objectivity*:

   1) "Individual objectivity means the internal auditors perform engagements in such a manner that they have an honest belief in their work product and that no significant quality compromises are made. Internal auditors are not to be placed in situations that could impair their ability to make objective professional judgments" (para. 1).

   2) "Individual objectivity involves the chief audit executive (CAE) organizing staff assignments that prevent potential and actual conflict of interest and bias, periodically obtaining information from the internal audit staff concerning potential conflict of interest and bias, and, when practicable, rotating internal audit staff assignments periodically" (para. 2).

   3) "Review of internal audit work results before the related engagement communications are released assists in providing reasonable assurance that the work was performed objectively" (para. 3).

   4) "The internal auditor's objectivity is not adversely affected when the auditor recommends standards of control for systems or reviews procedures before they are implemented. The auditor's objectivity is considered to be impaired if the auditor designs, installs, drafts procedures for, or operates such systems" (para. 4).

   5) "The occasional performance of non-audit work by the internal auditor, with full disclosure in the reporting process, would not necessarily impair objectivity. However, it would require careful consideration by management and the internal auditor to avoid adversely affecting the internal auditor's objectivity" (para. 5).

b. Within a business environment, certain activities lead to the presumption that objectivity is impaired.

1) These activities include designing, installing, or drafting procedures for operating systems.

a) The appearance of objectivity cannot be maintained when an internal auditor both (1) designs, installs, or drafts procedures for an operating system and (2) audits or reviews that system.

2) The following chart contains examples of what may or may not be presumed to impair the objectivity of an internal auditor:

Recommending standards of control for a new information system application.	Is **not** presumed to impair objectivity
Performing reviews of the procedures for retiring capital equipment.	Is **not** presumed to impair objectivity
Drafting procedures for a new hiring system.	Is presumed to impair objectivity

4. **Assess Individual Objectivity**

    a. The CAE must establish policies and procedures to assess the objectivity of individual internal auditors.

    1) These can take the form of periodic reviews of conflicts of interest or as-needed assessments during the staffing requirements phase of each engagement.

5. **Maintain Individual Objectivity**

    a. The responsibility to maintain objectivity rests with the CAE and with internal auditors themselves.

    1) Internal auditors should be aware of the possibility of new conflicts of interest that may arise owing to changes in personal circumstances or the particular auditees to which an auditor may be assigned.

Stop and review! You have completed the outline for this subunit. Study multiple-choice questions 4 through 8 beginning on page 47.

2.3 IMPAIRMENT TO INDEPENDENCE AND OBJECTIVITY

Attribute Standard 1130
Impairment to Independence or Objectivity

If independence or objectivity is impaired in fact or appearance, the details of the impairment must be disclosed to appropriate parties. The nature of the disclosure will depend upon the impairment.

Interpretation of Standard 1130

Impairment to organizational independence and individual objectivity may include, but is not limited to, personal conflict of interest, scope limitations, restrictions on access to records, personnel, and properties, and resource limitations, such as funding.

The determination of appropriate parties to which the details of an impairment to independence or objectivity must be disclosed is dependent upon the expectations of the internal audit activity's and the chief audit executive's responsibilities to senior management and the board as described in the internal audit charter, as well as the nature of the impairment.

SU 2: Independence, Objectivity, and Due Care 35

1. **Specific Circumstances**

    a. The IIA provides examples of and responses to impairments to both independence and objectivity in Practice Advisory 1130-1, *Impairment to Independence or Objectivity*:

        1) "Internal auditors are to report to the chief audit executive (CAE) any situations in which an actual or potential impairment to independence or objectivity may reasonably be inferred, or if they have questions about whether a situation constitutes an impairment to objectivity or independence. If the CAE determines that impairment exists or may be inferred, he or she needs to reassign the auditor(s)" (para. 1).

        2) "A scope limitation is a restriction placed on the internal audit activity that precludes the activity from accomplishing its objectives and plans. Among other things, a scope limitation may restrict the:

            - Scope defined in the internal audit charter.
            - Internal audit activity's access to records, personnel, and physical properties relevant to the performance of engagements.
            - Approved engagement work schedule.
            - Performance of necessary engagement procedures.
            - Approved staffing plan and financial budget" (para. 2).

        3) "A scope limitation, along with its potential effect, needs to be communicated, preferably in writing, to the board. The CAE needs to consider whether it is appropriate to inform the board regarding scope limitations that were previously communicated to and accepted by the board. This may be necessary particularly when there have been organization, board, senior management, or other changes" (para. 3).

        4) "Internal auditors are not to accept fees, gifts, or entertainment from an employee, client, customer, supplier, or business associate that may create the appearance that the auditor's objectivity has been impaired. The appearance that objectivity has been impaired may apply to current and future engagements conducted by the auditor. The status of engagements is not to be considered as justification for receiving fees, gifts, or entertainment. The receipt of promotional items (such as pens, calendars, or samples) that are available to employees and the general public and have minimal value do not hinder internal auditors' professional judgments. Internal auditors are to report immediately the offer of all material fees or gifts to their supervisors" (para. 4).

EXAMPLE

An internal audit activity was recently engaged to audit the final balance of inventory for the financial statements. During the audit, senior management contacted the lead auditor and stated that the internal audit activity would not be given access to the physical inventory.

The denial of access to the inventory is a scope limitation of the engagement. In accordance with PA1130-1, the internal audit activity needs to communicate the nature of the scope limitation and its potential effects to the board. This communication should preferably be in writing.

---

2. **Objectivity Impaired by Previous Assignment of Internal Audit Personnel**

    a. Employees often hold several different positions within the organization in sequence, on both temporary and permanent bases.

        1) Organizations build competence and gain the advantages of new perspectives by such cross-training.

b. On occasion, departments or functions in which current internal audit personnel were employed may be scheduled for an engagement in the internal audit work plan. These situations are addressed in the following Implementation Standard:

> **Implementation Standard 1130.A1**
>
> Internal auditors must refrain from assessing specific operations for which they were previously responsible. Objectivity is presumed to be impaired if an auditor provides assurance services for an activity for which the auditor had responsibility within the previous year.

c. More specific guidance is found in Practice Advisory 1130.A1-1, *Assessing Operations for Which Internal Auditors Were Previously Responsible*:

1) "Persons transferred to, or temporarily engaged by, the internal audit activity should not be assigned to audit those activities they previously performed or for which they had management responsibility until at least one year has elapsed. Such assignments are presumed to impair objectivity, and additional consideration should be exercised when supervising the engagement work and communicating engagement results" (para. 1).

3. **Objectivity Impaired by Assignment of Nonaudit Functions to Internal Audit Personnel**

    a. The CAE may be assigned responsibility for one or more functions outside the scope of internal auditing. The following Implementation Standard provides guidance for these situations:

> **Implementation Standard 1130.A2**
>
> Assurance engagements for functions over which the chief audit executive has responsibility must be overseen by a party outside the internal audit activity.

b. More detailed guidance is found in Practice Advisory 1130.A2-1, *Internal Audit's Responsibility for Other (Non-audit) Functions*:

1) "Internal auditors are not to accept responsibility for non-audit functions or duties that are subject to periodic internal audit assessments. If they have this responsibility, then they are not functioning as internal auditors" (para. 1).

2) "When the internal audit activity, chief audit executive (CAE), or individual internal auditor is responsible for, or management is considering assigning, an operational responsibility that the internal audit activity might audit, the internal auditor's independence and objectivity may be impaired" (para. 2).

3) "If the internal audit charter contains specific restrictions or limiting language regarding the assignment of non-audit functions to the internal auditor, then disclosure and discussion with management of such restrictions is necessary. If management insists on such an assignment, then disclosure and discussion of this matter with the board is necessary. If the internal audit charter is silent on this matter, the guidance noted in the points below are to be considered" (para. 3).

Stop and review! You have completed the outline for this subunit. Study multiple-choice questions 9 through 11 beginning on page 48.

2.4 AUDITOR PROFICIENCY

> **Attribute Standard 1200**
> **Proficiency and Due Professional Care**
>
> Engagements must be performed with proficiency and due professional care.

1. **Definitions**
   a. **Proficiency** - The knowledge, skills, and other competencies needed to fulfill internal audit responsibilities.
   b. **Due Professional Care** - The care and skill expected of a reasonably prudent and competent internal auditor.
2. **Shared and Ultimate Responsibility**
   a. The CAE's ultimate responsibility for, and the ethical necessity of, proficiency are described in Practice Advisory 1200-1, *Proficiency and Due Professional Care*:
      1) "Proficiency and due professional care are the responsibility of the chief audit executive (CAE) and each internal auditor. As such, the CAE ensures that persons assigned to each engagement collectively possess the necessary knowledge, skills, and other competencies to conduct the engagement appropriately" (para. 1).
      2) "Due professional care includes conforming with the Code of Ethics . . ." (para. 2).
   b. The attributes of proficiency and due care also are covered individually in the *Standards*.

> **Attribute Standard 1210**
> **Proficiency**
>
> Internal auditors must possess the knowledge, skills, and other competencies needed to perform their individual responsibilities. The internal audit activity collectively must possess or obtain the knowledge, skills, and other competencies needed to perform its responsibilities.

   1) This Standard requires only that the internal audit activity as a whole, not each auditor individually, be proficient in all necessary areas. This aspect is discussed in more detail in Subunit 2.5.

3. **Components of Auditor Proficiency**
   a. The IIA describes four levels of professional competence in Practice Advisory 1210-1, *Proficiency*: proficiency, knowledge, understanding, and appreciation.
      1) **Proficiency** is the ability to apply knowledge to situations likely to be encountered and to deal with them appropriately without extensive recourse to technical research and assistance.
         a) All internal auditors must have proficiency in applying
            i) Internal audit standards, procedures, and techniques in performing engagements.
            ii) Accounting principles and techniques if internal auditors work extensively with financial records and reports (para. 1).
      2) **Knowledge**
         a) The internal auditor must have knowledge of
            i) The indicators of fraud sufficient to identify them.
            ii) Key information technology risks and controls and available technology-based audit techniques (para. 1).

3) An **understanding** is the ability to apply broad knowledge to situations likely to be encountered, to recognize significant deviations, and to research reasonable solutions.

   a) The internal auditor must have an understanding of management principles to recognize and evaluate the materiality and significance of deviations from good business practices (para. 1).

4) An **appreciation** means the ability to recognize the existence of problems or potential problems and to identify the additional research to be undertaken or the assistance to be obtained.

   a) The internal auditor must have an appreciation of the fundamentals of business subjects such as (1) accounting, (2) economics, (3) commercial law, (4) taxation, (5) finance, (6) quantitative methods, (7) fraud, (8) risk management, and (9) information technology (para. 1).

Memory aids: The following should help you associate the appropriate subject matter with the requisite level of recognition.

P = Proficiency in	Paul
I = Internal	Is
A = Audit	A
S = Standards, etc.	Student

K = Knowledge of	Katie
F = Fraud and	Fixes
I = Information	Information
T = Technology	Technology

U = Understanding of	Under
M = Management	My
P = Principles	Pillow

A = Appreciation of	An
A = Accounting,	Accounting
E = Economics,	Education
L = Commercial Law,	Lets
T = Taxation,	Tim
F = Fraud, and	Feel
I = Information Technology	Intelligent

b. Practice Advisory 1210-1 also lists specific **skills** expected of the internal auditor.

   1) "Skills in dealing with people, understanding human relations, and maintaining satisfactory relationships with engagement clients.

   2) "Skills in oral and written communications to clearly and effectively convey such matters as engagement objectives, evaluations, conclusions, and recommendations" (para. 1).

Stop and review! You have completed the outline for this subunit. Study multiple-choice questions 12 and 13 beginning on page 49.

2.5 INTERNAL AUDIT RESOURCES

1. **Internal Resources**

   a. The CAE must ensure that the internal audit activity is able to fulfill its responsibilities.

      1) Identifying the available knowledge, skills, and competencies within the internal audit activity will help the CAE determine whether the current staff is sufficient to satisfy those responsibilities.

   b. The following practices help the CAE identify the available resources:

      1) Hiring practices are an essential part of understanding the background of the internal audit staff. During this process, the CAE identifies the internal auditor's education, previous experience, and specialized areas of knowledge.

2) The CAE should conduct periodic skills assessments to determine the specific resources available. Assessments should be performed at least annually. The IIA's Competency Framework is a useful tool for identifying the current level of knowledge, skills, and competencies available. This framework evaluates the following competency areas:

 a) Interpersonal skills
 b) Tools and techniques
 c) Internal audit standards, theory, and methodology
 d) Knowledge areas

3) Staff performance appraisals are completed at the end of any major internal audit engagement. These appraisals help the CAE assess future training needs and current staff abilities.

4) Continuing professional development encourages continued growth (see more detail in Subunit 2.6). Acquired training also should be considered when identifying internal audit resources.

c. If the internal audit staff is not able to fulfill internal audit responsibilities, the use of external service providers must be considered (see more detail in item 2. on the following page).

d. Databases can be used to store internal audit background information. The information stored can include lists of relevant skills, completed projects, acquired training, and development needs.

e. Further guidance can be found in Practice Advisory 1210-1, *Proficiency*, which states the following:

1) "Suitable criteria of education and experience for filling internal audit positions is established by the chief audit executive (CAE) who gives due consideration to the scope of work and the level of responsibility and obtains reasonable assurance as to each prospective auditor's qualifications and proficiency" (para. 2).

2) "The internal audit activity needs to collectively possess the knowledge, skills, and other competencies essential to the practice of the profession within the organization. Performing an annual analysis of an internal audit activity's knowledge, skills, and other competencies helps identify areas of opportunity that can be addressed by continuing professional development, recruiting, or co-sourcing" (para. 3).

3) "Continuing professional development is essential to help ensure internal audit staff remains proficient" (para. 4).

4) "The CAE may obtain assistance from experts outside the internal audit activity to support or complement areas where the internal audit activity is not sufficiently proficient" (para. 5).

2. **External Resources**

 a. **Outsourcing and Cosourcing**

 1) An organization may outsource none, all, or some of the functions of the internal audit activity. However, oversight of and responsibility for the internal audit activity must **not** be outsourced.

 a) Regardless of the degree of outsourcing, services must still be performed in accordance with the *Standards*, and the guidance for obtaining external service providers should be followed.

2) Outsourcing alternatives include the following:
   a) Partial or total external sourcing on an ongoing basis
   b) Cosourcing for a specific engagement or on an ongoing basis
      i) Cosourcing is performance by internal audit staff of joint engagements with external service providers (Position Paper, *The Role of Internal Auditing in Resourcing the Internal Audit Activity*).

b. **CAE's Responsibility**
   1) The following Implementation Standard requires the use of expertise from outside the internal audit activity during assurance engagements when the internal auditors lack the necessary expertise.

> **Implementation Standard 1210.A1**
>
> The chief audit executive must obtain competent advice and assistance if the internal auditors lack the knowledge, skills, or other competencies needed to perform all or part of the engagement.

   a) Not all internal audit staff are proficient in all areas. When necessary, the CAE can obtain necessary knowledge, skills, and competencies from external service providers.

c. **Guidelines for Use of Non-Internal Audit Personnel**
   1) The IIA provides comprehensive guidance in Practice Advisory 1210.A1-1, *Obtaining External Service Providers to Support or Complement the Internal Audit Activity*:
      a) "Each member of the internal audit activity need not be qualified in all disciplines. The internal audit activity may use external service providers or internal resources that are qualified in disciplines such as accounting, auditing, economics, finance, statistics, information technology, engineering, taxation, law, environmental affairs, and other areas as needed to meet the internal audit activity's responsibilities" (para. 1).

d. **External Service Providers**
   1) Qualified external service providers may be recruited from many sources, such as the external audit firm, an external consulting firm, or a university.
   2) However, an external service provider associated with the engagement client is unacceptable because the person would not be independent or objective.

Stop and review! You have completed the outline for this subunit. Study multiple-choice questions 14 through 16 on page 50.

2.6 DUE PROFESSIONAL CARE AND CONTINUING PROFESSIONAL DEVELOPMENT

> **Attribute Standard 1220**
> **Due Professional Care**
>
> Internal auditors must apply the care and skill expected of a reasonably prudent and competent internal auditor. Due professional care does not imply infallibility.

1. **Due Care in Practice**
    a. The IIA provides specifics about the application of due care in Practice Advisory 1220-1, *Due Professional Care*:
        1) "Exercising due professional care involves internal auditors being alert to the possibility of fraud, intentional wrongdoing, errors and omissions, inefficiency, waste, ineffectiveness, and conflicts of interest, as well as being alert to those conditions and activities where irregularities are most likely to occur" (para. 1).
        2) "Due professional care implies reasonable care and competence, not infallibility or extraordinary performance. As such, due professional care requires the internal auditor to conduct examinations and verifications to a reasonable extent. Accordingly, internal auditors cannot give absolute assurance that noncompliance or irregularities do not exist. Nevertheless, the possibility of material irregularities or noncompliance needs to be considered whenever an internal auditor undertakes an internal audit assignment" (para. 2).
    b. The following Implementation Standards provide guidance for the application of due care during assurance engagements:

Implementation Standard 1220.A1

Internal auditors must exercise due professional care by considering the:

- Extent of work needed to achieve the engagement's objectives;
- Relative complexity, materiality, or significance of matters to which assurance procedures are applied;
- Adequacy and effectiveness of governance, risk management, and control processes;
- Probability of significant errors, fraud, or noncompliance; and
- Cost of assurance in relation to potential benefits.

Implementation Standard 1220.A2

In exercising due professional care internal auditors must consider the use of technology-based audit and other data analysis techniques.

Implementation Standard 1220.A3

Internal auditors must be alert to the significant risks that might affect objectives, operations, or resources. However, assurance procedures alone, even when performed with due professional care, do not guarantee that all significant risks will be identified.

---

    c. Any unexpected results from analytical procedures should be investigated and adequately explained.
    d. Due professional care can be demonstrated if the auditor applied the care and skill of a reasonably competent and prudent internal auditor in the same or similar circumstances.

2. **Continuing Professional Development**
    a. The IIA requires internal auditors to continue expanding their knowledge and abilities throughout their careers.

Attribute Standard 1230
Continuing Professional Development

Internal auditors must enhance their knowledge, skills, and other competencies through continuing professional development.

b. More guidance is found in Practice Advisory 1230-1, *Continuing Professional Development*, which encourages internal auditors to continue their education to enhance their proficiency. Internal auditors are encouraged to

1) Stay informed about improvements and developments in internal audit standards, procedures, and techniques;
2) Pursue continuing professional education; and
3) Obtain professional certifications, such as CIA and other designations related to internal auditing.

c. Continuing professional development is the responsibility of each internal auditor. However, the CAE is uniquely able to encourage internal audit staff in this pursuit.

Stop and review! You have completed the outline for this subunit. Study multiple-choice questions 17 through 19 on page 51.

2.7 QUALITY ASSURANCE AND IMPROVEMENT PROGRAM

> **Attribute Standard 1300**
> **Quality Assurance and Improvement Program**
> The chief audit executive must develop and maintain a quality assurance and improvement program that covers all aspects of the internal audit activity.

1. **Quality Assurance and Improvement Program (QAIP)**

    a. To provide guidance for internal audit activities in the continuous examination of their processes and efforts to meet the needs of stakeholders, The IIA has issued Practice Advisory 1300-1, *Quality Assurance and Improvement Program*:

    1) "The chief audit executive (CAE) is responsible for establishing an internal audit activity whose scope of work includes the activities in the *Standards* and in the Definition of Internal Auditing. To ensure that this occurs, Standard 1300 requires that the CAE develop and maintain a quality assurance and improvement program (QAIP)" (para. 1).

    2) "The CAE is accountable for implementing processes designed to provide reasonable assurance to the various stakeholders that the internal audit activity:

    - Performs in accordance with the internal audit charter, which is consistent with the Definition of Internal Auditing, the Code of Ethics, and the *Standards*.
    - Operates in an effective and efficient manner.
    - Is perceived by those stakeholders as adding value and improving the organization's operations.

    These processes include appropriate supervision, periodic internal assessments and ongoing monitoring of quality assurance, and periodic external assessments" (para. 2).

> **Attribute Standard 1310**
> **Requirements of the Quality Assurance and Improvement Program**
> The quality assurance and improvement program must include both internal and external assessments.

SU 2: Independence, Objectivity, and Due Care   43

   b. Further guidance is provided in Practice Advisory 1310-1, *Requirements of the Quality Assurance and Improvement Program*:
      1) "A quality assurance and improvement program (QAIP) is an ongoing and periodic assessment of the entire spectrum of audit and consulting work performed by the internal audit activity. These ongoing and periodic assessments are composed of rigorous, comprehensive processes; continuous supervision and testing of internal audit and consulting work; and periodic validations of conformance with the Definition of Internal Auditing, the Code of Ethics, and the *Standards*. This also includes ongoing measurements and analyses of performance metrics (e.g., internal audit plan accomplishment, cycle time, recommendations accepted, and customer satisfaction). If the assessments' results indicate areas for improvement by the internal audit activity, the chief audit executive (CAE) will implement the improvements through the QAIP" (para. 1).
      2) "Assessments evaluate and conclude on the quality of the internal audit activity and lead to recommendations for appropriate improvements. QAIPs include an evaluation of:
         - Conformance with the Definition of Internal Auditing, the Code of Ethics, and the *Standards*, including timely corrective actions to remedy any significant instances of nonconformance.
         - Adequacy of the internal audit activity's charter, goals, objectives, policies, and procedures.
         - Contribution to the organization's governance, risk management, and control processes.
         - Compliance with applicable laws, regulations, and government or industry standards.
         - Effectiveness of continuous improvement activities and adoption of best practices.
         - The extent to which the internal audit activity adds value and improves the organization's operations" (para. 2).
      3) "The QAIP efforts also include follow-up on recommendations involving appropriate and timely modification of resources, technology, processes, and procedures" (para. 3).

Stop and review! You have completed the outline for this subunit. Study multiple-choice questions 20 and 21 on page 52.

2.8 REPORTING ON QUALITY ASSURANCE

1. **Reporting Results**
   a. Senior management and the board must be kept informed about the degree to which the internal audit activity achieves the degree of professionalism required by The IIA.

Attribute Standard 1320
Reporting on the Quality Assurance and Improvement Program

The chief audit executive must communicate the results of the quality assurance and improvement program to senior management and the board.

---

b. The IIA addresses the frequency of reporting on the QAIP in the following excerpt from the Interpretation of Standard 1320:

"To demonstrate conformance with the Definition of Internal Auditing, the Code of Ethics, and the Standards, the results of external and periodic internal assessments are communicated upon completion of such assessments and the results of ongoing monitoring are communicated at least annually."

2. **Importance of Conforming with the Standards**

a. The internal audit activity cannot claim to comply with the *Standards* unless it has a successfully functioning QAIP.

Attribute Standard 1321
Use of "Conforms with the *International Standards for the Professional Practice of Internal Auditing*"

The chief audit executive may state that the internal audit activity conforms with the *International Standards for the Professional Practice of Internal Auditing* only if the results of the quality assurance and improvement program support this statement.

---

3. **Importance of Reporting Nonconformance**

a. The internal audit activity is a crucial part of the modern complex organization's governance processes. Senior management and the board must be informed when an assessment discovers a significant degree of nonconformance.

Attribute Standard 1322
Disclosure of Nonconformance

When nonconformance with the Definition of Internal Auditing, the Code of Ethics, or the *Standards* impacts the overall scope or operation of the internal audit activity, the chief audit executive must disclose the nonconformance and the impact to senior management and the board.

---

b. Nonconformance of this type refers to the overall internal audit activity and not to specific engagements.

Stop and review! You have completed the outline for this subunit. Study multiple-choice questions 22 and 23 on page 52.

2.9 INTERNAL AND EXTERNAL ASSESSMENTS

Attribute Standard 1311
Internal Assessments

Internal assessments must include:
- Ongoing monitoring of the performance of the internal audit activity; and
- Periodic self-assessments or assessments by other persons within the organization with sufficient knowledge of internal audit practices.

---

1. **Internal Assessments**
    a. Further specifics are provided in Practice Advisory 1311-1, *Internal Assessments*:
        1) "The processes and tools used in ongoing internal assessments include:
            - Engagement supervision,
            - Checklists and procedures (e.g., in an audit and procedures manual) are being followed,
            - Feedback from audit customers and other stakeholders,
            - Selective peer reviews of workpapers by staff not involved in the respective audits,
            - Project budgets, timekeeping systems, audit plan completion, and cost recoveries, and/or
            - Analyses of other performance metrics (such as cycle time and recommendations accepted)" (para. 1).
        2) "The chief audit executive (CAE) establishes a structure for reporting results of internal assessments that maintains appropriate credibility and objectivity. Generally, those assigned responsibility for conducting ongoing and periodic reviews report to the CAE while performing the reviews and communicate results directly to the CAE" (para. 7).
        3) "At least annually, the CAE reports the results of internal assessments, necessary action plans, and their successful implementation to senior management and the board" (para. 8).

> **Attribute Standard 1312**
> **External Assessments**
>
> External assessments must be conducted at least once every five years by a qualified, independent assessor or assessment team from outside the organization. The chief audit executive must discuss with the board:
> - The form and frequency of external assessments; and
> - The qualifications and independence of the external assessor or assessment team, including any potential conflict of interest.

2. **External Assessments**
    a. External assessments provide an independent and objective evaluation of the internal audit activity's compliance with the *Standards* and Code of Ethics.
    b. The relevant guidance is provided in Practice Advisory 1312-1, *External Assessments*:
        1) "External assessments cover the entire spectrum of audit and consulting work performed by the internal audit activity and should not be limited to assessing its quality assurance and improvement program" (para. 1).
        2) "External assessments of an internal audit activity contain an expressed opinion as to the entire spectrum of assurance and consulting work performed (or that should have been performed based on the internal audit charter) by the internal audit activity, including its conformance with the Definition of Internal Auditing, the Code of Ethics, and the *Standards* and, as appropriate, includes recommendations for improvement" (para. 2).
        3) "On completion of the review, a formal communication is to be given to senior management and the board" (para. 3).
        4) "Individuals who perform the external assessment are free from any obligation to, or interest in, the organization whose internal audit activity is the subject of the external assessment or the personnel of such organization" (para. 5).

5) "The external assessment consists of a broad scope of coverage that includes the following elements of the internal audit activity:

- Conformance with the Definition of Internal Auditing; the Code of Ethics; and the *Standards*; and the internal audit activity's charter, plans, policies, procedures, practices, and applicable legislative and regulatory requirements,
- Expectations of the internal audit activity expressed by the board, senior management, and operational managers,
- Integration of the internal audit activity into the organization's governance process, including the relationships between and among the key groups involved in the process,
- Tools and techniques employed by the internal audit activity,
- Mix of knowledge, experience, and disciplines within the staff, including staff focus on process improvement, and
- Determination as to whether or not the internal audit activity adds value and improves the organization's operations" (para. 10).

c. External assessors must have no real or apparent **conflict of interest** due to current or past relationships with the organization.

1) Matters relating to independence include conflicts of **former employees** or of **firms** providing (a) the financial statement audit, (b) significant consulting services, or (c) assistance to the internal audit activity.
2) An individual in another part of the organization or in a related organization (e.g., a parent or an affiliate) is not independent.
3) **Peer review** among three unrelated organizations (but not between two) may satisfy the independence requirement.
4) Given concerns about independence, one or more **independent individuals** may provide separate validation.

Stop and review! You have completed the outline for this subunit. Study multiple-choice questions 24 and 25 on page 53.

QUESTIONS

2.1 Independence of the Internal Audit Activity

1. The reporting relationship within the organization's management structure that facilitates the day-to-day operations of the internal audit activity is

A. Administrative reporting.
B. Financial reporting.
C. Management reporting.
D. Functional reporting.

Answer (A) is correct.
REQUIRED: The type of reporting that facilitates the day-to-day operations of the internal audit activity.
DISCUSSION: Administrative reporting is the reporting relationship within the organization's management structure that facilitates the day-to-day operations of the internal audit activity. Administrative reporting typically includes (1) budgeting and management accounting; (2) human resource administration, including personnel evaluations and compensation; (3) internal communications and information flows; and (4) administration of the organization's internal policies and procedures (PA 1110-1, para. 4).
Answer (B) is incorrect. Financial reporting focuses primarily on reporting information about performance provided by measures of earnings and its components. Answer (C) is incorrect. A form of management reporting is issuance of financial statements, which report on the organization's performance to external parties. Answer (D) is incorrect. Functional reporting involves reporting to the board to facilitate the internal audit activity's independence.

SU 2: Independence, Objectivity, and Due Care

2. The CAE should report functionally to the board. The board is responsible for which of the following activities?

1. Internal communication and information flows
2. Approval of the internal audit risk assessment and related audit plan
3. Approval of annual compensation and salary adjustments for the CAE

    A. 1 and 2 only.
    B. 2 and 3 only.
    C. 1 and 3 only.
    D. 1, 2, and 3.

Answer (B) is correct.
    REQUIRED: The activities for which the board is responsible.
    DISCUSSION: Organizational independence is effectively achieved when the CAE reports functionally to the board. Examples of functional reporting to the board involve the board

- Approving the internal audit charter
- Approving the risk-based internal audit plan
- Receiving communications from the CAE on the internal audit activity's performance
- Approving decisions regarding the appointment and removal of the CAE
- Making appropriate inquiries of management and the CAE to determine whether there are inappropriate scope or resource limitations (Inter. Attr. Std. 1110)

    Answer (A) is incorrect. Internal communication and information flows are administrative reporting items. Administrative reporting is the reporting relationship within the management structure. Furthermore, functional reporting also involves the board's approval of annual compensation and salary adjustments for the CAE. Answer (C) is incorrect. Internal communication and information flows are administrative reporting items. Moreover, functional reporting also involves the board's approval of the internal audit risk assessment and related audit plan. Answer (D) is incorrect. Internal communication and information flows are administrative reporting items.

3. The optimal administrative reporting line of the CAE is to

    A. The audit committee.
    B. Line management.
    C. Board of directors.
    D. CEO or equivalent.

Answer (D) is correct.
    REQUIRED: The individual or group to whom the CAE should report administratively.
    DISCUSSION: Administrative reporting is the reporting relationship within the organization's management structure that facilitates the day-to-day operations of the internal audit activity. Administrative reporting typically includes (1) budgeting and management accounting; (2) human resource administration, including personnel evaluations and compensation; (3) internal communications and information flows; and (4) administration of the organization's internal policies and procedures (PA 1110-1, para. 4). Reporting functionally to the board and administratively to the CEO facilitates organizational independence (PA 1110-1, para. 2).
    Answer (A) is incorrect. Functional reporting is to the board. Answer (B) is incorrect. Administrative reporting preferably is to the CEO. Answer (C) is incorrect. The CAE must communicate and interact directly with the board. Functional reporting needs to be to the board.

2.2 Objectivity of Internal Auditors

4. Assessing individual objectivity of internal auditors is the responsibility of

    A. The chief executive officer.
    B. The board.
    C. The audit committee.
    D. The chief audit executive.

Answer (D) is correct.
    REQUIRED: The party responsible for assessing the individual objectivity of internal auditors.
    DISCUSSION: The CAE must establish policies and procedures to assess the objectivity of individual internal auditors.

5. Internal auditors should be objective. Objectivity

   A. Requires internal auditors not to subordinate their judgment on audit matters to that of others.
   B. Is required only in assurance engagements.
   C. Is freedom from threats to the ability to perform audit work without bias.
   D. Prohibits internal auditors from providing consulting services relating to operations for which they had previous responsibility.

Answer (A) is correct.
REQUIRED: The true statement regarding objectivity.
DISCUSSION: Objectivity is "an unbiased mental attitude that allows internal auditors to perform engagements in such a manner that they believe in their work product and that no quality compromises are made. Objectivity requires that internal auditors do not subordinate their judgment on audit matters to others" (The IIA Glossary).
Answer (B) is incorrect. Objectivity also is required in a consulting engagement. Answer (C) is incorrect. Independence is freedom from threats to the ability to perform audit work without bias. Answer (D) is incorrect. Internal auditors may provide consulting services relating to operations for which they had previous responsibility.

6. The CAE bears the responsibility to do which of the following?

   A. Assess the level of independence of the board.
   B. Assess the level of knowledge, skills, and competencies of the chief financial officer.
   C. Foster collective objectivity.
   D. Foster individual objectivity.

Answer (D) is correct.
REQUIRED: The responsibility of the chief audit executive.
DISCUSSION: The CAE must establish policies and procedures to assess the objectivity of individual internal auditors.
Answer (A) is incorrect. Independence is a quality of the internal audit activity, not the board. Answer (B) is incorrect. The concept of knowledge, skills, and competencies applies to individual internal auditors. Answer (C) is incorrect. Objectivity is an individual, not a collective, quality.

7. Which of the following actions is required of the CAE in regard to the objectivity of internal auditors?

   A. Maximize.
   B. Prioritize.
   C. Manage.
   D. Assess.

Answer (D) is correct.
REQUIRED: The CAE's responsibility with regard to internal auditor objectivity.
DISCUSSION: The CAE must establish policies and procedures to assess the objectivity of individual internal auditors.

8. Maintaining individual objectivity of internal auditors is the responsibility of

   A. The chairperson of the board of directors.
   B. The chairperson of the audit committee.
   C. The external assessment team.
   D. The chief audit executive.

Answer (D) is correct.
REQUIRED: The party(ies) responsible for maintaining the objectivity of internal auditors.
DISCUSSION: The responsibility rests with the CAE and with internal auditors themselves to maintain a sense of objectivity.

2.3 Impairment to Independence and Objectivity

9. The internal audit activity should be free to audit and report on any activity that also reports to its administrative head if it considers such coverage to be appropriate for its audit plan. Any limitation in scope or reporting of results of these activities needs to be brought to the attention of the

   A. Chief executive officer.
   B. Chief financial officer.
   C. External auditor.
   D. Board.

Answer (D) is correct.
REQUIRED: The person or group to be notified when a scope or reporting limitation exists.
DISCUSSION: A scope limitation, along with its potential effect needs to be communicated, preferably in writing, to the board (PA 1130-1, para. 3).
Answer (A) is incorrect. The CEO may be the administrative head of the internal audit activity. Answer (B) is incorrect. The CFO is also responsible for the organization's accounting functions. Thus, when a scope or reporting limitation exists, the CFO may be responsible for it. Answer (C) is incorrect. The external auditor should not be notified unless the board believes it is necessary.

SU 2: Independence, Objectivity, and Due Care

10. An internal auditor has recently received an offer from the manager of the marketing department of a weekend's free use of his beachfront condominium. No engagement is currently being conducted in the marketing department, and none is scheduled. The internal auditor

- A. Should reject the offer and report it to the appropriate supervisor.
- B. May accept the offer because its value is immaterial.
- C. May accept the offer because no engagement is being conducted or planned.
- D. May accept the offer if approved by the appropriate supervisor.

Answer (A) is correct.
REQUIRED: The true statement about the offer of a gift by a nonclient member of the organization.
DISCUSSION: An internal auditor is not to accept fees, gifts, or entertainment from an employee, client, customer, supplier, or business associate. Accepting a fee or gift may imply that the auditor's objectivity has been impaired. Even though an engagement is not being conducted in the applicable area at that time, a future engagement may result in the appearance of impairment of objectivity. Thus, no consideration should be given to the engagement status as justification for receiving fees or gifts. The receipt of promotional items (such as pens, calendars, or samples) that are available to the general public and have minimal value do not hinder internal auditors' professional judgments (PA 1130-1, para. 4). Impairment of independence or objectivity, in fact or appearance, must be disclosed to appropriate parties (Attr. Std. 1130).
Answer (B) is incorrect. The value of a weekend vacation is not immaterial. Answer (C) is incorrect. The status of engagements is not a justification for receiving fees or gifts. Answer (D) is incorrect. A supervisor may not approve unethical behavior.

11. George is the new internal auditor for XYZ Corporation. George was in charge of payroll for XYZ just 10 months ago. Performing what services in regard to payroll is considered an impairment of independence or objectivity if performed by George?

- A. Consulting services.
- B. Assurance services.
- C. Assurance or consulting services.
- D. Neither assurance nor consulting services.

Answer (B) is correct.
REQUIRED: The services that will impair independence or objectivity.
DISCUSSION: Objectivity is presumed to be impaired if an internal auditor provides assurance services for an activity for which the internal auditor had responsibility within the previous year (PA 1130.A1-1, para. 1). Thus, if George provides assurance services for payroll, his objectivity is presumed to be impaired. However, internal auditors may provide consulting services relating to operations for which they had previous responsibilities (Impl. Std. 1130.C1).
Answer (A) is incorrect. Providing assurance services but not consulting services regarding payroll will impair the independence or objectivity of George. Answer (C) is incorrect. Providing assurance services regarding payroll will impair the independence or objectivity of George. Answer (D) is incorrect. Providing consulting services regarding payroll will not impair the objectivity of George.

2.4 Auditor Proficiency

12. Your organization has selected you to develop an internal audit activity. Your approach will most likely be to hire

- A. Internal auditors, each of whom possesses all the skills required to handle all engagements.
- B. Inexperienced personnel and train them the way the organization wants them trained.
- C. Degreed accountants because most internal audit work is accounting related.
- D. Internal auditors who collectively have the knowledge and skills needed to perform the responsibilities of the internal audit activity.

Answer (D) is correct.
REQUIRED: The personnel required by an internal audit activity.
DISCUSSION: The internal audit activity collectively must possess or obtain the knowledge, skills, and other competencies needed to perform its responsibilities (Attr. Std. 1210).
Answer (A) is incorrect. The scope of internal auditing is so broad that one individual cannot have the requisite expertise in all areas. Answer (B) is incorrect. The internal audit activity should have personnel with various skill levels to permit appropriate matching of internal auditors with varying engagement complexities. Furthermore, experienced internal auditors should be available to train and supervise less experienced staff members. Answer (C) is incorrect. Many skills are needed in internal auditing. For example, computer skills are needed in engagements involving information technology.

13. Internal auditors must possess the knowledge, skills, and other competencies essential to the performance of their individual responsibilities. Consequently, all internal auditors should be proficient in applying

A. Internal auditing standards.
B. Quantitative methods.
C. Management principles.
D. Structured systems analysis.

Answer (A) is correct.
REQUIRED: The component of professional competence in which all internal auditors should be proficient.
DISCUSSION: All internal auditors should be proficient in applying internal auditing standards, procedures, and techniques required in performing engagements. Proficiency means the ability to apply knowledge to situations likely to be encountered and to deal with them without extensive recourse to technical research and assistance (PA 1210-1, para. 1).
Answer (B) is incorrect. Internal auditors must have an appreciation of, not proficiency in, the fundamentals of business subjects such as quantitative methods. Answer (C) is incorrect. Internal auditors must have an understanding of, not proficiency in, management principles to recognize and evaluate the materiality and significance of deviations from good business practices. Answer (D) is incorrect. Internal auditors must have an appreciation of, not proficiency in, the fundamentals of business subjects such as accounting, economics, commercial law, taxation, finance, quantitative methods, information technology, risk management, and fraud.

2.5 Internal Audit Resources

14. Which one of the following is responsible for determining the appropriate levels of education and experience needed for the internal audit staff?

A. Human resource manager.
B. Chief audit executive.
C. Chief executive officer.
D. Treasurer.

Answer (B) is correct.
REQUIRED: The person responsible for determining the internal audit knowledge, skills, and other competencies.
DISCUSSION: The CAE must ensure that the internal audit activity is able to fulfill its responsibilities. The CAE must determine the appropriate levels of education and experience needed for the internal audit staff to fulfill that responsibility.
Answer (A) is incorrect. Hiring practices are an essential part of understanding the internal audit staff's background, but the human resource manager is not responsible for determining the appropriate levels of education and experience needed for the internal audit staff. Answer (C) is incorrect. The chief executive officer is not directly responsible for determining the appropriate levels of education and experience needed for the internal audit staff. Answer (D) is incorrect. The treasurer is not responsible for determining the appropriate levels of education and experience needed for the internal audit staff.

15. All of the following will help the CAE identify the available knowledge, skills, and competencies of the internal audit staff **except**

A. Hiring practices.
B. Periodic skills assessment.
C. External service provider.
D. Staff performance appraisals.

Answer (C) is correct.
REQUIRED: The item that does not help the CAE identify internal audit resources.
DISCUSSION: External service providers are used when the internal audit staff does not have the necessary knowledge, skills, and competencies to fulfill the responsibilities of the internal audit activity.
Answer (A) is incorrect. Hiring practices are an essential part of understanding the background of the internal audit staff. Answer (B) is incorrect. The CAE should conduct periodic skills assessments to determine the specific resources available. Answer (D) is incorrect. Staff performance appraisals are completed at the end of any major internal audit engagement. These appraisals help the CAE assess future training needs and current staff abilities.

16. At a minimum, how often should the skills of the internal audit staff be assessed?

A. Annually.
B. Every 5 years.
C. Quarterly.
D. Semi-annually.

Answer (A) is correct.
REQUIRED: The frequency with which assessments should be performed.
DISCUSSION: The CAE should conduct periodic skills assessments to determine the specific resources available. Assessments should be performed at least annually.
Answer (B) is incorrect. Periodic skills assessments should be performed more frequently than every 5 years. Answer (C) is incorrect. Periodic skills assessments do not need to be performed quarterly. Answer (D) is incorrect. Periodic skills assessments do not need to be performed semiannually.

2.6 Due Professional Care and Continuing Professional Development

17. An internal auditor judged an item to be immaterial when planning an assurance engagement. However, the assurance engagement may still include the item if it is subsequently determined that

A. Sufficient staff is available.
B. Adverse effects related to the item are likely to occur.
C. Related information is reliable.
D. Miscellaneous income is affected.

Answer (B) is correct.
REQUIRED: The basis for including an item in the engagement although it is immaterial.
DISCUSSION: Internal auditors must exercise due professional care by considering the relative complexity, materiality, or significance of matters to which assurance procedures are applied (Impl. Std. 1220.A1). Materiality judgments are made in the light of all the circumstances and involve qualitative as well as quantitative considerations. Moreover, internal auditors also must consider the interplay of risk with materiality. Consequently, engagement effort may be required for a quantitatively immaterial item if adverse effects are likely to occur, for example, a material contingent liability arising from an illegal payment that is otherwise immaterial.
Answer (A) is incorrect. In the absence of other considerations, devoting additional engagement effort to an immaterial item is inefficient. Answer (C) is incorrect. Additional engagement procedures might not be needed if related information is reliable. Answer (D) is incorrect. The item is more likely to be included if it affects recurring income items rather than miscellaneous income.

18. Due professional care calls for

A. Detailed reviews of all transactions related to a particular function.
B. Infallibility and extraordinary performance when the system of internal control is known to be weak.
C. Consideration of the possibility of material irregularities during every engagement.
D. Testing in sufficient detail to give absolute assurance that noncompliance does not exist.

Answer (C) is correct.
REQUIRED: The implication of due care.
DISCUSSION: Due care implies reasonable care and competence, not infallibility or extraordinary performance. Due care requires the internal auditor to conduct examinations and verifications to a reasonable extent, but does not require detailed reviews of all transactions. Accordingly, internal auditors cannot give absolute assurance that noncompliance or irregularities do not exist. Nevertheless, the possibility of material irregularities or noncompliance should be considered whenever an internal auditor undertakes an internal auditing assignment (PA 1220-1, para. 2).
Answer (A) is incorrect. Detailed reviews of all transactions are not required. Answer (B) is incorrect. Reasonable care and skill, not infallibility or extraordinary performance, are necessary. Answer (D) is incorrect. Only reasonable, not absolute, assurance can be given.

19. A certified internal auditor performed an assurance engagement to review a department store's cash function. Which of the following actions will be deemed lacking in due professional care?

A. Organizational records were reviewed to determine whether all employees who handle cash receipts and disbursements were bonded.
B. A flowchart of the entire cash function was developed, but only a sample of transactions was tested.
C. The final engagement communication included a well-supported recommendation for the reduction in staff, although it was known that such a reduction would adversely affect morale.
D. Because of a highly developed system of internal control over the cash function, the final engagement communication assured senior management that no irregularities existed.

Answer (D) is correct.
REQUIRED: The action deemed lacking in due professional care.
DISCUSSION: Internal auditors cannot give absolute assurance that noncompliance or irregularities do not exist (PA 1220-1, para. 2).
Answer (A) is incorrect. Reviewing records to determine whether all employees who handle cash receipts and disbursements were bonded is a standard procedure. Answer (B) is incorrect. Sampling is permissible. Detailed reviews of all transactions are often not required or feasible. Answer (C) is incorrect. In exercising due professional care, internal auditors should be alert to inefficiency.

2.7 Quality Assurance and Improvement Program

20. Assessment of a quality assurance and improvement program should include evaluation of all of the following **except**

A. Adequacy of the oversight of the work of external auditors.
B. Conformance with the *Standards* and Code of Ethics.
C. Adequacy of the internal audit activity's charter.
D. Contribution to the organization's governance processes.

Answer (A) is correct.
REQUIRED: The element not required in the assessment of a QAIP.
DISCUSSION: Oversight of the work of external auditors, including coordination with the internal audit activity, is the responsibility of the board (PA 2050-1, para. 1). It is not within the scope of the process for monitoring and assessing the quality program.
Answer (B) is incorrect. Conformance with the Definition of Internal Auditing, *Standards*, and Code of Ethics, including timely corrective actions to remedy any significant instances of nonconformance, is an element of the assessment of a quality program. Answer (C) is incorrect. Adequacy of the internal audit activity's charter, goals, objectives, policies, and procedures is an element of the assessment of a quality program. Answer (D) is incorrect. Contribution to the organization's governance, risk management, and control processes is an element of the assessment of a quality program.

21. The internal audit activity's quality assurance and improvement program is the responsibility of

A. External auditors.
B. The chief audit executive.
C. The board.
D. The audit committee.

Answer (B) is correct.
REQUIRED: The individual(s) responsible for the quality assurance reviews of the internal audit activity.
DISCUSSION: The chief audit executive must develop and maintain a quality assurance and improvement program that covers all aspects of the internal audit activity (Attr. Std. 1300).
Answer (A) is incorrect. External auditors may perform an external assessment, but the CAE is responsible for it. Answer (C) is incorrect. The CAE may report results to the board, but the program is the CAE's responsibility. Answer (D) is incorrect. The CAE may report results to the audit committee, but the program is the CAE's responsibility.

2.8 Reporting on Quality Assurance

22. At what minimal required frequency does the chief audit executive report the results of internal assessments in the form of ongoing monitoring to senior management and the board?

A. Monthly.
B. Quarterly.
C. Annually.
D. Biennially.

Answer (C) is correct.
REQUIRED: The frequency of reporting the results of internal assessments.
DISCUSSION: To demonstrate conformance with the mandatory IIA guidance, the results of external and periodic internal assessments are communicated upon completion of such assessments and the results of ongoing monitoring are communicated at least annually (Inter. Std. 1320).

23. Following an external assessment of the internal audit activity, who is (are) responsible for communicating the results to the board?

A. Internal auditors.
B. Audit committee.
C. Chief audit executive.
D. External auditors.

Answer (C) is correct.
REQUIRED: The individual or group responsible for communicating the results of external assessments to the board.
DISCUSSION: The chief audit executive must communicate the results of the QAIP to senior management and the board (Attr. Std. 1320).
Answer (A) is incorrect. The chief audit executive (not internal auditors) is responsible for communicating the results of external assessments to the board. Answer (B) is incorrect. The chief audit executive (not the audit committee) is responsible for communicating the results of external assessments to the board. Answer (D) is incorrect. The chief audit executive (not external auditors) is responsible for communicating the results of external assessments to the board.

2.9 Internal and External Assessments

24. As a part of a quality program, internal assessment teams most likely will examine which of the following to evaluate the quality of engagement planning and documentation for individual engagements?

A. Written engagement work programs.
B. Project assignment documentation.
C. Weekly status reports.
D. The long-range engagement work schedule.

Answer (A) is correct.
REQUIRED: The item(s) most likely examined to evaluate the quality of planning and documentation for individual engagements.
DISCUSSION: Internal assessments must include ongoing monitoring of the performance of the internal audit activity and periodic self-assessments or assessments by other persons within the organization with sufficient knowledge of internal auditing practices (Attr. Std. 1311). The processes and tools used in ongoing internal assessments include, among other things, selective peer reviews of working papers by staff not involved in the respective audits (PA 1311-1, para. 1).
Answer (B) is incorrect. Project assignment documentation contains less relevant information for assessment purposes than work programs. Answer (C) is incorrect. Status reports do not bear directly on planning. Answer (D) is incorrect. The long-range engagement work schedule does not relate to planning and documentation for individual engagements.

25. An external assessment of an internal audit activity contains an expressed opinion. The opinion applies

A. Only to the internal audit activity's conformance with the *Standards*.
B. Only to the effectiveness of the internal auditing coverage.
C. Only to the adequacy of internal control.
D. To the entire spectrum of assurance and consulting work.

Answer (D) is correct.
REQUIRED: The subject of the opinion expressed in a communication after an external assessment of a quality program.
DISCUSSION: External assessments of an internal audit activity contain an expressed opinion as to the entire spectrum of assurance and consulting work performed (or that should have been performed under its charter), including (but not limited to) conformance with the Definition of Internal Auditing, the Code of Ethics, and the *Standards*. An external assessment also includes, as appropriate, recommendations for improvement (PA 1312-1, para. 2).
Answer (A) is incorrect. An opinion is expressed on all assurance and consulting work performed (or that should have been performed under its charter). Answer (B) is incorrect. The scope of an external assessment extends to more than the effectiveness of the internal auditing coverage. Answer (C) is incorrect. An external assessment addresses the internal audit activity, not the adequacy of the organization's controls.

Practice even more exam-emulating questions in **Gleim CIA Test Prep**!

GLEIM
What makes us different?

- ✓ Materials written by experts
- ✓ Commitment to excellent customer care
- ✓ Tried and true review systems and study plans
- ✓ 40-year history of helping candidates pass their exams.
- ✓ All these things and more make Gleim the experts in CIA Review.

Call **800.874.5346** or visit **gleim.com/GoCIA** to learn more.

STUDY UNIT THREE
CONTROL FRAMEWORKS AND FRAUD

(19 pages of outline)

3.1	Control Frameworks	55
3.2	Enterprise Risk Management	65
3.3	Risk Management Processes	68
3.4	Fraud -- Nature, Prevention, and Detection	70
3.5	Fraud -- Indicators	72

This study unit is the first of two covering **Section II: Internal Control / Risk** from The IIA's CIA Exam Syllabus. This section makes up 25% to 35% of Part 1 of the CIA exam and is tested at the **awareness level**. The relevant portion of the syllabus is highlighted below. (The complete syllabus is in Appendix B.)

II. **INTERNAL CONTROL / RISK (25%–35%)**
   A. Types of Controls (e.g., preventive, detective, input, output, etc.)
   B. Management Control Techniques

   C. **Internal Control Framework Characteristics and Use (e.g., COSO, Cadbury)**
      1. Develop and implement an organization-wide risk and control framework
   D. **Alternative Control Frameworks**
   E. **Risk Vocabulary and Concepts**
   F. **Fraud Risk Awareness**
      1. Types of fraud
      2. Fraud red flags

3.1 CONTROL FRAMEWORKS

1. **Available Control Frameworks**

   a. Several bodies have published control frameworks that provide a comprehensive means of ensuring that the organization has considered all relevant aspects of internal control.

   1) The use of a particular model or control design not mentioned here may be specified by regulatory or legal requirements.
   2) Some of the better-known frameworks are described below and on the following page.

   b. **United States**

   1) *Internal Control – Integrated Framework* is widely accepted as the standard for the design and operation of internal control systems.
   2) The Watergate investigations of 1973-74 revealed that U.S. companies were bribing government officials, politicians, and political parties in foreign countries. The result was the Foreign Corrupt Practices Act of 1977.
   3) The private sector also responded by forming the National Commission on Fraudulent Financial Reporting (NCFFR) in 1985.

      a) The NCFFR is known as the Treadway Commission because James C. Treadway was its first chair.
      b) The Treadway Commission was originally sponsored and funded by five professional accounting organizations based in the United States.

             c) This group of five became known as the Committee of Sponsoring Organizations of the Treadway Commission (COSO).
             d) The Commission recommended that this group of five organizations cooperate in creating guidance for internal control.
        4) The result was *Internal Control – Integrated Framework*, published in 1992, which was modified in 1994 and again in 2013.
   c. **Canada**
        1) *Guidance on Control* (commonly referred to as CoCo based on its original title *Criteria of Control*), published by the Canadian Institute of Chartered Accountants (CICA).
   d. **United Kingdom**
        1) *Internal Control: Guidance for Directors on the Combined Code* (commonly referred to as the Turnbull Report after Nigel Turnbull, chair of the committee that drafted the report), published by the Financial Reporting Council (FRC) of the UK and re-released as *Internal Control: Revised Guide for Directors on the Combined Code*.
        2) The UK Committee on the Financial Aspects of Corporate Governance (known informally as the Cadbury Committee after its chairman Sir Adrian Cadbury) issued its report about the same time as the Treadway Commission in the U.S.
        3) It was subsequently blended with the reports of two other organizations. The resulting *Combined Code* includes such recommendations for sound governance as requiring that the CEO and chairperson be separate individuals.
   e. **Information Technology**
        1) COBIT is the best-known framework specifically for IT controls. When originally published, COBIT was an acronym for *Control Objectives for Information and Related Technology*. COBIT 5 is the most recent version.
        2) *Electronic Systems Assurance and Control* (eSAC), published by The Institute of Internal Auditors Research Foundation, is an alternative control model for IT.
2. **COSO Framework**
   a. **Definition of Internal Control**
        1) The COSO model defines internal control as follows:

            Internal control is a process, effected by an entity's board of directors, management, and other personnel, designed to provide reasonable assurance regarding the achievement of objectives relating to operations, reporting, and compliance.

        2) Thus, internal control is
             a) Intended to achieve three classes of objectives
             b) An ongoing process
             c) Effected by people at all organizational levels, e.g., the board, management, and all other employees
             d) Able to provide reasonable, but not absolute, assurance
             e) Adaptable to an entity's structure

b. **Objectives**

1) The three classes of objectives direct organizations to the different (but overlapping) elements of control.

   a) **Operations**

      i) Operations objectives relate to achieving the entity's mission.
         - Appropriate objectives include improving (1) financial performance, (2) productivity, (3) quality, (4) innovation, and (5) customer satisfaction.

      ii) Operations objectives also include **safeguarding of assets**.
         - Objectives related to protecting and preserving assets assist in risk assessment and development of mitigating controls.
         - Avoidance of waste, inefficiency, and bad business decisions relates to broader objectives than safeguarding of assets.

   b) **Reporting**

      i) To make sound decisions, stakeholders must have reliable, timely, and transparent financial information.

      ii) Reports may be prepared for use by the organization and stakeholders.

      iii) Objectives may relate to
         - Financial and nonfinancial reporting.
         - Internal or external reporting.

   c) **Compliance**

      i) Entities are subject to laws, rules, and regulations that set minimum standards of conduct.
         - Examples include taxation, environmental protection, and employee relations.
         - Compliance with internal policies and procedures is an operational matter.

   d) The following is a useful memory aid for the COSO classes of objectives:

      O = **O**perations
      R = **R**eporting
      C = **C**ompliance

2) Achievement of Objectives

   a) An internal control system is more likely to provide reasonable assurance of achieving the reporting and compliance objectives than the operational objectives.

   b) Reporting and compliance objectives are responses to standards established by external parties, such as regulators.

      i) Thus, achieving these objectives depends on actions almost entirely within the entity's control.

   c) However, operational effectiveness may not be within the entity's control because it is affected by human judgment and many external factors.

c. **Components of Internal Control**

1) Supporting the organization in its efforts to achieve objectives are the following five components of internal control:

    a) Control environment
    b) Risk assessment
    c) Control activities
    d) Information and communication
    e) Monitoring

2) A useful memory aid for the COSO components of internal control is, "Controls stop **CRIME**."

    C = **C**ontrol activities
    R = **R**isk assessment
    I = **I**nformation and communication
    M = **M**onitoring
    E = Control **e**nvironment

d. **Control Environment**

1) The control environment is a set of standards, processes, and structures that pervasively affects the system of internal control. Five principles relate to the control environment.

    a) The organization demonstrates a commitment to **integrity and ethical values** by

        i) Setting the tone at the top. Through words and actions, the board of directors and management communicate their attitude toward integrity and ethical values.
        ii) Establishing standards of conduct. The board and management create expectations that should be understood at all organizational levels and by outside service providers and business partners.
        iii) Evaluating the performance of individuals and teams based on the established standards of conduct.
        iv) Correcting deviations in a timely and consistent manner.

    b) The board demonstrates independence from management and exercises **oversight** for internal control. The board

        i) Establishes oversight responsibility. The board identifies and accepts its oversight responsibilities.
        ii) Applies relevant experience by defining, maintaining, and periodically evaluating the skills and expertise needed among its members to ask difficult questions of management and take appropriate actions.
        iii) Operates independently. The board includes enough members who are independent and objective in evaluations and decision making.

            • For example, in some jurisdictions, all members of the audit committee must be outside directors.

        iv) Provides oversight. The board is responsible for oversight of management's design, implementation, and conduct of internal control.

c) Management establishes, with board oversight, **structures, reporting lines, and appropriate authorities and responsibilities**. Management
    i) Considers all structures of the entity. Variables considered in establishing organizational structures include the following:
        - Nature of the business
        - Size and geographic scope of the entity
        - Risks, some of them outsourced, and connections with outside service providers and partners
        - Assignment of authority to different management levels
        - Definition of reporting lines
        - Reporting requirements
    ii) Establishes and evaluates reporting lines. The trend in corporate governance has been to allow employees closer to day-to-day operations to make decisions.
    iii) Designs, assigns, and limits authorities and responsibilities.
d) The organization demonstrates a **commitment to attract, develop, and retain competent individuals** in alignment with objectives.
    i) Policies and practices reflect expectations of competence. Internal control is strengthened when management specifies what competencies are needed for particular jobs.
    ii) The board and management evaluate competence and address shortcomings. Employees and outside service providers have the appropriate skills and knowledge to perform their jobs.
    iii) The organization attracts, develops, and retains individuals. The organization is committed to hiring individuals who are competent and have integrity. Ongoing training and mentoring are necessary to adapt employees to the control requirements of a changing environment.
    iv) Senior management and the board plan and prepare for succession.
e) The **organization holds individuals accountable** for their internal control responsibilities in pursuit of objectives. Management and the board
    i) Enforce accountability through structures, authorities, and responsibilities
    ii) Establish performance measures, incentives, and rewards
    iii) Evaluate performance measures, incentives, and rewards for ongoing relevance
    iv) Consider excessive pressures
    v) Evaluate performance and reward or discipline individuals

e. **Risk Assessment**
  1) The risk assessment process encompasses an assessment of the risks themselves and the need to manage organizational change. This process is a basis for determining how the risks should be managed. Four principles relate to risk assessment.
      a) The organization **specifies objectives** with sufficient clarity to enable the identification and assessment of risks relating to five types of objectives.
          i) Operations
          ii) External financial reporting
          iii) External nonfinancial reporting
          iv) Internal reporting
          v) Compliance

b) The organization **identifies** risks to the achievement of its objectives across the entity and **analyzes** risks to determine how the risks should be managed. Management must focus carefully on risks at all levels of the entity and take the necessary actions to manage them.

c) The organization considers the potential for fraud in **assessing fraud risks** to the achievement of objectives. The organization must

   i) Consider various types of fraud,
   ii) Assess incentives and pressures,
   iii) Assess opportunities, and
   iv) Assess attitudes and rationalizations.

d) The organization **identifies and assesses changes** that could significantly affect the system of internal control.

   i) Significant changes could occur in an organization's external environment, business model, and leadership. Thus, internal controls must be adapted to the entity's changing circumstances.

f. **Control Activities**

1) These policies and procedures help ensure that management directives are carried out. Whether automated or manual, they are applied at various levels of the entity and stages of processes. They may be preventive or detective, and segregation of duties is usually present. Three principles relate to control activities.

   a) The organization **selects and develops control activities** that contribute to the mitigation of risks to the achievement of objectives to acceptable levels.

   b) The organization selects and develops **general control activities** over technology to support the achievement of objectives.

   c) The organization **deploys control activities** through **policies** that establish what is expected and **procedures** that put policies into action.

g. **Information and Communication**

1) Information systems enable the organization to obtain, generate, use, and communicate information to (a) maintain accountability and (b) measure and review performance. Three principles relate to information and communication.

   a) The organization obtains or generates and uses **relevant, quality information** to support the functioning of internal control.

   b) The organization **internally communicates** information, including objectives and responsibilities for internal control, necessary to support the function of internal control.

   c) The organization **communicates with external parties** regarding matters affecting the functioning of internal control.

h. **Monitoring Activities**

1) Control systems and the way controls are applied change over time. Monitoring is a process that assesses the quality of internal control performance over time to ensure that controls continue to meet the needs of the organization. The following are two principles related to monitoring activities:

   a) The organization selects, develops, and performs **ongoing or separate evaluations (or both)** to determine whether the components of internal control are present and functioning.

   b) The organization **evaluates and communicates control deficiencies** in a timely manner.

i. **Relationship of Objectives, Components, and Organizational Structure**

1) The COSO model may be displayed as a cube with rows, slices, and columns. The rows are the five components, the slices are the three objectives, and the columns represent an entity's organizational structure.

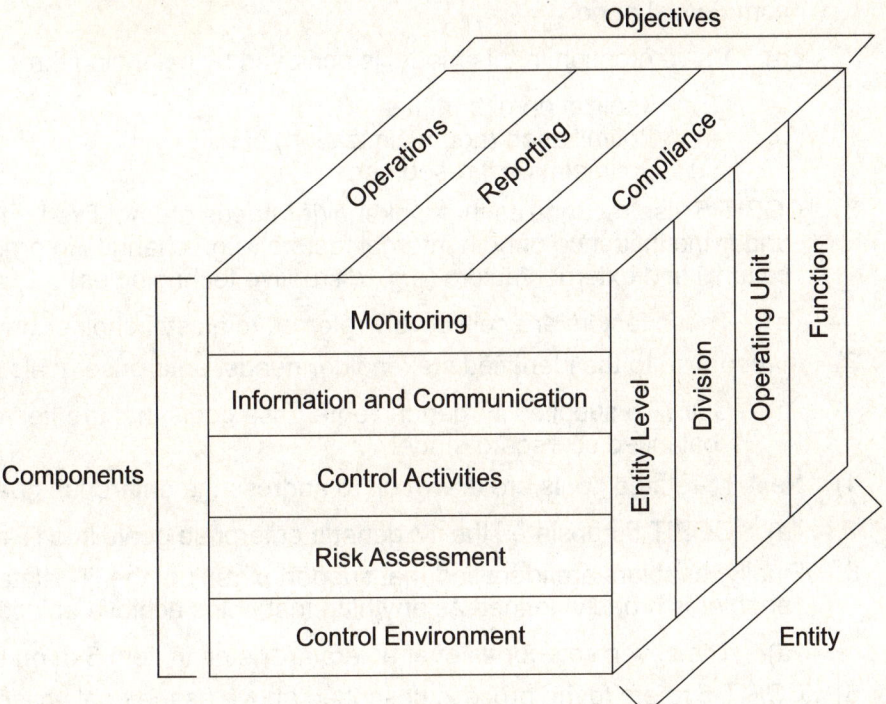

Figure 3-1

3. **CoCo Model**

a. The CoCo model is thought to be more suited for internal auditing purposes. It consists of 20 criteria grouped into 4 components:

1) Purpose
2) Commitment
3) Capability
4) Monitoring and Learning

b. The following is a useful memory aid for the components of the CoCo model:

P = Purpose	**P**olice
C = Commitment	**C**an
C = Capability	**C**atch
M = Monitoring	**M**any
L = Learning	**L**awbreakers

4. **COBIT -- A Framework for IT Governance and Management**

a. COBIT is the best-known control and governance framework that addresses information technology.

1) In its original version, COBIT was focused on controls for specific IT processes.
2) Over the years, information technology has gradually come to pervade every facet of the organization's operations. IT can no longer be viewed as a function distinct from other aspects of the organization.

a) The evolution of COBIT has reflected this change in the nature of IT within the organization.

5. **COBIT 5 -- Five Key Principles**
   a. **Principle 1: Meeting Stakeholder Needs**
      1) COBIT 5 asserts that value creation is the most basic stakeholder need. Thus, the creation of stakeholder value is the fundamental goal of any enterprise, commercial or not.
         a) Value creation in this model is achieved by balancing three components:
            i) Realization of benefits
            ii) Optimization (not minimization) of risk
            iii) Optimal use of resources
      2) COBIT 5 also recognizes that stakeholder needs are not fixed. They evolve under the influence of both internal factors (e.g., changes in organizational culture) and external factors (e.g., disruptive technologies).
         a) These factors are collectively referred to as stakeholder drivers.
      3) In response to the identified stakeholder needs, enterprise goals are established.
         a) COBIT 5 supplies 17 generic enterprise goals that are tied directly to the balanced scorecard model.
      4) Next, IT-related goals are drawn up to address the enterprise goals.
         a) COBIT 5 translates the 17 generic enterprise goals into IT-related goals.
      5) Finally, enablers are identified that support pursuit of the IT-related goals. An enabler is broadly defined as anything that helps achieve objectives.
         a) The seven categories of enablers are listed in item 5.d. on the next page.
      6) COBIT 5 refers to the process described above as the goals cascade. It can be depicted graphically as follows:

COBIT 5 Goals Cascade

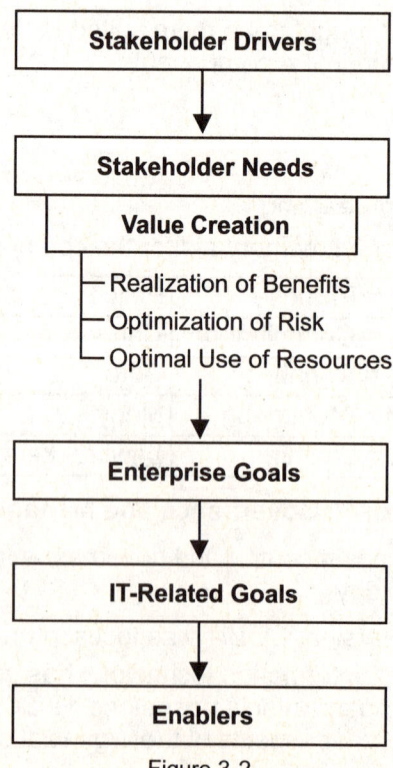

Figure 3-2

b. **Principle 2: Covering the Enterprise End-to-End**
   1) COBIT 5 takes a comprehensive view of all of the enterprise's functions and processes. Information technology pervades them all; it cannot be viewed as a function distinct from other enterprise activities.
      a) Thus, IT governance must be integrated with enterprise governance.
   2) IT must be considered enterprise-wide and end-to-end, i.e., all functions and processes that govern and manage information "wherever that information may be processed."

c. **Principle 3: Applying a Single, Integrated Framework**
   1) In acknowledgment of the availability of multiple IT-related standards and best practices, COBIT 5 provides an overall framework for enterprise IT within which other standards can be consistently applied.
   2) COBIT 5 was developed to be an overarching framework that does not address specific technical issues; i.e., its principles can be applied regardless of the particular hardware and software in use.

d. **Principle 4: Enabling a Holistic Approach**
   1) COBIT 5 describes seven categories of enablers that support comprehensive IT governance and management:
      a) Principles, policies, and frameworks
      b) Processes
      c) Organizational structures
      d) Culture, ethics, and behavior
      e) Information
      f) Services, infrastructure, and applications
      g) People, skills, and competencies
   2) The last three of these enablers also are classified as resources, the use of which must be optimized.
   3) Enablers are interconnected because they
      a) Need the input of other enablers to be fully effective and
      b) Deliver output for the benefit of other enablers.

e. **Principle 5: Separating Governance from Management**
   1) The complexity of the modern enterprise requires governance and management to be treated as distinct activities.
      a) In general, governance is the setting of overall objectives and the monitoring of progress toward those objectives. COBIT 5 associates governance with the board of directors.
         i) Within any governance process, three practices must be addressed: evaluate, direct, and monitor.
      b) Management is the carrying out of activities in pursuit of enterprise goals. COBIT 5 associates these activities with executive management under the leadership of the CEO.
         i) Within any management process, four responsibility areas must be addressed: plan, build, run, and monitor.

6. **The eSAC Model**
   a. In the eSAC (*Electronic Systems Assurance and Control*) model, the entity's internal processes accept inputs and produce outputs.
      1) **Inputs:** Mission, values, strategies, and objectives
      2) **Outputs:** Results, reputation, and learning

b. The eSAC model's **broad control objectives** are influenced by the COSO Framework:

1) Operating effectiveness and efficiency
2) Reporting of financial and other management information
3) Compliance with laws and regulations
4) Safeguarding of assets

c. The following are eSAC's IT **business assurance objectives**:

1) Availability. The entity must ensure that information, processes, and services are available at all times.
2) Capability. The entity must ensure reliable and timely completion of transactions.
3) Functionality. The entity must ensure that systems are designed to user specifications to fulfill business requirements.
4) Protectability. The entity must ensure that a combination of physical and logical controls prevents unauthorized access to system data.
5) Accountability. The entity must ensure that transactions are processed under firm principles of data ownership, identification, and authentication.

d. The following is a useful memory aid for the eSAC IT business assurance objectives:

A = Availability	**A**
C = Capability	**C**ourt
F = Functionality	**F**inds
P = Protectability	**P**eople
A = Accountability	**A**ccountable

7. **Soft Controls**

a. The COSO and CoCo models emphasize soft controls (see Roth, "Taking a Hard Look at Soft Controls," *Internal Auditor*, February 1998). For example, the communication of ethical values and the fostering of mutual trust are soft controls in the CoCo model. In the COSO model, soft controls are part of the control environment.

1) Soft controls should be distinguished from hard controls, such as compliance with specific policies and procedures imposed upon employees from above.

b. Soft controls have become more necessary as technology advances have empowered employees. Technology has given them access to large amounts of critical information and enabled them to make decisions formerly made by those higher in the organizational structure.

1) In addition to making many hard controls obsolete, technology advances also have permitted the automation of hard controls, for example, the embedding of audit modules in computer programs.

c. One approach to auditing soft controls is **control self-assessment (CSA)**. It is the involvement of management and staff in the assessment of internal controls within their workgroup.

d. Hard and soft controls can be associated with particular risks and measured. The vulnerability addressed can be stated as the product of the probability of occurrence and the significance of the occurrence ($V = P \times S$).

Stop and review! You have completed the outline for this subunit. Study multiple-choice questions 1 through 3 on page 74.

3.2 ENTERPRISE RISK MANAGEMENT

1. **The COSO ERM Framework**
    a. *Enterprise Risk Management – Integrated Framework* describes a model that incorporates the earlier COSO control framework while extending it to the broader subject of enterprise risk management (ERM).
        1) ERM is based on key concepts applicable to many types of organizations. The emphasis is on (a) the objectives of a specific entity and (b) establishing a means for evaluating the effectiveness of ERM.
    b. The COSO Framework defines ERM as follows:
        > *Enterprise risk management is a process, effected by an entity's board of directors, management, and other personnel, applied in strategy setting and across the enterprise, designed to identify potential events that may affect the entity, and manage risk to be within its risk appetite, to provide reasonable assurance regarding the achievement of entity objectives.*

2. **COSO Risk Vocabulary**
    a. **Risk** is the possibility that an event will occur and adversely affect the achievement of objectives.
        1) **Inherent risk** is the risk in the absence of a risk response.
        2) **Residual risk** is the risk after a risk response.
        3) **Risk universe** refers to all risks that could possibly affect an entity.
            a) In a financial statement audit, **audit risk** is the risk that the auditor expresses an inappropriate opinion on materially misstated financial statements.
    b. **Risk appetite** is the amount of risk an entity is willing to accept in pursuit of value. It reflects the entity's risk management philosophy and influences the entity's culture and operating style.
        1) Risk appetite is considered in evaluating strategies, setting objectives, and developing risk management methods.
    c. An opportunity is the possibility that an event will positively affect the achievement of objectives.

3. **ERM Components**
    a. The internal environment reflects the entity's (1) risk management philosophy, (2) risk appetite, (3) integrity, (4) ethical values, and (5) overall environment. It sets the tone of the entity.
    b. Objective setting precedes event identification. ERM ensures that (1) a process is established and (2) objectives align with the mission and the risk appetite.
    c. Event identification relates to internal and external events affecting the organization. It differentiates between opportunities and risks. Impact factors are potential results of an event.
    d. Risk assessment considers likelihood and impact (see the definitions of risk in The IIA Glossary) as a basis for risk management. The assessment considers the inherent risk and the residual risk.
    e. Risk responses are actions taken to reduce the impact or likelihood of adverse events. They include control activities. They should be consistent with the entity's risk tolerances and appetite.
    f. Control activities are policies and procedures to ensure the effectiveness of risk responses.

g. The information and communication component identifies, captures, and communicates relevant and timely information.
h. Monitoring involves ongoing management activities or separate evaluations. The full ERM process is monitored.

4. **Five Strategies for Risk Response**
    a. Risk avoidance ends the activity from which the risk arises. For example, the risk of having a pipeline sabotaged in an unstable region can be avoided by simply selling the pipeline.
    b. Risk acceptance acknowledges the risks of an activity and no action is taken to affect risk likelihood or impact. This term is synonymous with self-insurance.
    c. Risk reduction (mitigation) lowers the level of risk associated with an activity. For example, the risk of systems penetration can be reduced by maintaining a robust information security function within the entity.
    d. Risk sharing transfers some loss potential to another party. Examples are purchasing insurance, hedging, and entering into joint ventures.
    e. Risk exploitation seeks risk to pursue a high return on investment.

5. **Responsibilities**
    a. **Senior Management**
        1) The CEO sets the tone at the top of the entity and has ultimate responsibility for ERM.
        2) Senior management should ensure that sound risk management processes are in place and functioning.
        3) Senior management also determines the entity's risk management philosophy. For example, officers who issue definitive policy statements, insist on written procedures, and closely monitor performance indicators exhibit one type of risk management philosophy. Officers who manage informally and take a relaxed approach to performance monitoring exhibit a different philosophy.
            a) If senior management establishes a consistent risk management philosophy, all parts of the entity can respond to risk appropriately.
    b. **Board of Directors**
        1) The board has an oversight role. It should determine that risk management processes are in place, adequate, and effective.
        2) Directors' attitudes are a key component of the internal environment. They must possess certain qualities for them to be effective.
            a) A majority of the board should be outside directors.
            b) Directors generally should have years of experience either in the industry or in corporate governance.
            c) Directors must be willing to challenge management's choices. Complacent directors increase the chances of adverse consequences.
    c. **Risk Committee and Chief Risk Officer**
        1) Larger entities may wish to establish a risk committee composed of directors that also includes managers, the individuals most familiar with entity processes.
            a) A chief risk officer (CRO) may be appointed to coordinate the entity's risk management activities. The CRO is a member of, and reports to, the risk committee.
    d. **Internal Auditing**
        1) According to The IIA, internal auditors may be directed by the board to evaluate the effectiveness and contribute to the improvement of risk management processes.

2) The internal auditors' determination of whether risk management processes are effective is a judgment resulting from the assessment that

    a) Entity objectives support and align with its mission.
    b) Significant risks are identified and assessed.

        i) Appropriate risk responses are selected that align risks and the entity's risk appetite.
        ii) Relevant risk information is captured and communicated in a timely manner across the entity, enabling staff, management, and the board to carry out their responsibilities.

6. **Graphical Depiction**

    a. The COSO ERM Framework is depicted as a matrix in the form of a cube with rows, slices, and columns.

        1) The rows are the eight components, the slices are the four categories of objectives, and the columns are the organizational units of the entity.

    b. The entity should make the appropriate response at each intersection of the Framework, such as control activities for achieving reporting objectives at the division level.

COSO ERM Framework

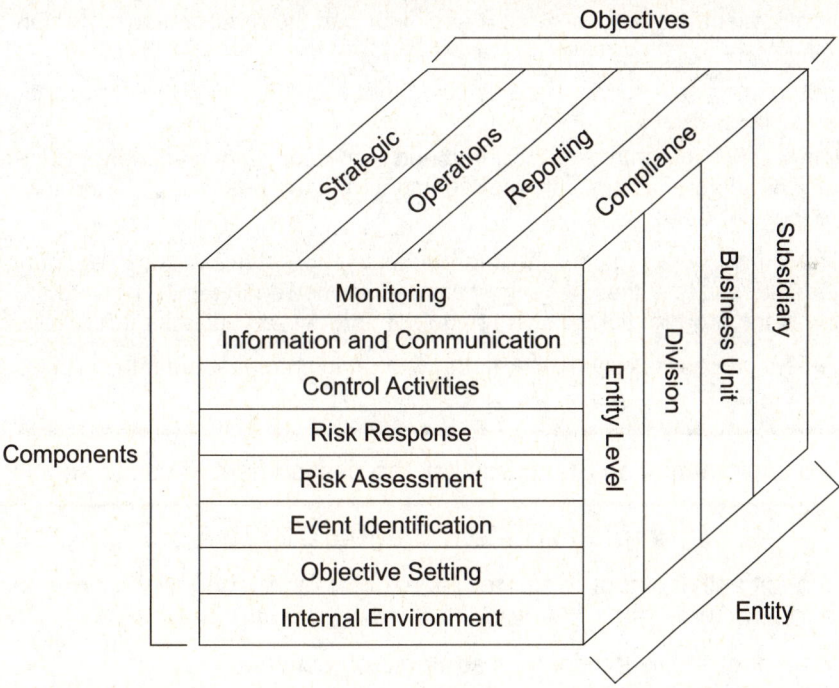

Figure 3-3

7. **ERM Limitations**

    a. Limitations of ERM arise from the possibility of

        1) Faulty human judgment,
        2) Cost-benefit considerations,
        3) Simple errors or mistakes,
        4) Collusion, and
        5) Management override of ERM decisions.

Stop and review! You have completed the outline for this subunit. Study multiple-choice questions 4 through 8 beginning on page 74.

3.3 RISK MANAGEMENT PROCESSES

 At one time, external audit professionals thought of risk only in the context of an audit (e.g., the probability of not discovering a material financial statement misstatement). Today, after extensive research and many scholarly publications, risk is recognized as something that must be examined and mitigated in every aspect of an organization's operations. Thus, CIA candidates should understand the distinct responsibilities of (1) the internal audit activity and (2) senior management and the board for enterprise-wide risk.

Performance Standard 2120
Risk Management

The internal audit activity must evaluate the effectiveness and contribute to the improvement of risk management processes.

1. **Importance of Internal Audit's Role in Risk Management**

    a. The IIA issued the following Interpretation to clarify internal audit's role:

    ### Interpretation of Standard 2120

    Determining whether risk management processes are effective is a judgment resulting from the internal auditor's assessment that:

    - Organizational objectives support and align with the organization's mission;
    - Significant risks are identified and assessed;
    - Appropriate risk responses are selected that align risks with the organization's risk appetite; and
    - Relevant risk information is captured and communicated in a timely manner across the organization, enabling staff, management, and the board to carry out their responsibilities.

    The internal audit activity may gather the information to support this assessment during multiple engagements. The results of these engagements, when viewed together, provide an understanding of the organization's risk management processes and their effectiveness.

    Risk management processes are monitored through ongoing management activities, separate evaluations, or both.

    b. Two Implementation Standards link the assessment of risk to specific risk areas.

    ### Implementation Standard 2120.A1

    The internal audit activity must evaluate risk exposures relating to the organization's governance, operations, and information systems regarding the:

    - Achievement of the organization's strategic objectives;
    - Reliability and integrity of financial and operational information;
    - Effectiveness and efficiency of operations and programs;
    - Safeguarding of assets; and
    - Compliance with laws, regulations, policies, procedures, and contracts.

    ### Implementation Standard 2120.A2

    The internal audit activity must evaluate the potential for the occurrence of fraud and how the organization manages fraud risk.

    c. Establishing a risk-based audit model and participating in the organization's risk management processes are both ways in which the internal audit activity adds value.

2. **Responsibility for Aspects of Organizational Risk Management**
    a. The division of responsibility is described in detail in Practice Advisory 2120-1, *Assessing the Adequacy of Risk Management Processes*.
        1) "Risk management is a key responsibility of senior management and the board. To achieve its business objectives, management ensures that sound risk management processes are in place and functioning. Boards have an oversight role to determine that appropriate risk management processes are in place and that these processes are adequate and effective. In this role, they may direct the internal audit activity to assist them by examining, evaluating, reporting, and/or recommending improvements to the adequacy and effectiveness of management's risk processes" (para. 1).
        2) "Management and the board are responsible for their organization's risk management and control processes. However, internal auditors acting in a consulting role can assist the organization in identifying, evaluating, and implementing risk management methodologies and controls to address those risks" (para. 2).
        3) "In situations where the organization does not have formal risk management processes, the chief audit executive (CAE) formally discusses with management and the board their obligations to understand, manage, and monitor risks within the organization and the need to satisfy themselves that there are processes operating within the organization, even if informal, that provide the appropriate level of visibility into the key risks and how they are being managed and monitored" (para. 3).
        4) "The CAE is to obtain an understanding of senior management's and the board's expectations of the internal audit activity in the organization's risk management process. This understanding is then codified in the charters of the internal audit activity and the board. Internal auditing's responsibilities are to be coordinated between all groups and individuals within the organization's risk management process. The internal audit activity's role in the risk management process of an organization can change over time and may encompass:
            a) No role.
            b) Auditing the risk management process as part of the internal audit plan.
            c) Active, continuous support and involvement in the risk management process such as participation on oversight committees, monitoring activities, and status reporting.
            d) Managing and coordinating the risk management process" (para. 4).
        5) "Ultimately, it is the role of senior management and the board to determine the role of internal audit in the risk management process. Their view on internal audit's role is likely to be determined by factors such as the culture of the organization, ability of the internal audit staff, and local conditions and customs of the country. However, taking on management's responsibility regarding the risk management process and the potential threat to the internal audit activity's independence requires a full discussion and board approval." (para. 5).
        6) "The techniques used by various organizations for their risk management practices can vary significantly. Depending on the size and complexity of the organization's business activities, risk management processes can be:
            a) Formal or informal.
            b) Quantitative or subjective.
            c) Embedded in the business units or centralized at a corporate level" (para. 6).

7) "The organization designs processes based on its culture, management style, and business objectives. [Author's note: The assumption is that the objective of the choices made is to maximize stakeholder (shareholder) value.] For example, the use of derivatives or other sophisticated capital markets products by the organization could require the use of quantitative risk management tools. Smaller, less complex organizations could use an informal risk committee to discuss the organization's risk profile and to initiate periodic actions. The internal auditor determines that the methodology chosen is sufficiently comprehensive and appropriate for the nature of the organization's activities" (para. 7).

8) "Internal auditors need to obtain sufficient and appropriate evidence to determine that the key objectives of the risk management processes are being met to form an opinion on the adequacy of risk management processes" (para. 8).

Stop and review! You have completed the outline for this subunit. Study multiple-choice questions 9 through 14 beginning on page 76.

3.4 FRAUD -- NATURE, PREVENTION, AND DETECTION

1. **Definition from The IIA Glossary** (see Appendix A for the complete Glossary)

   a. Fraud is "any illegal act characterized by deceit, concealment, or violation of trust. These acts are not dependent upon the threat of violence or physical force. Frauds are perpetrated by parties and organizations to obtain money, property, or services; to avoid payment or loss of services; or to secure personal or business advantage."

2. **Effects of Fraud**

   a. Monetary losses from fraud are significant, but its full cost is immeasurable in terms of time, productivity, and reputation, including customer relationships.

   b. Thus, an organization should have a fraud program that includes awareness, prevention, and detection programs. It also should have a fraud risk assessment process to identify fraud risks.

3. **Causative Factors of Fraud**

   a. Pressure or incentive is the need the fraudster is trying to satisfy by committing the fraud.

   b. Opportunity is the fraudster's ability to commit the fraud.

      1) This characteristic is the one that the organization can most influence, e.g., by means of controls and procedures.

   c. Rationalization is the fraudster's ability to justify the fraud.

4. **Examples of Fraud**

   a. Asset misappropriation is stealing cash or other assets (supplies, inventory, equipment, and information). The theft may be concealed, e.g., by adjusting records. An example is embezzlement, the intentional appropriation of property entrusted to one's care.

   b. Skimming is theft of cash before it is recorded, for example, accepting payment from a customer but not recording the sale.

   c. Disbursement fraud involves payment for fictitious goods or services, overstatement of invoices, or use of invoices for personal reasons.

   d. Expense reimbursement is payment for fictitious or inflated expenses, for example, an expense report for personal travel, nonexistent meals, or extra mileage.

   e. Payroll fraud is a false claim for compensation, for example, overtime for hours not worked or payments to fictitious employees.

f. Financial statement misrepresentation often overstates assets or revenue or understates liabilities and expenses. Management may benefit by selling stock, receiving bonuses, or concealing another fraud.

g. Information misrepresentation provides false information, usually to outsiders in the form of fraudulent financial statements.

h. Corruption is an improper use of power, e.g., bribery. It often leaves little accounting evidence. These crimes usually are uncovered through tips or complaints from third parties. Corruption often involves the purchasing function.

i. Bribery is offering, giving, receiving, or soliciting anything of value to influence an outcome. Bribes may be offered to key employees such as purchasing agents. Those paying bribes tend to be intermediaries for outside vendors.

j. A conflict of interest is an undisclosed personal economic interest in a transaction that adversely affects the organization or its shareholders.

k. A diversion redirects to an employee or outsider a transaction that would normally benefit the organization.

l. Wrongful use of confidential or proprietary information is fraudulent.

m. A related party fraud is receipt of a benefit not obtainable in an arm's-length transaction.

n. Tax evasion is intentionally falsifying a tax return.

5. **Division of Responsibilities**

   a. Control is the principal means of preventing fraud.

      1) Management is primarily responsible for establishing and maintaining control.
      2) Internal auditors are primarily responsible for preventing fraud by examining and evaluating the adequacy and effectiveness of control.

         a) They are not responsible for designing and implementing fraud prevention controls.

   b. Internal auditors are not expected to detect all fraud.

> **Implementation Standard 1210.A2**
>
> Internal auditors must have sufficient knowledge to evaluate the risk of fraud and the manner in which it is managed by the organization, but are not expected to have the expertise of a person whose primary responsibility is detecting and investigating fraud.

      1) According to Implementation Standard 1220.A1, internal auditors must exercise due professional care by considering, among other things, the "probability of significant errors, fraud, or noncompliance."
      2) Thus, internal auditors must consider the probability of fraud when developing engagement objectives (Implementation Standard 2210.A2).

6. **Components of a Fraud Prevention System**

   a. Fraud prevention involves actions to discourage fraud and limit the exposure when it occurs. A strong ethical culture and setting the correct tone at the top are essential to prevention.

   b. Overlapping control elements of a fraud prevention program are presented below and on the next page. They are based on the COSO control framework described in Subunit 3.1.

      1) The control environment includes such elements as a code of conduct, ethics policy, or fraud policy.

2) A fraud risk assessment generally includes the following:
    a) Identifying and prioritizing fraud risk factors and fraud schemes
    b) Mapping existing controls to potential fraud schemes and identifying gaps
    c) Testing operating effectiveness of fraud prevention and detection controls
    d) Documenting and reporting the fraud risk assessment
3) Control activities are policies and procedures for business processes that include authority limits and segregation of duties.
4) Fraud-related information and communication practices promote the fraud risk management program and the organization's position on risk. The means used include fraud awareness training and confirming that employees comply with the organization's policies.
    a) A fraud hotline can open the channel of communication for employees to report suspected improprieties.
5) Monitoring evaluates antifraud controls through independent evaluations of the fraud risk management program and use of it.

7. **Responsibility for Detection**
    a. Internal auditors are not responsible for the detection of all fraud, but they always must be alert to the possibility of fraud.

> **Implementation Standard 2120.A2**
>
> The internal audit activity must evaluate the potential for the occurrence of fraud and how the organization manages fraud risk.

b. An internal auditor's responsibilities for detecting fraud include evaluating fraud indicators and deciding whether any additional action is necessary or whether an investigation should be recommended.

Stop and review! You have completed the outline for this subunit. Study multiple-choice questions 15 through 20 beginning on page 77.

3.5 FRAUD -- INDICATORS

1. **Low-Level Fraud vs. Executive Fraud**
    a. Fraud committed by staff or line employees most often consists of theft of property or embezzlement of cash. The incentive might be relief of economic hardship, the desire for material gain, or a drug or gambling habit.
        1) Stealing petty cash or merchandise, lapping accounts receivable, and creating nonexistent vendors are common forms of low-level fraud.
    b. Fraud at the executive level is very different. The incentive is usually either maintaining or increasing the stock price, receiving a large bonus, or both.
        1) This type of fraud consists most often of producing false or misleading financial statements.

2. **Terminology of Fraud Indicators**

   a. A document symptom is any kind of tampering with the accounting records to conceal a fraud. Keeping two sets of books or forcing the books to reconcile are examples.

   b. Situational pressure can be personal (e.g., financial difficulties in an employee's personal life) or organizational (e.g., the desire to release positive news to the financial media).

   c. Opportunity to commit is especially a factor in low-level employee fraud. Poor controls over cash, merchandise, and other organizational property, as well as lack of compensating accounting controls, are enabling factors.

   d. A lifestyle symptom is an unexplained rise in an employee's social status or level of material consumption.

   e. Rationalization occurs when a person attributes his or her actions to rational and creditable motives without analysis of the true and especially unconscious motives. Feeling underpaid is a common rationalization for low-level fraud.

   f. A behavioral symptom (i.e., a drastic change in an employee's behavior) may indicate the presence of fraud. The guilt and the other forms of stress associated with perpetrating and concealing the fraud may cause noticeable changes in behavior.

3. **Procedures for Detection**

   a. The nature and extent of the procedures performed to detect fraud depend on the circumstances of the engagement, including the features of the organization and the internal auditor's risk assessment.

      1) Accordingly, no text can feasibly present lists of all procedures relative to fraud. However, analytical procedures are routinely performed in many engagements. They may provide an early indication of fraud.

         a) Analytical procedures are performed to assess information collected in an engagement. The assessment compares information with expectations identified or developed by the internal auditor.

4. **Some Indicators of Possible Fraud**

   a. Frauds and their indicators (often called "red flags") take different forms:

      1) Lack of employee rotation in sensitive positions such as cash handling
      2) Inappropriate combination of job duties
      3) Unclear lines of responsibility and accountability
      4) Unrealistic sales or production goals
      5) An employee who refuses to take vacations or refuses promotion
      6) Established controls not applied consistently
      7) High reported profits when competitors are suffering from an economic downturn
      8) High turnover among supervisory positions in finance and accounting areas
      9) Excessive or unjustifiable use of sole-source procurement
      10) An increase in sales far out of proportion to the increase in cost of goods sold

Stop and review! You have completed the outline for this subunit. Study multiple-choice questions 21 through 25 beginning on page 79.

QUESTIONS

3.1 Control Frameworks

1. Which of the following are included in the control environment described in the COSO internal control framework?

A. Organizational structure, management philosophy, and planning.
B. Integrity and ethical values, assignment of authority, and human resource policies.
C. Competence of personnel, backup facilities, laws, and regulations.
D. Risk assessment, assignment of responsibility, and human resource practices.

Answer (B) is correct.
REQUIRED: The elements of the control environment.
DISCUSSION: The control environment is a set of standards, processes, and structures that includes

- Integrity and ethical values
- Commitment to competence
- Board of directors or audit committee
- Management's philosophy and operating style
- Organizational structure
- Assignment of authority and responsibility
- Human resource policies and practices

Answer (A) is incorrect. Planning is not an element of the control environment. Answer (C) is incorrect. Backup facilities, laws, and regulations are not elements of the control environment. Answer (D) is incorrect. Risk assessment is part of planning the internal audit activity and specific engagements.

2. The COSO framework treats internal control as a process designed to provide reasonable assurance regarding the achievement of objectives related to

A. Reliability of financial reporting.
B. Effectiveness and efficiency of operations.
C. Compliance with applicable laws and regulations.
D. All of the answers are correct.

Answer (D) is correct.
REQUIRED: The true statement regarding COSO's objectives in relation to internal control.
DISCUSSION: The COSO framework treats internal control as a process designed to provide reasonable assurance regarding the achievement of objectives related to reliability of financial reporting, effectiveness and efficiency of operations, and compliance with applicable laws and regulations.

3. The policies and procedures helping to ensure that management directives are executed and actions are taken to address risks to achievement of objectives are best described as

A. Risk assessments.
B. Control environments.
C. Control activities.
D. Monitoring activities.

Answer (C) is correct.
REQUIRED: The definition of control activities.
DISCUSSION: The COSO model for internal control describes control activities as the policies and procedures helping to ensure that management directives are executed and actions are taken to address risks to achievement of objectives.
Answer (A) is incorrect. Risk assessment identifies and analyzes external or internal risks to achievement of the objectives at the activity level as well as the entity level. Answer (B) is incorrect. The control environment reflects the attitude and actions of the board and management regarding the significance of control within the organization. Answer (D) is incorrect. Monitoring is a process that assesses the quality of the system's performance over time.

3.2 Enterprise Risk Management

4. Which of the following is a factor affecting risk?

A. New personnel.
B. New or revamped information systems.
C. Rapid growth.
D. All of the answers are correct.

Answer (D) is correct.
REQUIRED: The item that is a factor affecting risk.
DISCUSSION: New personnel, new or revamped information systems, and rapid growth are all factors that affect risk.

SU 3: Control Frameworks and Fraud

5. Components of enterprise risk management (ERM) are integrated with the management process. Which of the following correctly states four of the eight components of ERM according to the COSO's framework?

A. Event identification, risk assessment, control activities, and objective setting.
B. Internal environment, risk responses, monitoring, and risk minimization.
C. External environment, information and communication, monitoring, and event identification.
D. Objective setting, response to opportunities, risk assessment, and control activities.

Answer (A) is correct.
REQUIRED: The item identifying four components of ERM.
DISCUSSION: ERM ensures that (1) a process is established and (2) objectives align with the mission and the risk appetite. Event identification, risk assessment, control activities, and objective setting are components of ERM. Event identification relates to internal and external events affecting the organization. Risk assessment considers likelihood and impact (see the definitions of risk in The IIA Glossary) as a basis for risk management. Control activities are policies and procedures to ensure the effectiveness of risk responses. Objective setting precedes event identification.
Answer (B) is incorrect. Risk assessment, not minimization, is a component of ERM. Answer (C) is incorrect. The internal, not external, environment is a component of ERM. Answer (D) is incorrect. Response to opportunities is a capability of ERM.

6. Limitations of enterprise risk management (ERM) may arise from

A. Faulty human judgment.
B. Cost-benefit considerations.
C. Collusion.
D. All of the answers are correct.

Answer (D) is correct.
REQUIRED: The limitations of ERM.
DISCUSSION: The limitations of ERM are the same as those for control in general. They arise from the possibility of (1) faulty human judgment, (2) cost-benefit considerations, (3) simple errors or mistakes, (4) collusion, and (5) management override.
Answer (A) is incorrect. Limitations of ERM can also arise from cost-benefit considerations and collusion. Answer (B) is incorrect. Limitations of ERM can also arise from faulty human judgment and collusion. Answer (C) is incorrect. Limitations of ERM can also arise from faulty human judgment and cost-benefit considerations.

7. Management considers risk appetite for all of the following reasons **except**

A. Evaluating strategic options.
B. Setting objectives.
C. Developing risk management techniques.
D. Increasing the net present value of investments.

Answer (D) is correct.
REQUIRED: The item not a reason for considering risk appetite.
DISCUSSION: As described in the COSO ERM framework, risk appetite should be considered in

1. Evaluating strategies,
2. Setting related objectives, and
3. Developing risk management methods.

Increasing the net present value of investments is an operational objective. It would be determined after consideration of the entity's risk appetite and other strategic factors.

8. Inherent risk is

A. A potential event that will adversely affect the organization.
B. Risk response risk.
C. The risk after management takes action to reduce the impact or likelihood of an adverse event.
D. The risk when management has not taken action to reduce the impact or likelihood of an adverse event.

Answer (D) is correct.
REQUIRED: The definition of inherent risk.
DISCUSSION: Inherent risk is the risk when management has not taken action to reduce the impact or likelihood of an adverse event. Thus, it is risk in the absence of a risk response.
Answer (A) is incorrect. A risk event is a potential event that will affect the entity adversely. Answer (B) is incorrect. A risk response is an action taken to reduce the impact or likelihood of an adverse event, including a control activity. "Risk response risk" is a nonsense term. Answer (C) is incorrect. The risk after management takes action to reduce the impact or likelihood of an adverse event in responding to a risk is residual risk.

3.3 Risk Management Processes

9. In the risk management process, management's view of the internal audit activity's role is likely to be determined by all of the following factors **except**

A. Organizational culture.
B. Preferences of the independent auditor.
C. Ability of the internal audit staff.
D. Local conditions and customs of the country.

Answer (B) is correct.
REQUIRED: The factor not influencing management's view on the role of internal auditing.
DISCUSSION: Ultimately, the role of internal auditing in the risk management process is determined by senior management and the board. Their view on internal auditing's role is likely to be determined by factors such as the culture of the organization, ability of the internal audit staff, and local conditions and customs (PA 2120-1, para. 5).
Answer (A) is incorrect. Organizational culture is a factor that influences management's view of the role of internal auditing. Answer (C) is incorrect. The ability of the internal audit staff is a factor that influences management's view of the role of internal auditing. Answer (D) is incorrect. Local conditions and customs of the country influence management's view of the role of internal auditing.

10. Which of the following threatens the independence of an internal auditor who had participated in the initial establishment of a risk management process?

A. Developing assessments and reports on the risk management process.
B. Managing the identified risks.
C. Evaluating the adequacy and effectiveness of management's risk processes.
D. Recommending controls to address the risks identified.

Answer (B) is correct.
REQUIRED: The activity that threatens independence.
DISCUSSION: Assuming management's responsibility for the risk management process is a potential threat to the internal audit activity's independence. It requires a full discussion and board approval (PA 2120-1, para. 5).
Answer (A) is incorrect. Developing assessments and reports on the organization's risk management processes is not only an internal audit role but normally also a high audit priority. Answer (C) is incorrect. Internal auditors assist both management and the board by examining, evaluating, reporting, and recommending improvements on the adequacy and effectiveness of risk management processes. Answer (D) is incorrect. Internal auditors may recommend controls.

11. The board's expectations of the internal audit activity regarding the risk management process is

A. Noted in the work programs for formal consulting engagements.
B. Included in the business continuity plan.
C. Codified in the charters of the internal audit activity and the board.
D. Reviewed by the internal auditors immediately following a disaster.

Answer (C) is correct.
REQUIRED: The treatment of the board's expectations of the internal audit activity regarding the risk management process.
DISCUSSION: The chief audit executive (CAE) is to obtain an understanding of senior management's and the board's expectations of the internal audit activity in the organization's risk management process. This understanding is then codified in the charters of the internal audit activity and the board (PA 2120-1, para. 4).
Answer (A) is incorrect. A work program is a listing of specific procedures. Answer (B) is incorrect. Business continuity planning is just one element of risk management. Answer (D) is incorrect. The internal audit activity's role needs to be understood before a crisis.

12. Which of the following is the most accurate term for a process to identify, assess, manage, and control potential events or situations to provide reasonable assurance regarding the achievement of the organization's objectives?

A. The internal audit activity.
B. Control process.
C. Risk management.
D. Consulting service.

Answer (C) is correct.
REQUIRED: The process to identify, assess, manage, and control potential events or situations.
DISCUSSION: Risk management is "a process to identify, assess, manage, and control potential events or situations to provide reasonable assurance regarding the achievement of the organization's objectives" (The IIA Glossary).
Answer (A) is incorrect. The internal audit activity assists in risk management; it is not the same thing as risk management. Answer (B) is incorrect. Control processes are "the policies, procedures, and activities that are part of a control framework designed to ensure that risks are contained within the risk tolerances established by the risk management process" (The IIA Glossary). Answer (D) is incorrect. Consulting services are "advisory and related client service activities, the nature and scope of which are agreed with the client" (The IIA Glossary).

13. Risk management is the responsibility of management. The role of the internal audit activity in the risk management process may include which of the following?

1. Monitoring activities.
2. Evaluating the risk management process as part of the engagement plan.
3. Participating on oversight committees, monitoring of activities, and status reporting.
4. Managing and coordinating the process.

A. 1 only.
B. 2 only.
C. 1, 2, and 3 only.
D. 1, 2, 3, and 4.

Answer (D) is correct.
REQUIRED: The role of the internal audit activity in the risk management process.
DISCUSSION: The internal audit activity's role in the risk management process of an organization can change over time and may include responsibilities along a continuum that extends from (1) no role; (2) auditing the risk management process as part of the internal audit plan; (3) active, continuous support and involvement in the risk management process, such as participation on oversight committees, monitoring activities, and status reporting; and (4) managing and coordinating the process (PA 2120-1, para. 4).
Answer (A) is incorrect. The internal audit activity's role in the risk management process may extend on a continuum from no role to managing and coordinating the process. Answer (B) is incorrect. The internal audit activity's role in the risk management process also may extend to monitoring activities; participating on oversight committees, monitoring of activities, and status reporting; and managing and coordinating the process. Answer (C) is incorrect. The internal audit activity's role in the risk management process also may extend to managing and coordinating the process.

14. The internal audit activity must evaluate the effectiveness and contribute to the improvement of risk management processes. With respect to evaluating the adequacy of risk management processes, internal auditors most likely should

A. Recognize that organizations should use similar techniques for managing risk.
B. Determine that the key objectives of risk management processes are being met.
C. Determine the level of risks acceptable to the organization.
D. Treat the evaluation of risk management processes in the same manner as the risk analysis used to plan engagements.

Answer (B) is correct.
REQUIRED: The responsibility of internal auditors for assessing the adequacy of risk management processes.
DISCUSSION: Internal auditors need to obtain sufficient and appropriate evidence to determine that key objectives of the risk management processes are being met to form an opinion on the adequacy of risk management processes (PA 2120-1, para. 8).
Answer (A) is incorrect. Risk management processes vary with the size and complexity of an organization's business activities. Answer (C) is incorrect. Management and the board determine the level of acceptable organizational risks. Answer (D) is incorrect. Evaluating management's risk processes differs from the internal auditors' risk assessment used to plan an engagement, but information from a comprehensive risk management process is useful in such planning.

3.4 Fraud -- Nature, Prevention, and Detection

15. In the course of their work, internal auditors must be alert for fraud and other forms of white-collar crime. The important characteristic that distinguishes fraud from other varieties of white-collar crime is that

A. Fraud is characterized by deceit, concealment, or violation of trust.
B. Unlike other white-collar crimes, fraud is always perpetrated against an outside party.
C. White-collar crime is usually perpetrated for the benefit of an organization, but fraud benefits an individual.
D. White-collar crime is usually perpetrated by outsiders to the detriment of an organization, but fraud is perpetrated by insiders to benefit the organization.

Answer (A) is correct.
REQUIRED: The trait distinguishing fraud from other white-collar crimes.
DISCUSSION: Fraud is defined in The IIA Glossary as "any illegal act characterized by deceit, concealment, or violation of trust. These acts are not dependent upon the threat of violence or physical force."
Answer (B) is incorrect. Fraud may be perpetrated internally. Answer (C) is incorrect. Fraud may be perpetrated for the organization's benefit or for otherwise unselfish reasons. Answer (D) is incorrect. Fraud may be perpetrated by insiders and outsiders, and it may be either beneficial or detrimental to an organization.

16. In an organization with a separate division that is primarily responsible for the prevention of fraud, the internal audit activity is responsible for

A. Examining and evaluating the adequacy and effectiveness of that division's actions taken to prevent fraud.
B. Establishing and maintaining that division's system of internal control.
C. Planning that division's fraud prevention activities.
D. Controlling that division's fraud prevention activities.

Answer (A) is correct.
REQUIRED: The responsibility of the internal audit activity in an organization with a separate fraud prevention division.
DISCUSSION: Control is the principal means of preventing fraud. Management is primarily responsible for the establishment and maintenance of control. Internal auditors are primarily responsible for preventing fraud by examining and evaluating the adequacy and effectiveness of control.
Answer (B) is incorrect. Establishing and maintaining control is a responsibility of management. Answer (C) is incorrect. Planning fraud prevention activities is a responsibility of management. Answer (D) is incorrect. Controlling fraud prevention activities is a responsibility of management.

17. The internal audit activity's responsibility for preventing fraud is to

A. Establish internal control.
B. Maintain internal control.
C. Evaluate the system of internal control.
D. Exercise operating authority over fraud prevention activities.

Answer (C) is correct.
REQUIRED: The internal audit activity's responsibility for preventing fraud.
DISCUSSION: Control is the principal means of preventing fraud. Management, in turn, is primarily responsible for the establishment and maintenance of control. Internal auditors are primarily responsible for preventing fraud by examining and evaluating the adequacy and effectiveness of control.
Answer (A) is incorrect. Establishing internal control is management's responsibility. Answer (B) is incorrect. Maintaining internal control is management's responsibility. Answer (D) is incorrect. Operating authority is a management function.

18. Internal auditors have a responsibility for helping to deter fraud. Which of the following best describes how this responsibility is usually met?

A. By coordinating with security personnel and law enforcement agencies in the investigation of possible frauds.
B. By testing for fraud in every engagement and following up as appropriate.
C. By assisting in the design of control systems to prevent fraud.
D. By evaluating the adequacy and effectiveness of controls in light of the potential exposure or risk.

Answer (D) is correct.
REQUIRED: The responsibility of internal auditing to deter fraud.
DISCUSSION: Control is the principal means of preventing fraud. Management is primarily responsible for the establishment and maintenance of control. Internal auditors are primarily responsible for preventing fraud by examining and evaluating the adequacy and effectiveness of control.
Answer (A) is incorrect. Investigating possible frauds involves detection, not deterrence. Answer (B) is incorrect. Testing for fraud in every engagement is not required. Answer (C) is incorrect. Designing control systems impairs an internal auditor's objectivity.

19. Internal auditors are more likely to detect fraud by developing/strengthening their ability to

A. Recognize and question changes that occur in organizations.
B. Interrogate fraud perpetrators to discover why the fraud was committed.
C. Develop internal controls to prevent the occurrence of fraud.
D. Document computerized operating system programs.

Answer (A) is correct.
REQUIRED: The ability that should be developed or strengthened to detect fraud.
DISCUSSION: An internal auditor's responsibilities for detecting fraud include evaluating fraud indicators and deciding whether any additional action is necessary or whether an investigation should be recommended.
Answer (B) is incorrect. Interrogation of fraud perpetrators occurs after detection. The danger signals of fraud often involve negative organizational changes. Answer (C) is incorrect. The controls mentioned are preventive, not detective. Answer (D) is incorrect. Documentation of operating systems is not within the scope of internal auditing and would do little to enhance fraud detection skills.

20. An internal auditor's field work uncovers a series of transactions that indicate a possible embezzlement. Which of the following actions should the chief audit executive take?

A. Confront the suspected embezzler to determine that the facts are correct.
B. Review the finding with the suspect's fellow workers to see whether the workers can furnish additional evidence.
C. Decide whether to recommend an investigation.
D. Discuss the case with the board.

Answer (C) is correct.
REQUIRED: The appropriate action when wrongdoing is suspected.
DISCUSSION: An internal auditor's responsibilities for detecting fraud include evaluating fraud indicators and deciding whether any additional action is necessary or whether an investigation should be recommended.
Answer (A) is incorrect. The internal auditor should avoid confronting suspected employees. Employees suspected of theft or fraud have certain common law and statutory rights that, if infringed upon, can be costly to the organization. Answer (B) is incorrect. Fellow workers may also be involved in the embezzlement. Answer (D) is incorrect. The CAE should determine the extent, if any, of the fraud before presenting it to the board.

3.5 Fraud -- Indicators

21. Which of the following policies is most likely to result in an environment conducive to the occurrence of fraud?

A. Budget preparation input by the employees who are responsible for meeting the budget.
B. Unreasonable sales and production goals.
C. The division's hiring process frequently results in the rejection of adequately trained applicants.
D. The application of some accounting controls on a sample basis.

Answer (B) is correct.
REQUIRED: The policy most likely to result in an environment conducive to the occurrence of fraud.
DISCUSSION: Unrealistically high sales or production quotas can be an incentive to falsify the records or otherwise take inappropriate action to improve performance measures so that the quotas appear to have been met.
Answer (A) is incorrect. Participatory budgeting can reduce resistance to budgets and reduce the likelihood of inappropriate means being taken to meet the budget. Answer (C) is incorrect. Hiring policies should be based on factors other than adequate training, such as the applicants' personal integrity. Furthermore, hiring of all adequately trained applicants is unlikely to be necessary. Answer (D) is incorrect. Under the reasonable assurance concept, the cost of controls should not exceed their benefits. The cost of applying controls to all relevant transactions rather than a sample may be greater than the resultant savings.

22. Internal auditors have been advised to consider red flags to determine whether management is involved in a fraud. Which of the following does **not** represent a difficulty in using the red flags as fraud indicators?

A. Many common red flags are also associated with situations in which no fraud exists.
B. Some red flags are difficult to quantify or to evaluate.
C. Red flag information is not gathered as a normal part of an engagement.
D. The red flags literature is not well enough established to have a positive impact on internal auditing.

Answer (D) is correct.
REQUIRED: The item not a difficulty in using red flags as fraud indicators.
DISCUSSION: The state of red flags literature is an aid, not a difficulty, in internal auditing. It is well established and will be refined in the future as research is done.
Answer (A) is incorrect. Red flags are developed by correlation analysis, not necessarily by causation analysis. Answer (B) is incorrect. Many red flags, such as management's attitude, are difficult to quantify. Answer (C) is incorrect. Internal auditors should be able to identify fraud indicators and should be alert to opportunities that could allow fraud. However, internal auditors do not normally perform procedures specifically to gather red flag information.

23. Which of the following is most likely to be considered an indication of possible fraud?

A. The replacement of the management team after a hostile takeover.
B. Rapid turnover of the organization's financial executives.
C. Rapid expansion into new markets.
D. A government audit of the organization's tax returns.

Answer (B) is correct.
REQUIRED: The indication of possible fraud.
DISCUSSION: Even the most effective internal control can sometimes be circumvented, perhaps by collusion of two or more employees. Thus, an auditor must be sensitive to certain conditions that might indicate the existence of fraud, including high personnel turnover. In the case of financial executives, high turnover may suggest a pattern of inflation of profits to obtain bonuses or other benefits, to secure advantages in the marketplace, or to conceal incompetence or rash actions.
Answer (A) is incorrect. The replacement of the management team after a hostile takeover is not unusual. Answer (C) is incorrect. Rapid expansion into new markets is not unusual. Answer (D) is incorrect. A government audit of the organization's tax returns is not unusual.

24. An internal auditor should be concerned about the possibility of fraud if

A. Cash receipts, net of the amounts used to pay petty cash-type expenditures, are deposited in the bank daily.
B. The monthly bank statement reconciliation is performed by the same employee who maintains the perpetual inventory records.
C. The accounts receivable subsidiary ledger and accounts payable subsidiary ledger are maintained by the same person.
D. One person, acting alone, has sole access to the petty cash fund (except for a provision for occasional surprise counts by a supervisor or auditor).

Answer (A) is correct.
REQUIRED: The reason an internal auditor should be concerned about the possibility of fraud.
DISCUSSION: Paying petty cash expenditures from cash receipts facilitates the unauthorized removal of cash before deposit. All cash receipts should be deposited intact daily. Petty cash expenditures should be handled through an imprest fund.
Answer (B) is incorrect. The monthly bank reconciliation should not be performed by a person who makes deposits or writes checks, but the inventory clerk has no such responsibilities. Answer (C) is incorrect. There is no direct relationship between the transactions posted to the accounts receivable and accounts payable subsidiary ledgers; having the same person maintain both does not create a control weakness. Answer (D) is incorrect. To establish accountability for petty cash, only one person should have access to the fund.

25. The most common motivation for management fraud is the existence of

A. Vices, such as a gambling habit.
B. Job dissatisfaction.
C. Financial pressures on the organization.
D. The challenge of committing the perfect crime.

Answer (C) is correct.
REQUIRED: The most common motivation for management fraud.
DISCUSSION: Management fraud benefits organizations rather than individuals, so the existence of financial pressures is the most common motivation. Management perpetrators attempt to make their financial statements appear more attractive because of the financial pressures of restrictive loan covenants, a poor cash position, loss of significant customers, etc.
Answer (A) is incorrect. Vices are an example of motivators of fraud perpetrated for the benefit of individuals and to the organization's detriment. Answer (B) is incorrect. Job dissatisfaction is an example of motivators of fraud perpetrated for the benefit of individuals and to the organization's detriment. Answer (D) is incorrect. The challenge of committing the perfect crime is an example of motivators of fraud perpetrated for the benefit of individuals and to the organization's detriment.

Practice even more exam-emulating questions in **Gleim CIA Test Prep!**

STUDY UNIT FOUR
CONTROL: TYPES AND TECHNIQUES

(24 pages of outline)

4.1	Overview of Control	82
4.2	Classifying Controls	82
4.3	Flowcharts and Process Mapping	86
4.4	Accounting Cycles and Associated Controls	90
4.5	Management Controls	101

This study unit is the second of two covering **Section II: Internal Control / Risk** from The IIA's CIA Exam Syllabus. This section makes up 25% to 35% of Part 1 of the CIA exam and is tested at the **awareness level**. The relevant portion of the syllabus is highlighted below. (The complete syllabus is in Appendix B.)

II. INTERNAL CONTROL / RISK (25%–35%)

   A. Types of Controls (e.g., preventive, detective, input, output, etc.)
   B. Management Control Techniques
   C. Internal Control Framework Characteristics and Use (e.g., COSO, Cadbury)
   D. Alternative Control Frameworks
   E. Risk Vocabulary and Concepts
   F. Fraud Risk Awareness

III. CONDUCTING INTERNAL AUDIT ENGAGEMENTS – AUDIT TOOLS AND TECHNIQUES (25%–35%)

   A. Data Gathering (Collect and analyze data on proposed engagements)
   B. Data Analysis and Interpretation
   C. Data Reporting
   D. Documentation / Work Papers
   E. Process Mapping, Including Flowcharting
   F. Evaluate Relevance, Sufficiency, and Competence of Evidence

Many questions on the CIA exam address controls. Few such questions are answerable based on memorization of lists. Moreover, no text can feasibly present comprehensive lists of procedures. Thus, candidates must be able to apply reasoning processes and knowledge of auditing concepts to unfamiliar situations involving controls. By answering our questions, you will be able to synthesize, understand, and apply internal control theory. **Analysis** results in an understanding of a situation, set of circumstances, or process. **Synthesis** involves developing standards and generalizations for a situation, set of circumstances, or a process. It is a means of combining individual components or parts to produce a whole. Synthesis requires inductive reasoning, which is reaching a generalized conclusion from particular instances. **Evaluation** is relating a situation, set of circumstances, or process to predetermined or synthesized standards. Evaluation usually includes both analysis and synthesis. This skill set will allow you to answer any question on the CIA exam with confidence.

4.1 OVERVIEW OF CONTROL

1. **Definitions from the IIA Glossary** (see Appendix A for the complete IIA Glossary)

   a. **Control** is "any action taken by management, the board, and other parties to manage risk and increase the likelihood that established objectives and goals will be achieved. Management plans, organizes, and directs the performance of sufficient actions to provide reasonable assurance that objectives and goals will be achieved."

   b. **Control processes** are "the policies, procedures (both manual and automated), and activities that are part of a control framework, designed and operated to ensure that risks are contained within the level that an organization is willing to accept."

2. **The Control Process**

   a. Control requires feedback on the results of organizational activities for the purposes of measurement and correction.

   b. The control process includes

   1) Establishing standards for the operation to be controlled,
   2) Measuring performance against the standards,
   3) Examining and analyzing deviations,
   4) Taking corrective action, and
   5) Reappraising the standards based on experience.

   c. An evaluation-reward system should be implemented to encourage compliance with the control system.

   d. The cost of internal control must not be greater than its benefits.

Stop and review! You have completed the outline for this subunit. Study multiple-choice questions 1 through 4 beginning on page 105.

4.2 CLASSIFYING CONTROLS

1. **Primary Controls**

   a. **Preventive controls** deter the occurrence of unwanted events.

   1) Storing petty cash in a locked safe and segregating duties are examples of this type of control.
   2) IT examples include (a) designing a database so that users cannot enter a letter in the field that stores a Social Security number and (b) requiring the number of invoices in a batch to be entered before processing begins.

   b. **Detective controls** alert the proper people after an unwanted event. They are effective when detection occurs before material harm occurs.

   1) For example, a batch of invoices submitted for processing may be rejected by the computer system if it includes identical payments to a single vendor. A detective control provides for automatic reporting of all rejected batches to the accounts payable department.
   2) A burglar alarm is another example.

   c. **Corrective controls** correct the negative effects of unwanted events.

   1) An example is a requirement that all cost variances over a certain amount be justified.

   d. **Directive controls** cause or encourage the occurrence of a desirable event. These include the following:

   1) Policy and procedure manuals
   2) Employee training
   3) Job descriptions

2. **Secondary Controls**
    a. **Compensatory (mitigative) controls** may reduce risk when the primary controls are ineffective. However, they do not, by themselves, reduce risk to an acceptable level.
        1) An example is the lack of segregation of duties when a store clerk is the only employee present at closing. Accordingly, the clerk counts cash at the end of the day without supervision. The compensating control performed the next morning is for a supervisor to reconcile the count with the cash register data.
    b. **Complementary controls** work with other controls to reduce risk to an acceptable level. In other words, their synergy is more effective than either control by itself.
        1) For example, separating the functions of accounting for and custody of cash receipts is complemented by obtaining deposit slips validated by the bank.
3. **Application Controls**
    a. Application controls are primary controls that relate to the business tasks performed by a particular system. They should provide reasonable assurance that the recording, processing, and reporting of data are properly performed. Application controls include input, processing, and output controls.
    b. **Input Controls.** The most economical point for correcting input errors in an application is at the time in which the data are entered into the system. For this reason, input controls are the focus of an internal auditor's activity. Each of the two major types of processing modes has its own controls.
        1) **Batch Input Controls**
            a) Financial totals summarize monetary amounts in an information field in a group of records. The total produced by the system after the batch has been processed is compared to the total produced manually beforehand.
            b) Record counts track the number of records processed by the system for comparison to the number that the user expected to be processed.
            c) Hash totals are control totals without a defined meaning, such as the total of vendor numbers or invoice numbers, that are used to verify the completeness of the data.
        2) **Online Input Controls**
            a) Preformatting of data entry screens, i.e., to make them imitate the layout of a printed form, can aid the operator in keying to the correct fields.
            b) Field checks are tests of the characters in a field to verify that they are of an appropriate type for that field. For example, the system is programmed to reject alphabetic characters entered in the field for Social Security number.
            c) Validity checks compare the data entered in a given field with a table of valid values for that field. For example, the vendor number on a request to cut a check must match the table of current vendors, and the invoice number must match the approved invoice table.
            d) Limit and range checks are based on known limits for given information. For example, hours worked per week must be between 0 and 100, with anything above that range requiring management authorization.
            e) Self-checking digits are used to detect incorrect identification numbers. The digit is generated by applying an algorithm to the ID number. During the input process, the check digit is recomputed by applying the same algorithm to the code actually entered.

c. **Processing controls** ensure that data are complete and accurate during updating.
d. **Output controls** ensure that processing results are complete, accurate, and properly distributed. An important output control is user review. Users should be able to determine when output is incomplete or unreasonable, particularly when the user prepared the input. Thus, users as well as computer personnel have a quality assurance function.

4. **Time-Based Classification**

   a. **Feedback controls** report information about completed activities. They permit improvement in future performance by learning from past mistakes. Thus, corrective action occurs after the fact. Inspection of completed goods is an example.
   b. **Concurrent controls** adjust ongoing processes. These real-time controls monitor activities in the present to prevent them from deviating too far from standards. An example is close supervision of production-line workers.
   c. **Feedforward controls** anticipate and prevent problems. These controls require a long-term perspective. Organizational policies and procedures are examples.

5. **Financial vs. Operating Controls**

   a. **Financial controls** should be based on relevant established accounting principles.
      1) Objectives of financial controls may include (a) proper authorization; (b) appropriate recordkeeping; (c) safeguarding of assets; and (d) compliance with laws, regulations, and contracts.
   b. **Operating controls** apply to production and support activities.
      1) Because they may lack established criteria or standards, they should be based on management principles and methods. They also should be designed with regard to the management functions of planning, organizing, directing, and controlling.

6. **People-Based vs. System-Based Controls**

   a. **People-based controls** are dependent on the intervention of humans for their proper operation, for example, regular performance of bank reconciliations.
      1) Checklists, such as lists of required procedures for month-end closing, can be valuable to ensure that people-based controls are executed when needed.
   b. **System-based controls** are executed whenever needed with no human intervention.
      1) An example is code in a computerized purchasing system that prevents any purchase order over a certain monetary threshold from being submitted to the vendor without managerial approval.

7. **Use of a Control Matrix**

   a. Controls do not necessarily match risks one-to-one. Certain controls may address more than one risk, and more than one control may be needed to adequately address a single risk.

   1) For example, assume all petty cash custodians must present expense vouchers periodically. This control helps ensure that (a) petty cash accounts are maintained at the established level and (b) petty cash expenditures are reviewed for appropriateness.

   2) A control matrix is useful for matching controls with risks in these circumstances. The following is an example:

Control Matrix

	Control A	Control B	Control C	Control D
Risk 1	●			
Risk 2	●			
Risk 3		●		
Risk 4		●	●	
Risk 5	●			
Risk 6				●

Figure 4-1

Stop and review! You have completed the outline for this subunit. Study multiple-choice questions 5 through 8 beginning on page 106.

4.3 FLOWCHARTS AND PROCESS MAPPING

1. **Uses of Flowcharts**
    a. Flowcharts are graphical representations of the step-by-step progression of information through preparation, authorization, flow, storage, etc. The system depicted may be manual, computerized, or a combination of the two.
        1) Flowcharting allows the internal auditor to analyze a system and to identify the strengths and weaknesses of internal controls and the appropriate areas of audit emphasis.
    b. Flowcharting is typically used during the preliminary survey to gain an understanding of the client's processes and controls.

2. **Flowchart Symbols**
    a. Commonly used document flowchart symbols include the following:

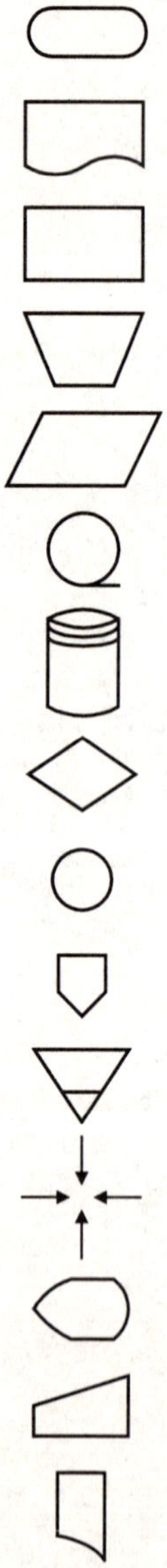

    ⬭ Starting or ending point or point of interruption

    ▱ Input or output of a document or report

    ▭ Computer operation or group of operations

    ⏢ Manual processing operation, e.g., prepare document

    ▱ Generalized symbol for input or output used when the medium is not specified

    ◯ Hard drive used for input or output

    🗄 Hard drive or other digital media used for storage

    ◇ Decision symbol indicating a branch in the flow

    ○ Connection between points on the same page

    ⬠ Connection between two pages of the flowchart

    ▽ Storage (file) that is not immediately accessible by computer

    ✢ Flow direction of data or processing

    ⬠ Display on a video terminal

    ▱ Manual input into a terminal or other online device

    ⬠ Adding machine tape (batch control)

Figure 4-2

SU 4: Control: Types and Techniques

3. **Horizontal Flowcharts**

   a. Horizontal flowcharts (sometimes called **system flowcharts**) depict areas of responsibility (departments or functions) arranged horizontally across the page in vertical columns. Accordingly, activities, controls, and document flows that are the responsibility of a given department or function are shown in the same column. The following is an example:

Horizontal (System) Flowchart

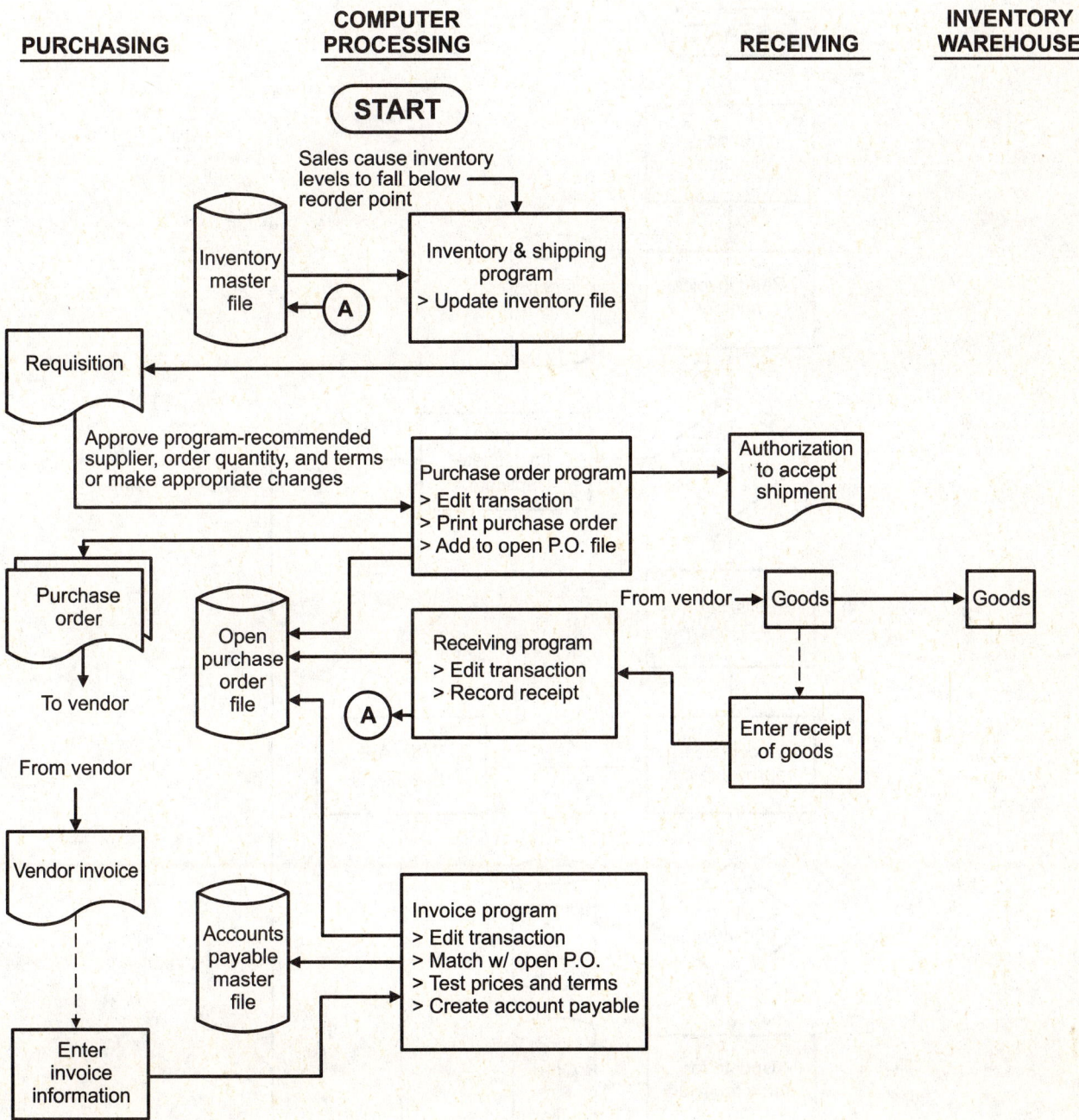

Figure 4-3

4. **Vertical Flowcharts**
    a. Vertical flowcharts, sometimes called **program flowcharts**, present successive steps in a top-to-bottom format.
        1) Their principal use is in the depiction of the specific actions carried out by a computer program.

Vertical (Program) Flowchart

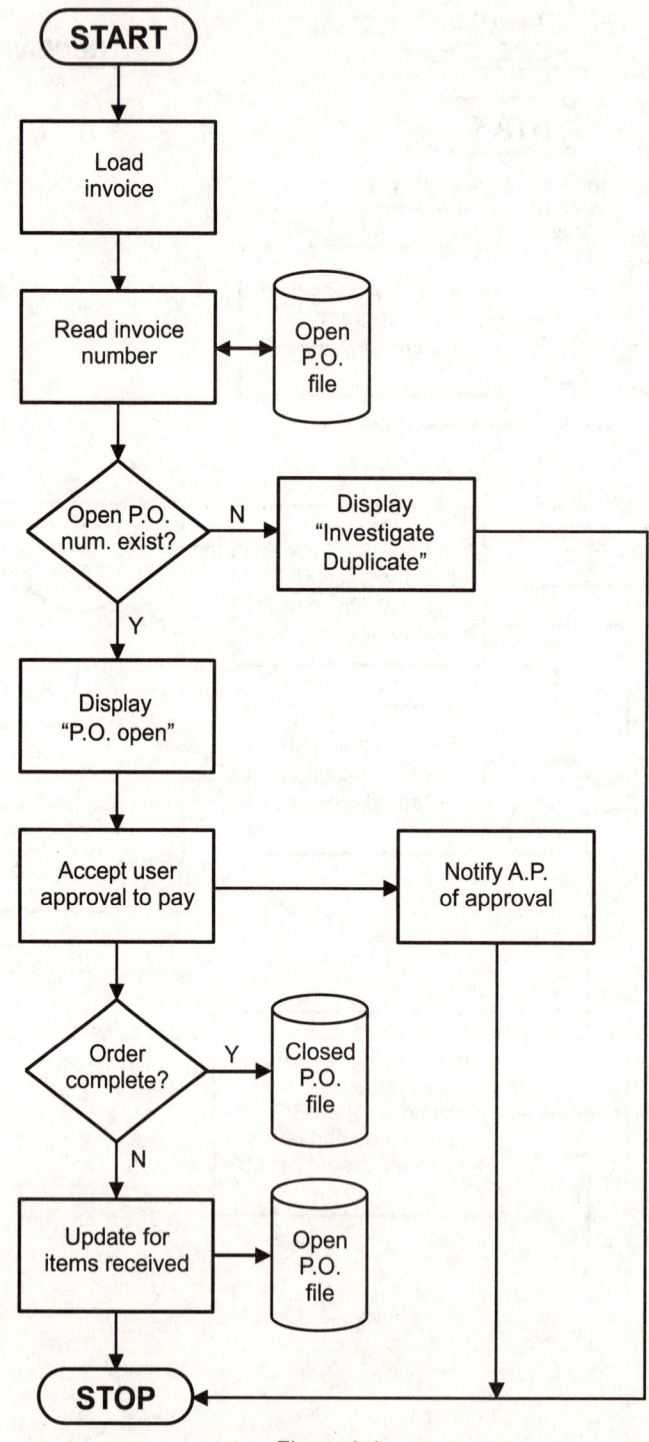

Figure 4-4

5. **Data Flow Diagrams**

    a. Data flow diagrams show how data flow to, from, and within an information system and the processes that manipulate the data. A data flow diagram can be used to depict lower-level details as well as higher-level processes.

        1) A system can be divided into subsystems, and each subsystem can be further subdivided at levels of increasing detail. Thus, any process can be expanded as many times as necessary to show the required level of detail.
        2) The symbols used in data flow diagrams are presented below:

Data Flow Diagram Symbols

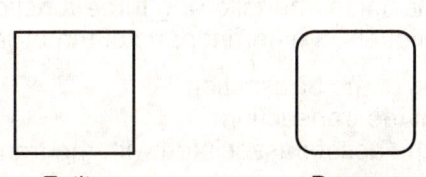

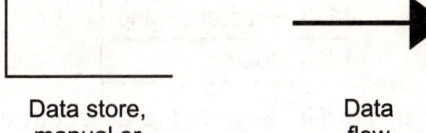

Figure 4-5

        a) No symbol is needed for documents or other output because data flow diagrams depict only the flow of data. For the same reason, no distinction is made between manual and online storage.

6. **Process Mapping**

    a. Process mapping is a simple form of flowcharting used to depict a client process. Below is an example of a process map. (P.O. is a purchase order, and A.P. is accounts payable.)

Process Map for Invoice Processing in Purchasing Department

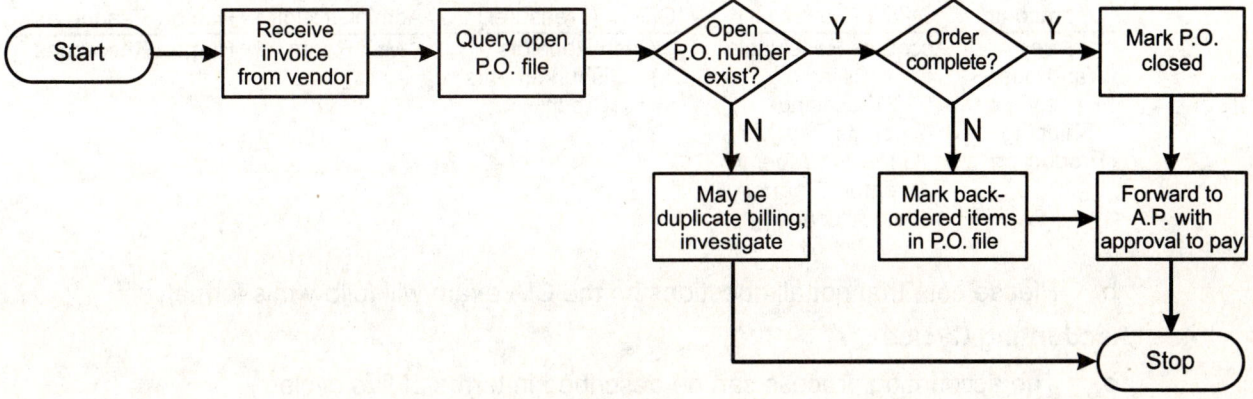

Figure 4-6

Stop and review! You have completed the outline for this subunit. Study multiple-choice questions 9 through 11 on page 107.

4.4 ACCOUNTING CYCLES AND ASSOCIATED CONTROLS

1. **Internal Controls**
    a. A properly designed system of internal controls should reduce the risk of errors and prevent an individual from perpetrating and concealing fraud. The structure of an organization and the assignment of job duties should be designed to segregate certain functions within this environment.
        1) Cost-benefit criteria must be considered.
2. **Segregation of Duties**
    a. For any given transaction, the following three functions preferably should be performed by separate individuals in different parts of the organization:
        1) Authorization of the transaction
        2) Recording of the transaction
        3) Custody of the assets associated with the transaction
            a) The following memory aid is for the functions that should be kept separate for proper segregation of duties:

A	Authorization
R	Recordkeeping
C	Custody

    b. The internal control system is designed to detect fraud by one person but not fraud by collusion or management override.

CIA candidates must understand segregation of duties, a basic principle of internal control. Expect multiple questions on this topic.

3. **Organizational Hierarchy**
    a. In a medium-sized or larger organization, adequate segregation of duties can be achieved by separating the responsibilities of the following corporate-level executives:

VP of Operations	Chief Accounting Officer (Controller)	Chief Financial Officer (Treasurer)	VP of Administration	VP of Human Resources
Sales	Accounts Receivable	Cash Receipts	Mail Room	Human Resources
Warehouse	Billing	Cash Disbursements		
Receiving	Purchasing	Credit		
Shipping	Accounts Payable			
Production	General Ledger			
	Inventory Control			
	Cost Accounting			
	Payroll			

    b. Please note that not all questions on the CIA exam will follow this format.

4. **Accounting Cycles**
    a. The accounting process can be described in terms of five cycles:
        1) Sales to customers on credit and recognition of receivables
        2) Collection of cash from customer receivables
        3) Purchases on credit and recognition of payables
        4) Payment of cash to satisfy trade payables
        5) Payment of employees for work performed and allocation of costs

SU 4: Control: Types and Techniques   91

   b. Below and on the following pages are five flowcharts and accompanying tables depicting the steps in the cycles and the controls in each step for an organization large enough to have an optimal segregation of duties.
      1) In small- and medium-sized organizations, some duties must be combined. The internal auditor must assess whether organizational segregation of duties is adequate.
5. Author's Note:
   a. Except for manual checks and remittance advices, the flowcharts presented do not assume use of either a paper-based or an electronic system. Each document symbol represents a business activity or control, whether manual or computerized.
   b. In the diagrams that follow, documents that originate outside the organization are separated by a thick border.
   c. The following detailed explanations of the accounting cycles do **not** need to be memorized. However, you should be able to understand them, and you may be able to relate these generic cycles to how the organization you work for handles them. If you understand these cycles and their respective control techniques, you should be able to answer any type of question about accounting cycles and their controls on the CIA exam.
   d. Please note that not all questions on the CIA exam will follow the exact cycles described on the following pages.

Sales-Receivables Cycle

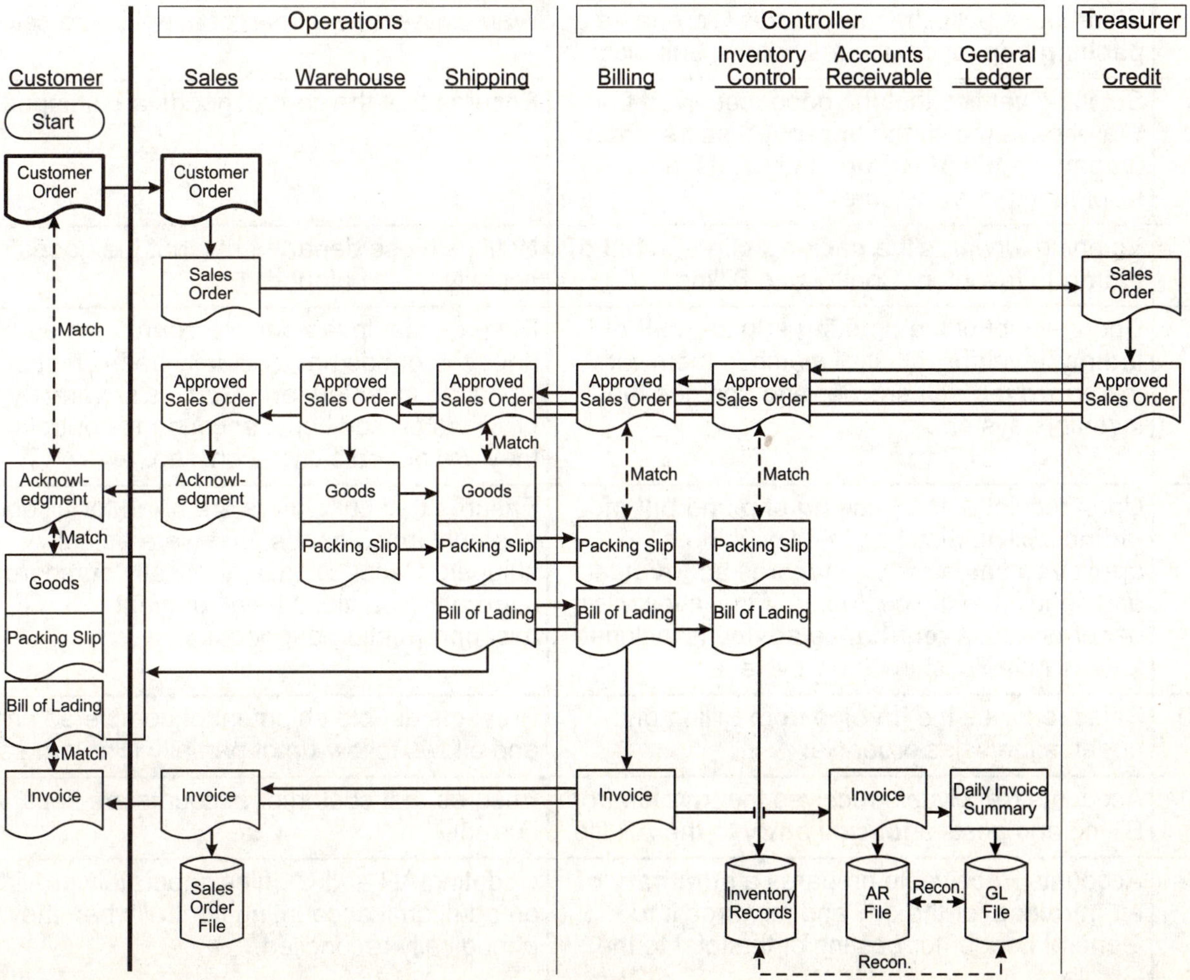

Figure 4-7

Sales-Receivables Cycle

Function:	Authorization				Custody		Recording		
Department:	Customer	Sales	Credit	Billing	Shipping	Warehouse	Inventory Control	Accounts Receivable	General Ledger

Step	Business Activity	Embedded Control
1	Sales receives a **customer order** for merchandise, prepares a **sales order**, and forwards it to Credit.	Reconciling sequentially numbered sales orders helps ensure that customer orders are legitimate.
2	Credit performs a credit check on the customer. If the customer is creditworthy, Credit approves the **sales order**.	Ensures that goods are shipped only to actual customers and that the account is unlikely to become delinquent.
3	Credit sends the **approved sales order** to Sales, Warehouse, Shipping, Billing, and Inventory Control.	Notifies these departments that a legitimate sale has been made.
4	Upon receipt of an **approved sales order**, Sales sends an acknowledgment to the customer.	The customer's expectation of receiving goods reduces the chances of misrouting or misappropriation.
5	Upon receipt of an **approved sales order**, Warehouse pulls the merchandise, prepares a **packing slip**, and forwards both to Shipping.	Ensures that merchandise is removed from Warehouse only as part of a legitimate sale.
6	Shipping verifies that the goods received from Warehouse match the **approved sales order**, prepares a **bill of lading**, and sends the shipment to the customer.	Ensures that the correct goods are shipped.
7	Shipping forwards the **packing slip** and **bill of lading** to Inventory Control and Billing.	Notifies these departments that the goods have actually been shipped.
8	Upon receipt of the **packing slip** and **bill of lading**, Inventory Control matches them with the **approved sales order** and updates the inventory system.	Ensures that inventory unit counts are updated once the goods have actually been shipped. Updating inventory and GL files separately provides an additional accounting control when they are periodically reconciled.
9	Upon receipt of the **packing slip** and **bill of lading**, Billing matches them with the **approved sales order**, prepares an **invoice**, and sends it to the customer. If the invoice is paper-based, a **remittance advice** is included for use in the cash receipts cycle.	Ensures that customers are billed for all goods, and only those goods, that were actually shipped. Reconciling sequentially numbered invoice transactions helps prevent misappropriation of goods.
10	Sales receives the **invoice** from Billing and updates the sales order file.	Prevents double shipment of completed orders and allows follow-up of partially filled orders.
11	Accounts Receivable receives the **invoice** from Billing and posts a **journal entry** to the AR file.	Ensures that customer accounts are kept current.
12	Accounts Receivable prepares a **summary of all invoices** for the day and forwards it to General Ledger for posting of the total to the GL file.	Updating AR and GL files separately provides an additional accounting control when they are periodically reconciled.

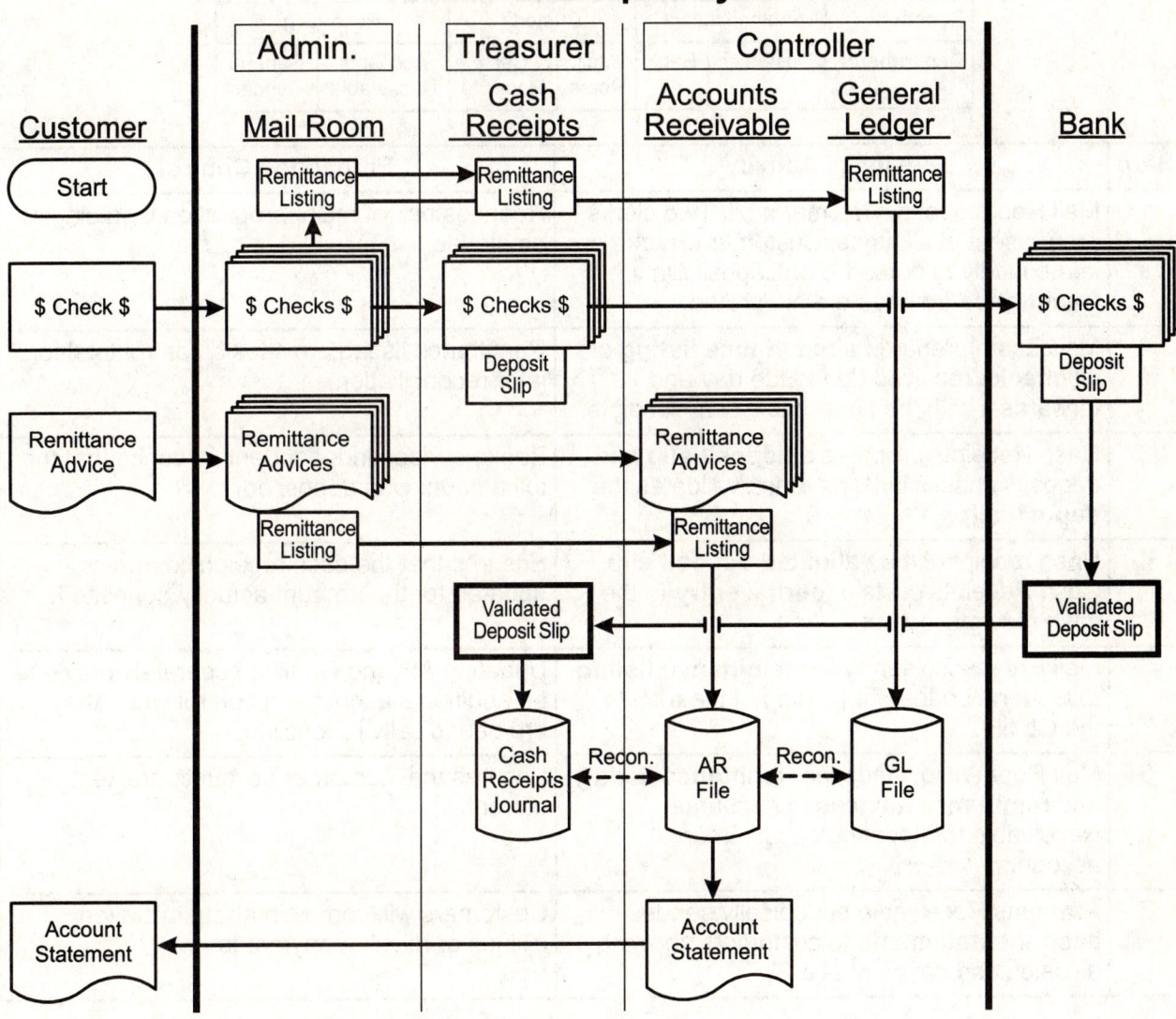

Figure 4-8

Cash Receipts Cycle

Function:	Authorization		Custody		Recording	
Department:	Customer	Bank	Mail Room	Cash Receipts	Accounts Receivable	General Ledger

Step	Business Activity	Embedded Control
1	Mail Room opens customer mail. Two clerks are present at all times. Customer **checks** are immediately endorsed "For Deposit Only." **Remittance advices** are separated.	Reduces risk of misappropriation by a single employee.
2	Mail Room prepares a **remittance listing** of all **checks** received during the day and forwards it with the checks to Cash Receipts.	Remittance listing provides a control total for later reconciliation.
3	Cash Receipts prepares a **deposit slip** and deposits checks in Bank. Bank validates the **deposit slip**.	Bank provides independent evidence that the full amount was deposited.
4	Upon receipt of the **validated deposit slip**, Cash Receipts posts a **journal entry** to the cash receipts journal.	Ensures that the cash receipts journal is updated for the amount actually deposited.
5	Mail Room also sends the **remittance listing** to General Ledger for posting of the total to the GL file.	Updating AR and GL files separately provides an additional accounting control when they are periodically reconciled.
6	Mail Room also sends the **remittance listing** and **remittance advices** to Accounts Receivable for updating of customer accounts.	Ensures that customer accounts are kept current.
7	Accounts Receivable periodically sends **account statements** to customers showing all sales and payment activity.	Customers will complain about mistaken billings or missing payments.

SU 4: Control: Types and Techniques

Purchases-Payables Cycle

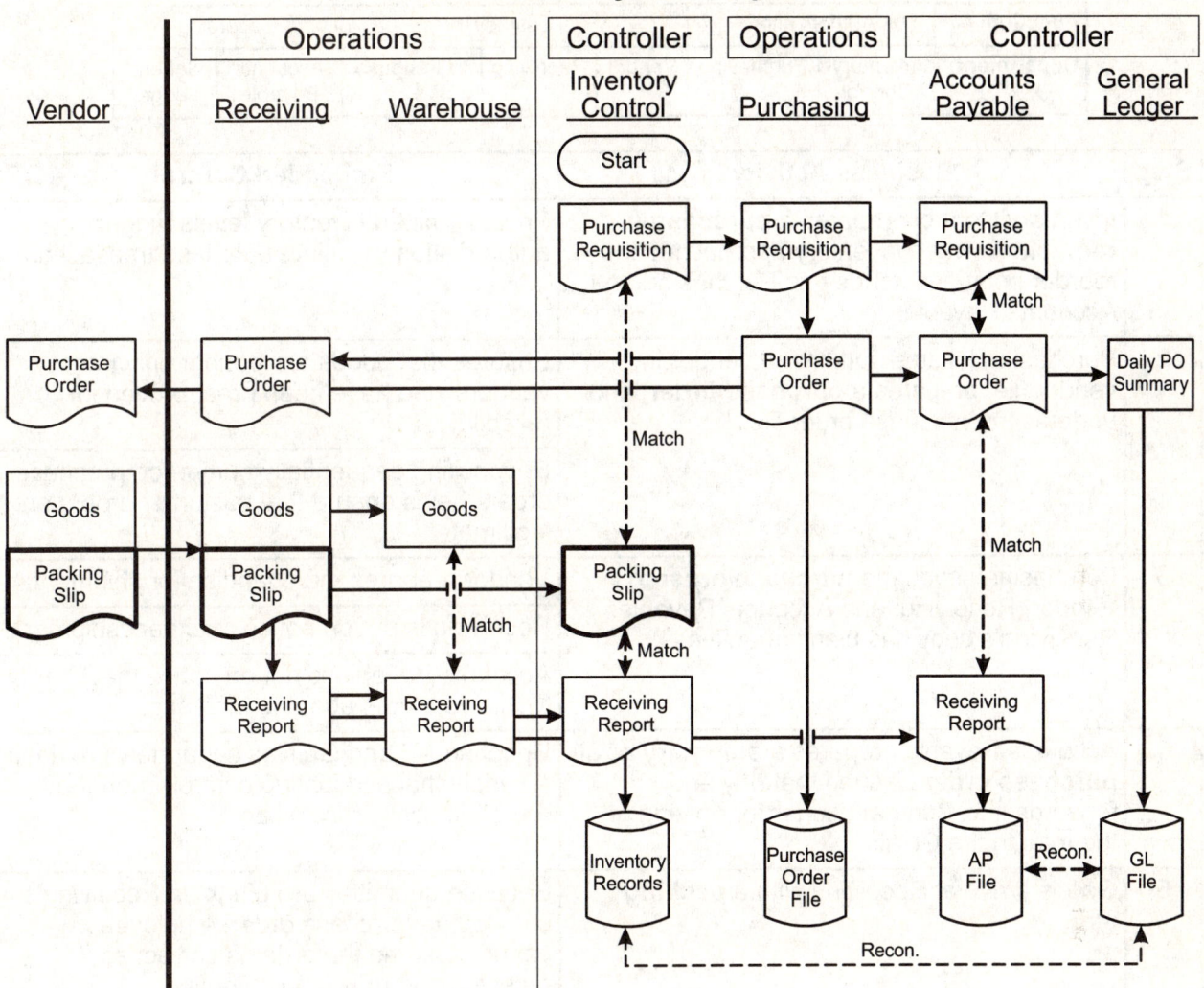

Figure 4-9

Purchases-Payables Cycle

Function:	Authorization		Custody			Recording	
Department:	Inventory Control	Purchasing	Vendor	Receiving	Warehouse	Accounts Payable	General Ledger

Step	Business Activity	Embedded Control
1	Inventory Control prepares a **purchase requisition** when inventory approaches the reorder point and sends it to Purchasing and Accounts Payable.	Predetermined inventory levels trigger authorization to initiate purchase transaction.
2	Purchasing locates authorized vendor in vendor file, prepares a **purchase order**, and updates the purchase order file.	Ensures that goods are bought only from vendors who have been preapproved for reliability.
		Reconciling sequentially numbered purchase orders helps ensure that customer orders are legitimate.
3	Purchasing sends the **purchase order** to Vendor, Receiving, and Accounts Payable. Receiving's copy has blank quantities.	Vendor prepares merchandise for shipment.
		Receiving is put on notice to expect shipment.
		Accounts Payable is put on notice that liability to this vendor is about to increase.
4	Accounts Payable prepares a **summary of all purchase orders** issued that day and forwards it to General Ledger for posting of the total to the GL file.	Updating AP and GL files separately provides an additional accounting control when they are periodically reconciled.
5	Goods arrive at Receiving with a **packing slip**.	Because quantities are blank on Receiving's copy of the purchase order, employees cannot assume the order is correct as received and must count items.
6	Receiving prepares a **receiving report** and forwards it with the goods to Warehouse.	Detects discrepancies between the vendor packing slip and actual goods received.
7	Warehouse verifies that goods received match those listed on the **receiving report**.	Detects any loss or damage between Receiving and Warehouse.
8	Receiving sends the **receiving report** and **packing slip** to Inventory Control for matching with the **purchase requisition** and updating of inventory records.	Ensures that inventory records are current. Updating inventory and GL files separately provides an additional accounting control when they are periodically reconciled.
9	Receiving also sends the **receiving report** to Accounts Payable for matching with the **purchase order** and **purchase requisition** and updating of the AP file.	Ensures that vendor accounts are current.

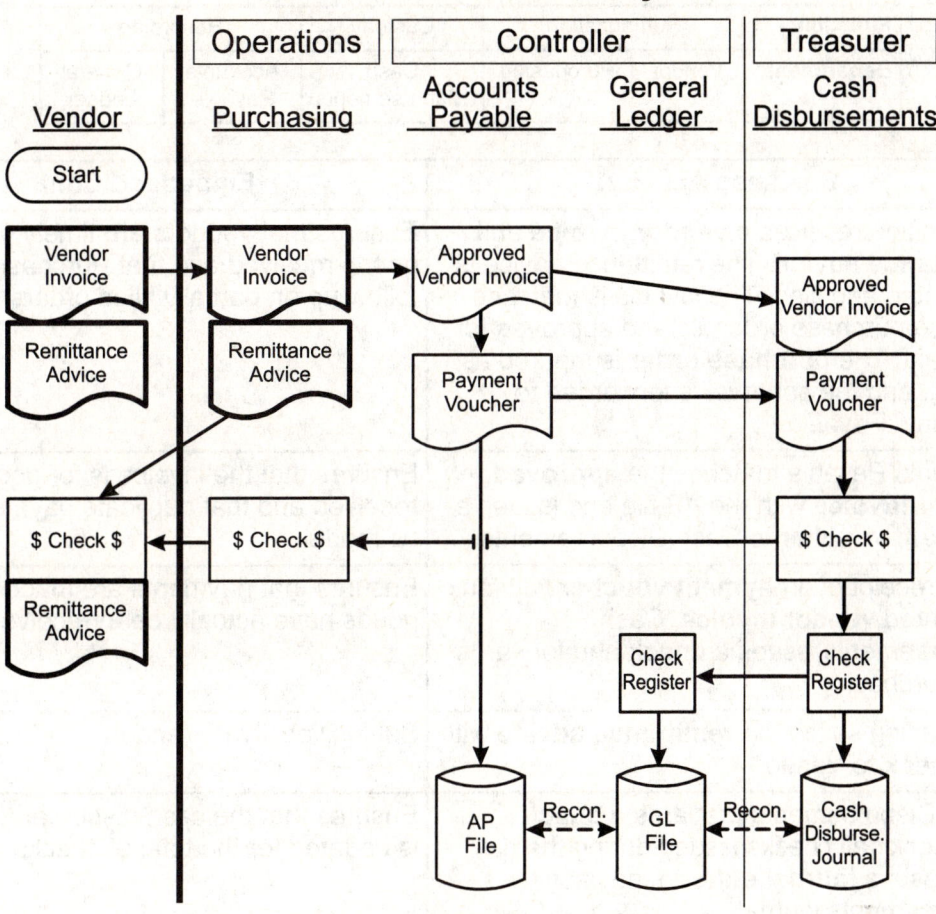

Figure 4-10

Cash Disbursements Cycle

Function:	Authorization		Custody	Recording	
Department:	Vendor	Purchasing	Cash Disbursements	Accounts Payable	General Ledger

Step	Business Activity	Embedded Control
1	Purchasing receives a **vendor invoice** and **remittance advice**. The remittance advice is separated and filed. The invoice is matched with the purchase order file and approved for payment. The **purchase order** is marked as closed, and the approval is forwarded to Accounts Payable.	Ensures that vendors are timely paid for goods received and that Purchasing can follow up on partially filled orders.
2	Accounts Payable matches the **approved vendor invoice** with the AP file and issues a **payment voucher** to Cash Disbursements.	Ensures that the invoice is for goods actually received and that duplicate payment cannot be made.
3	Upon receipt of a **payment voucher** with an **approved vendor invoice**, Cash Disbursements issues a **check** and forwards it to Purchasing.	Ensures that payments are made only when goods have actually been received.
4	Purchasing sends the **remittance advice** with the **check** to Vendor.	Settles liability to Vendor.
5	Cash Disbursements prepares a **check register** of all checks issued during the day and posts a **journal entry** to the cash disbursements journal.	Ensures that the cash disbursements journal is updated for the total of checks requested.
6	The check register is also forwarded to General Ledger for posting of the total to the GL file.	Updating AP and GL files separately provides an additional accounting control when they are periodically reconciled.

SU 4: Control: Types and Techniques

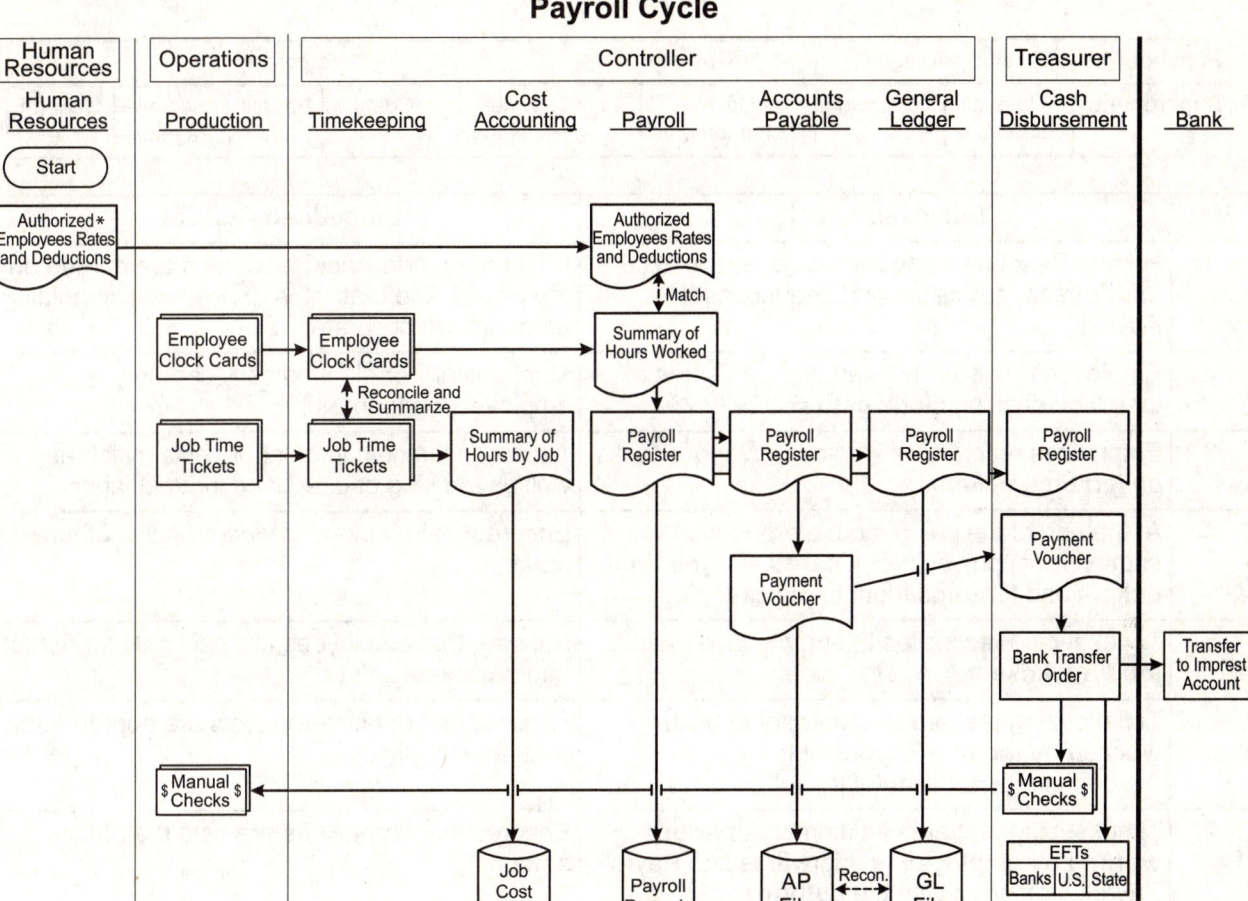

Figure 4-11

Payroll Cycle

Function:	Authorization		Custody		Recording				
Department:	Human Resources	Production	Cash Disbursements	Bank	Time-keeping	Cost Accounting	Payroll	Accounts Payable	General Ledger

Step	Business Activity	Embedded Control
1	Human Resources sends a **list of authorized employees**, pay rates, and deductions to Payroll.	Ensures that only actual persons are carried on the payroll and that rates of pay and withholding amounts are accurate.
2	Employees register the start and end times of their workdays on **clock cards**.	Mechanically or electronically captures employee work hours.
3	Employees record time worked on various tasks on **job time tickets**.	Allows accumulation of labor costs by job as well as tracking of direct and indirect labor.
4	At the end of the pay period, a production supervisor approves **clock cards** and **job time tickets** and forwards them to Timekeeping.	Ensures that employees worked only authorized hours.
5	Timekeeping reconciles the **clock cards** and **job time tickets**.	Ensures that employees are paid only for actual hours worked.
6	Timekeeping prepares a summary of **hours worked by job** and forwards it to Cost Accounting for updating of the job records.	Ensures that direct labor costs are appropriately assigned to jobs.
7	Timekeeping prepares a summary of **hours worked by employee** and forwards it to Payroll. Payroll matches it with the **authorized employee list**, prepares a **payroll register**, and updates the payroll records.	Ensures that employees are paid the proper amount.
8	Accounts Payable receives the **payroll register** from Payroll, prepares a **payment voucher**, and forwards it along with the payroll register to Cash Disbursements.	Ensures that a payable is accrued. Authorizes the movement of cash into the payroll imprest account.
9	Accounts Payable also forwards the **payroll register** to General Ledger for posting of the total to the GL file.	Updating AP and GL files separately provides an additional accounting control when they are periodically reconciled.
10	Cash Disbursements compares the **payment voucher** with the payroll register total and initiates appropriate **bank transfers**.	Ensures that the correct amount is transferred to the payroll imprest account and governmental authorities.
11	Cash Disbursements executes three **bank transfers**.	Use of an imprest payroll account allows idle funds to be invested and funds related to uncashed checks to be isolated.
		In the U.S., federal taxes withheld are transferred to the U.S. Treasury.
		In the U.S., state taxes withheld are transferred to the state government.
12	Employees paid by **manual check** are given checks by Treasury personnel, not by Payroll or their supervisors.	Ensures that Payroll or supervisory personnel cannot perpetrate fraud through the creation of fictitious employees.

Stop and review! You have completed the outline for this subunit. Study multiple-choice questions 12 through 19 beginning on page 108.

4.5 MANAGEMENT CONTROLS

1. **Control Techniques**

    a. Up to this point, we have covered the various types of controls. The remainder of this study unit describes the various control methods available to management.

2. **Roles and Responsibilities**

    a. **Management**

       1) The chief executive officer (CEO) should establish the tone at the top. Organizations reflect the ethical values and control consciousness of the CEO.
       2) The chief accounting officer also has a crucial role to play. Accounting staff have insight into activities across all levels of the organization.

    b. **Board of Directors**

       1) The entity's commitment to integrity and ethical values is reflected in the board's selections for senior management positions.
       2) To be effective, board members should be capable of objective judgment, have knowledge of the organization's industry, and be willing to ask the relevant questions about management's decisions.
       3) Important subcommittees of the board in organizations of sufficient size and complexity include the audit committee, the compensation committee, the finance committee, and the risk committee.

    c. **Internal Auditors**

       1) Management is ultimately responsible for the design and function of the system of internal controls. However, an organization's internal audit function may play an important consulting and advisory role.
       2) The internal audit function also evaluates the soundness of the system of internal control by performing systematic reviews according to professional standards.
       3) To remain independent in the conduct of these reviews, the internal audit function cannot be responsible for selecting and executing controls.

    d. **Other Personnel**

       1) Everyone in the entity must be involved in internal control and is expected to perform his or her appropriate control activities.
       2) In addition, all employees should understand that they are expected to inform those higher in the entity of instances of poor control when controls are not functioning as intended.

3. **Imposed Control and Self-Control**

    a. Imposed control is the traditional, mechanical approach. It measures performance against standards and then takes corrective action through the individual responsible for the function or area being evaluated.

       1) Though common, it has the drawback that corrective action tends to come after performance. The result may be a response to poor performance rather than its prevention.

    b. Self-control evaluates the entire process of management and the functions performed. Thus, it attempts to improve that process instead of simply correcting the specific performance of the manager. Management by objectives is an example.

4. **Alternative Definition of Control**

    a. Sawyer, Dittenhofer, and Scheiner, in *Sawyer's Internal Auditing* (Altamonte Springs, FL, The Institute of Internal Auditors, 5th ed., 2003, pages 82-86), define control and describe the means of achieving control. Their definition of control is as follows:

    > *The employment of all the means devised in an enterprise to promote, direct, restrain, govern, and check upon its various activities for the purpose of seeing that enterprise objectives are met. These means of control include, but are not limited to, form of organization, policies, systems, procedures, instructions, standards, committees, charts of accounts, forecasts, budgets, schedules, reports, records, checklists, methods, devices, and internal auditing.*

    b. Author's note: The concepts and definition of control have been constant for decades. This text quotes Sawyer's 5th edition rather than the 6th edition. It is a thorough yet concise explanation and is arguably more helpful to CIA candidates than the less thorough 6th edition.

5. **Organization**

    a. Organization, as a means of control, is an approved intentional structuring of roles assigned to people within the organization so that it can achieve its objectives efficiently and economically.

        1) Responsibilities should be divided so that no one person will control all phases of any transaction (this is discussed in further detail in Subunit 4.3).

        2) Managers should have the authority to take the action necessary to discharge their responsibilities.

        3) Individual responsibility always should be clearly defined so that it can be neither sidestepped nor exceeded.

        4) An official who assigns responsibility and delegates authority to subordinates should have an effective system of follow-up. Its purpose is to ensure that tasks assigned are properly carried out.

        5) The individuals to whom authority is delegated should be allowed to exercise that authority without close supervision. But they should check with their superiors in case of exceptions.

        6) People should be required to account to their superiors for the manner in which they have discharged their responsibilities.

        7) The organization should be flexible enough to permit changes in its structure when operating plans, policies, and objectives change.

        8) Organizational structures should be as simple as possible.

        9) Organization charts and manuals should be prepared. They help plan and control changes in, as well as provide better understanding of, the organization, chain of authority, and assignment of responsibilities.

6. **Policies**

    a. A policy is any stated principle that requires, guides, or restricts action. Policies should follow certain principles.

        1) Policies should be clearly stated in writing in systematically organized handbooks, manuals, or other publications and should be properly approved. But when the organizational culture is strong, the need for formal, written policies is reduced. In a strong culture, substantial training results in a high degree of acceptance of the organization's key values. Thus, such values are intensely held and widely shared.

        2) Policies should be systematically communicated to all officials and appropriate employees of the organization.

3) Policies must conform with applicable laws and regulations. They should be consistent with objectives and general policies prescribed at higher levels.
4) Policies should be designed to promote the conduct of authorized activities in an effective, efficient, and economical manner. They should provide a satisfactory degree of assurance that resources are suitably safeguarded.
5) Policies should be periodically reviewed. They should be revised when circumstances change.

7. **Procedures**
    a. Procedures are methods employed to carry out activities in conformity with prescribed policies. The same principles applicable to policies also are applicable to procedures. In addition,
        1) To reduce the possibility of fraud and error, procedures should be coordinated so that one employee's work is automatically checked by another who is independently performing separate prescribed duties. The extent to which automatic internal checks should be built into the system of control depends on many factors. Examples are (a) degree of risk, (b) cost of preventive procedures, (c) availability of personnel, (d) operational impact, and (e) feasibility.
        2) For nonmechanical operations, prescribed procedures should not be so detailed as to stifle the use of judgment.
        3) To promote maximum efficiency and economy, prescribed procedures should be as simple and as inexpensive as possible.
        4) Procedures should not be overlapping, conflicting, or duplicative.
        5) Procedures should be periodically reviewed and improved as necessary.

8. **Personnel**
    a. People hired or assigned should have the qualifications to do the jobs assigned to them. The best form of control over the performance of individuals is supervision. Hence, high standards of supervision should be established. The following practices help improve control:
        1) New employees should be investigated as to honesty and reliability.
        2) Employees should be given training that provides the opportunity for improvement and keeps them informed of new policies and procedures.
        3) Employees should be given information on the duties and responsibilities of other segments of the organization. They will better understand how and where their jobs fit into the organization as a whole.
        4) The performance of all employees should be periodically reviewed to see whether all essential requirements of their jobs are being met. Superior performance should be given appropriate recognition. Shortcomings should be discussed with employees so that they are given an opportunity to improve their performance or upgrade their skills.

9. **Accounting**
    a. Accounting is the indispensable means of financial control over activities and resources. It is a framework that can be fitted to assignments of responsibility. Moreover, it is the financial scorekeeper of the organization. The problem lies in what scores to keep. Some basic principles for accounting systems follow:
        1) Accounting should fit the needs of managers for rational decision making rather than the dictates of a textbook or check list.
        2) Accounting should be based on lines of responsibility.

3) Financial reports of operating results should parallel the organizational units responsible for carrying out operations.
4) Accounting should permit controllable costs to be identified.

10. **Budgeting**

    a. A budget is a statement of expected results expressed in numerical terms. As a control, it sets a standard for input of resources and what should be achieved as output and outcomes.

    1) Those who are responsible for meeting a budget should participate in its preparation.
    2) Those responsible for meeting a budget should be provided with adequate information that compares budgets with actual events and shows reasons for any significant variances.

        a) Management should ensure it receives prompt feedback on performance variances.

    3) All subsidiary budgets should tie into the overall budget.
    4) Budgets should set measurable objectives. Budgets are meaningless unless managers know why they have a budget.
    5) Budgets should help sharpen the organizational structure. Objective budgeting standards are difficult to set in a confused combination of subsystems. Budgeting is therefore a form of discipline and coordination.

11. **Reporting**

    a. In most organizations, management functions and makes decisions on the basis of reports it receives. Thus, reports should be timely, accurate, meaningful, and economical. The following are some principles for establishing a satisfactory internal reporting system:

    1) Reports should be made in accordance with assigned responsibilities.
    2) Individuals or units should be required to report only on those matters for which they are responsible.
    3) The cost of accumulating data and preparing reports should be weighed against the benefits to be obtained from them.
    4) Reports should be as simple as possible and consistent with the nature of the subject matter. They should include only information that serves the needs of the readers. Common classifications and terminology should be used as much as possible to avoid confusion.
    5) When appropriate, performance reports should show comparisons with predetermined standards of cost, quality, and quantity. Controllable costs should be segregated.
    6) When performance cannot be reported in quantitative terms, the reports should be designed to emphasize exceptions or other matters requiring management attention.
    7) For maximum value, reports should be timely. Timely reports based partly on estimates may be more useful than delayed reports that are more precise.
    8) Report recipients should be polled periodically to see whether they still need the reports they are receiving or whether the reports could be improved.

Stop and review! You have completed the outline for this subunit. Study multiple-choice questions 20 through 25 beginning on page 110.

SU 4: Control: Types and Techniques

QUESTIONS

4.1 Overview of Control

1. Which of the following statements best describes the relationship between planning and controlling?

A. Planning looks to the future; controlling is concerned with the past.

B. Planning and controlling are completely independent of each other.

C. Planning prevents problems; controlling is initiated by problems that have occurred.

D. Controlling cannot operate effectively without the tools provided by planning.

Answer (D) is correct.
REQUIRED: The best description of the relationship between planning and controlling.
DISCUSSION: Control is the process of making certain that plans are achieving the desired objectives. The elements of control include (1) establishing standards for the operation to be controlled, (2) measuring performance against the standards, (3) examining and analyzing deviations, (4) taking corrective action, and (5) reappraising the standards based on experience. Planning provides needed tools for the control process by establishing standards, i.e., the first step.
Answer (A) is incorrect. A control system looks to the future when it provides for corrective action and review and revision of standards. Answer (B) is incorrect. Planning and controlling overlap. Answer (C) is incorrect. Comprehensive planning includes creation of controls.

2. According to The IIA Glossary appended to the *Standards*, which of the following are most directly designed to ensure that risks are contained?

A. Risk management processes.

B. Internal audit activities.

C. Control processes.

D. Governance processes.

Answer (C) is correct.
REQUIRED: The term that is defined as the policies, procedures, and activities that are part of a control framework, designed to ensure that risks are contained within the established risk tolerances.
DISCUSSION: Control processes are the policies, procedures, and activities that are part of a control framework, designed to ensure that risks are contained within the risk tolerances established by the risk management process.
Answer (A) is incorrect. Risk management is a process to identify, assess, manage, and control potential events or situations to provide reasonable assurance regarding the achievement of the organization's objectives. Answer (B) is incorrect. An internal audit activity is a department, division, team of consultants, or other practitioner(s) that provides independent, objective assurance and consulting services designed to add value and improve an organization's operations. Answer (D) is incorrect. Governance is the combination of processes and structures implemented by the board to inform, direct, manage, and monitor the activities of the organization toward the achievement of its objectives.

3. Which of the following is **not** implied by the definition of control?

A. Measurement of progress toward goals.

B. Uncovering of deviations from plans.

C. Assignment of responsibility for deviations.

D. Indication of the need for corrective action.

Answer (C) is correct.
REQUIRED: The item not implied by the definition of control.
DISCUSSION: The elements of control include (1) establishing standards for the operation to be controlled, (2) measuring performance against the standards, (3) examining and analyzing deviations, (4) taking corrective action, and (5) reappraising the standards based on experience. Thus, assigning responsibility for deviations found is not a part of the controlling function.
Answer (A) is incorrect. Measurement of progress toward goals is implied by the definition of control. Answer (B) is incorrect. Uncovering of deviations from plans is implied by the definition of control. Answer (D) is incorrect. Indication of the need for corrective action is implied by the definition of control.

4. The actions taken to manage risk and increase the likelihood that established objectives and goals will be achieved are best described as

    A. Supervision.
    B. Quality assurance.
    C. Control.
    D. Compliance.

Answer (C) is correct.
REQUIRED: The term for actions taken to manage risk and increase the likelihood that established objectives and goals will be achieved.
DISCUSSION: Control is "any action taken by management, the board, and other parties to manage risk and increase the likelihood that established objectives and goals will be achieved" (The IIA Glossary).
Answer (A) is incorrect. Supervision is just one means of achieving control. Answer (B) is incorrect. Quality assurance relates to just one set of objectives and goals. It does not pertain to achievement of all established organizational objectives and goals. Answer (D) is incorrect. Compliance is "adherence to policies, plans, procedures, laws, regulations, contracts, or other requirements" (The IIA Glossary).

4.2 Classifying Controls

5. The requirement that purchases be made from suppliers on an approved vendor list is an example of a

    A. Preventive control.
    B. Detective control.
    C. Corrective control.
    D. Monitoring control.

Answer (A) is correct.
REQUIRED: The type of control requiring that purchases be made from suppliers on an approved vendor list.
DISCUSSION: Preventive controls are actions taken prior to the occurrence of transactions with the intent of stopping errors from occurring. Use of an approved vendor list is a control to prevent the use of unacceptable suppliers.
Answer (B) is incorrect. a detective control identifies errors after they have occurred. Answer (C) is incorrect. corrective controls correct the problems identified by detective controls. Answer (D) is incorrect. monitoring controls are designed to ensure the quality of the control system's performance over time.

6. Managerial control can be divided into feedforward, concurrent, and feedback controls. Which of the following is an example of a feedback control?

    A. Quality control training.
    B. Budgeting.
    C. Forecasting inventory needs.
    D. Variance analysis.

Answer (D) is correct.
REQUIRED: The example of a feedback control.
DISCUSSION: A feedback control measures actual performance, i.e., something that has already occurred, to ensure that a desired future state is attained. It is used to evaluate past activity to improve future performance. A variance is a deviation from a standard. Hence, variance analysis is a feedback control.
Answer (A) is incorrect. Quality control training is a feedforward, or future-directed, control. Answer (B) is incorrect. Budgeting is a feedforward, or future-directed, control. Answer (C) is incorrect. Forecasting inventory needs is a feedforward, or future-directed, control.

7. Which of the following is **not** a type of control?

    A. Preventive.
    B. Reactive.
    C. Detective.
    D. Directive.

Answer (B) is correct.
REQUIRED: The types of controls.
DISCUSSION: Controls may be preventive (to deter undesirable events from occurring), detective (to detect and correct undesirable events which have occurred), or directive (to cause or encourage a desirable event to occur). "Reactive" is not a specified type of control. However, controls may be reactive in the sense that they detect an undesirable event and react to it or correct it.
Answer (A) is incorrect. Controls may be preventive. Answer (C) is incorrect. Controls may be detective. Answer (D) is incorrect. Controls may be directive.

8. Which of the following is a feedback control?

   A. Preventive maintenance.
   B. Inspection of completed goods.
   C. Close supervision of production-line workers.
   D. Measuring performance against a standard.

Answer (B) is correct.
REQUIRED: The example of a feedback control.
DISCUSSION: Feedback controls obtain information about completed activities. They permit improvement in future performance by learning from past mistakes. Thus, corrective action occurs after the fact. Inspection of completed goods is an example of a feedback control.
Answer (A) is incorrect. Preventive maintenance is a feedforward control. It attempts to anticipate and prevent problems. Answer (C) is incorrect. The close supervision of production-line workers is a concurrent control. It adjusts an ongoing process. Answer (D) is incorrect. Measuring performance against a standard is a general aspect of control.

4.3 Flowcharts and Process Mapping

9. Which of the following tools would best give a graphical representation of a sequence of activities and decisions?

   A. Flowchart.
   B. Control chart.
   C. Histogram.
   D. Run chart.

Answer (A) is correct.
REQUIRED: The best tool for a graphical representation of a sequence of activities and decisions.
DISCUSSION: Flowcharting is an essential aid in the program development process that involves a sequence of activities and decisions. A flowchart is a pictorial diagram of the definition, analysis, or solution of a problem in which symbols are used to represent operations, data flow, equipment, etc.
Answer (B) is incorrect. A control chart is used to monitor deviations from desired quality measurements during repetitive operations. Answer (C) is incorrect. A histogram is a bar chart showing conformance to a standard bell curve. Answer (D) is incorrect. A run chart tracks the frequency or amount of a given variable over time.

10. Of the following, which is the most efficient source for an auditor to use to evaluate a company's overall control system?

    A. Control flowcharts.
    B. Copies of standard operating procedures.
    C. A narrative describing departmental history, activities, and forms usage.
    D. Copies of industry operating standards.

Answer (A) is correct.
REQUIRED: The most efficient source for an auditor to use to evaluate a company's overall control system.
DISCUSSION: Control flowcharting is a graphical means of representing the sequencing of activities and information flows with related control points. It provides an efficient and comprehensive method of describing relatively complex activities, especially those involving several departments.
Answer (B) is incorrect. Copies of procedures and related forms do not provide an efficient overview of processing activities. Answer (C) is incorrect. A narrative review covering the history and forms usage of the department is not as efficient or comprehensive as flowcharting for the purpose of communicating relevant information about controls. Answer (D) is incorrect. Industry standards do not provide a picture of existing practice for subsequent audit activity.

11. The diamond-shaped symbol is commonly used in flowcharting to show or represent a

    A. Process or a single step in a procedure or program.
    B. Terminal output display.
    C. Decision point, conditional testing, or branching.
    D. Predefined process.

Answer (C) is correct.
REQUIRED: The meaning of the diamond-shaped symbol used in flowcharting.
DISCUSSION: Flowcharts illustrate in pictorial fashion the flow of data, documents, and/or operations in a system. Flowcharts may summarize a system or present great detail, e.g., as found in program flowcharts. The diamond-shaped symbol represents a decision point or test of a condition in a program flowchart, that is, the point at which a determination must be made as to which logic path (branch) to follow.
Answer (A) is incorrect. The rectangle is the appropriate symbol for a process or a single step in a procedure or program. Answer (B) is incorrect. A terminal display is signified by a symbol similar to the shape of a cathode ray tube. Answer (D) is incorrect. A predefined processing step is represented by a rectangle with double lines on either side.

4.4 Accounting Cycles and Associated Controls

12. An adequate system of internal controls is most likely to detect a fraud perpetrated by a

A. Group of employees in collusion.
B. Single employee.
C. Group of managers in collusion.
D. Single manager.

Answer (B) is correct.
REQUIRED: The fraud most likely to be detected by an adequate system of internal controls.
DISCUSSION: Segregation of duties and other control processes serve to prevent or detect a fraud committed by an employee acting alone. One employee may not have the ability to engage in wrongdoing or may be subject to detection by other employees in the course of performing their assigned duties. However, collusion may circumvent controls. For example, comparison of recorded accountability for assets with the assets known to be held may fail to detect fraud if persons having custody of assets collude with recordkeepers.
Answer (A) is incorrect. A group has a better chance of successfully perpetrating a fraud than does an individual employee. Answer (C) is incorrect. Management can override controls. Answer (D) is incorrect. Even a single manager may be able to override controls.

13. Which of the following describes the most effective preventive control to ensure proper handling of cash receipt transactions?

A. Have bank reconciliations prepared by an employee not involved with cash collections and then have them reviewed by a supervisor.
B. One employee issues a prenumbered receipt for all cash collections; another employee reconciles the daily total of prenumbered receipts to the bank deposits.
C. Use predetermined totals (hash totals) of cash receipts to control posting routines.
D. The employee who receives customer mail receipts prepares the daily bank deposit, which is then deposited by another employee.

Answer (B) is correct.
REQUIRED: The most effective preventive control to ensure proper handling of cash receipt transactions.
DISCUSSION: Sequentially numbered receipts should be issued to maintain accountability for cash collected. Such accountability should be established as soon as possible because cash has a high inherent risk. Daily cash receipts should be deposited intact so that receipts and bank deposits can be reconciled. The reconciliation should be performed by someone independent of the cash custody function.
Answer (A) is incorrect. The bank reconciliation is a detective, not a preventive, control. Answer (C) is incorrect. Use of hash totals is a control over the completeness of posting routines, not cash receipts. Answer (D) is incorrect. A cash remittance list should be prepared before a separate employee prepares the bank deposit. The list and deposit represent separate records based on independent counts made by different employees.

14. Which of the following activities performed by a payroll clerk is a control weakness rather than a control strength?

A. Has custody of the check signature stamp machine.
B. Prepares the payroll register.
C. Forwards the payroll register to the chief accountant for approval.
D. Draws the paychecks on a separate payroll checking account.

Answer (A) is correct.
REQUIRED: The activity by a payroll clerk that is a control weakness.
DISCUSSION: Payroll checks should be signed by the treasurer, i.e., by someone who is not involved in timekeeping, recordkeeping, or payroll preparation. The payroll clerk performs a recordkeeping function.
Answer (B) is incorrect. Preparing the payroll register is one of the recordkeeping tasks of the payroll clerk. Answer (C) is incorrect. The payroll register should be approved by an officer of the organization. This control is a strength. Answer (D) is incorrect. Paychecks should be drawn on a separate payroll checking account. This control is a strength.

15. One payroll engagement objective is to determine whether segregation of duties is proper. Which of the following activities is incompatible?

A. Hiring employees and authorizing changes in pay rates.
B. Preparing the payroll and filing payroll tax forms.
C. Signing and distributing payroll checks.
D. Preparing attendance data and preparing the payroll.

Answer (D) is correct.
REQUIRED: The two activities that are incompatible.
DISCUSSION: Attendance data are accumulated by the timekeeping function. Preparing the payroll is a payroll department function. For control purposes, these two functions should be separated to avoid the perpetration and concealment of irregularities.
Answer (A) is incorrect. Hiring employees and authorizing changes in pay rates are both personnel functions. Answer (B) is incorrect. Preparing the payroll and filing payroll tax forms are both functions of the payroll department. Answer (C) is incorrect. Proper treasury functions include signing and distributing payroll checks.

16. Which of the following observations made during the preliminary survey of a local department store's disbursement cycle reflects a control strength?

   A. Individual department managers use prenumbered forms to order merchandise from vendors.
   B. The receiving department is given a copy of the purchase order complete with a description of goods, quantity ordered, and extended price for all merchandise ordered.
   C. The treasurer's office prepares checks for suppliers based on vouchers prepared by the accounts payable department.
   D. Individual department managers are responsible for the movement of merchandise from the receiving dock to storage or sales areas as appropriate.

Answer (C) is correct.
REQUIRED: The observation about the disbursement cycle indicating a control strength.
DISCUSSION: Accounting for payables is a recording function. The matching of the supplier's invoice, the purchase order, and the receiving report (and usually the purchase requisition) should be the responsibility of the accounting department. These are the primary supporting documents for the payment voucher prepared by the accounts payable section that will be relied upon by the treasurer in making payment.
Answer (A) is incorrect. The managers should submit purchase requisitions to the purchasing department. The purchasing function should be separate from operations. Answer (B) is incorrect. To encourage a fair count, the receiving department should receive a copy of the purchase order from which the quantity has been omitted. Answer (D) is incorrect. The receiving department should transfer goods directly to the storeroom to maintain security. A copy of the receiving report should be sent to the storeroom so that the amount stored can be compared with the amount in the report.

17. Which one of the following situations represents an internal control weakness in the payroll department?

   A. Payroll department personnel are rotated in their duties.
   B. Paychecks are distributed by the employees' immediate supervisor.
   C. Payroll records are reconciled with quarterly tax reports.
   D. The timekeeping function is independent of the payroll department.

Answer (B) is correct.
REQUIRED: The internal control weakness in the payroll department.
DISCUSSION: Paychecks should not be distributed by supervisors because an unscrupulous person could terminate an employee and fail to report the termination. The supervisor could then clock in and out for the employee and keep the paycheck. A person unrelated to either payroll recordkeeping or the operating department should distribute checks.
Answer (A) is incorrect. Periodic rotation of payroll personnel inhibits the perpetration and concealment of fraud. Answer (C) is incorrect. This analytical procedure may detect a discrepancy. Answer (D) is incorrect. Timekeeping should be independent of asset custody and employee records.

18. An auditor's flowchart of a client's accounting system is a diagrammatic representation that depicts the auditor's

   A. Assessment of the risks of material misstatement.
   B. Identification of weaknesses in the system.
   C. Assessment of the control environment's effectiveness.
   D. Understanding of the system.

Answer (D) is correct.
REQUIRED: The purpose of an auditor's flowchart.
DISCUSSION: The auditor should document (1) the understanding of the entity and its environment and the components of internal control, (2) the sources of information regarding the understanding, and (3) the risk assessment procedures performed. The form and extent of this documentation are influenced by the nature and complexity of the entity's controls (AU-C 315). For example, documentation of the understanding of internal control of a complex information system in which many transactions are electronically initiated, authorized, recorded, processed, or reported may include questionnaires, flowcharts, or decision tables.
Answer (A) is incorrect. The conclusions about the assessments of the RMMs should be documented. These are professional judgments of the auditor documented in the working papers. Answer (B) is incorrect. The flowchart is a tool to document the auditor's understanding of internal control, but it does not specifically identify weaknesses in the system. Answer (C) is incorrect. The auditor's judgment is the ultimate basis for concluding that controls are effective.

19. When documenting internal control, the independent auditor sometimes uses a systems flowchart, which can best be described as a

A. Pictorial presentation of the flow of instructions in a client's internal computer system.
B. Diagram that clearly indicates an organization's internal reporting structure.
C. Graphic illustration of the flow of operations that is used to replace the auditor's internal control questionnaire.
D. Symbolic representation of a system or series of sequential processes.

Answer (D) is correct.
REQUIRED: The best description of a systems flowchart.
DISCUSSION: A systems flowchart is a symbolic representation of the flow of documents and procedures through a series of steps in the accounting process of the client's organization.
Answer (A) is incorrect. A pictorial presentation of the flow of instructions in a client's internal computer system is a computer program flowchart. Answer (B) is incorrect. The organizational chart depicts the client's internal reporting structure. Answer (C) is incorrect. A flowchart does not necessarily replace the auditor's internal control questionnaire. Controls beyond those depicted on the systems flowchart must also be considered by the auditor, and information obtained from the questionnaire may be used to develop the flowchart.

4.5 Management Controls

20. The most appropriate method to prevent fraud or theft during the frequent movement of trailers loaded with valuable metal scrap from the manufacturing plant to the organization's scrap yard about 10 miles away would be to

A. Perform complete physical inventory of the scrap trailers before leaving the plant and upon arrival at the scrap yard.
B. Require existing security guards to log the time of plant departure and scrap yard arrival. The elapsed time should be reviewed by a supervisor for fraud.
C. Use armed guards to escort the movement of the trailers from the plant to the scrap yard.
D. Contract with an independent hauler for the removal of scrap.

Answer (B) is correct.
REQUIRED: The most appropriate method to prevent fraud or theft during the frequent movement of trailers loaded with valuable metal scrap.
DISCUSSION: Having the security guards record the times of departure and arrival is a cost-effective detective control because it entails no additional expenditures. Comparing the time elapsed with the standard time allowed and investigating material variances may detect a diversion of part of the scrap.
Answer (A) is incorrect. Performing a complete physical inventory of the scrap at both locations would not be economically feasible. Answer (C) is incorrect. Hiring armed guards to escort the scrap trailers is unlikely to be cost-effective unless the scrap is extremely valuable. Logging departures and arrivals will be sufficient in most cases. Answer (D) is incorrect. Using an independent hauler would provide no additional assurance of prevention or detection of wrongdoing.

21. Obsolete or scrap materials are charged to a predefined project number. The materials are segregated into specified bin locations and eventually transported to a public auction for sale. To reduce the risks associated with this process, an organization should employ which of the following procedures?

1. Require managerial approval for materials to be declared scrap or obsolete.
2. Permit employees to purchase obsolete or scrap materials prior to auction.
3. Limit obsolete or scrap materials sales to a pre-approved buyer.
4. Specify that a fixed fee, rather than a commission, be paid to the auction firm.

A. 2 and 3.
B. 1 only.
C. 2 and 4.
D. 1, 3, and 4.

Answer (B) is correct.
REQUIRED: The means of reducing risks associated with disposal of obsolete and scrap materials.
DISCUSSION: A preventive control is needed. Management approval for materials to be declared scrap or obsolete reduces the risk of misappropriation. Otherwise, materials may be more easily misclassified.
Answer (A) is incorrect. Permitting employees to purchase obsolete or scrap materials prior to auction provides even more incentive for misappropriation. Limiting obsolete or scrap materials sales to a pre-approved buyer does not mitigate the risk of misappropriation before the materials are sold. Moreover, these procedures may be less effective than an auction for obtaining the best price. Answer (C) is incorrect. Permitting employees to purchase obsolete or scrap materials prior to auction provides even more incentive for misappropriation. Specifying that a commission be paid to the auction firm creates an incentive to maximize the organization's return. Answer (D) is incorrect. Limiting obsolete or scrap materials sales to a pre-approved buyer does not mitigate the risk of misappropriation before the materials are sold. It also may be less effective than an auction for obtaining the best price. Specifying that a commission be paid to the auction firm creates an incentive to maximize the organization's return.

22. Which of the following control procedures does an internal auditor expect to find during an engagement to evaluate risk management and insurance?

A. Periodic internal review of the in-force list to evaluate the adequacy of insurance coverage.
B. Required approval of all new insurance policies by the organization's CEO.
C. Policy of repetitive standard journal entries to record insurance expense.
D. Cutoff procedures with regard to insurance expense reporting.

Answer (A) is correct.
REQUIRED: The control that should be found in an audit of risk management and insurance.
DISCUSSION: Obtaining insurance and periodically reviewing its adequacy are among management's responses to the findings of a risk assessment. Insurance coverage should be sufficient to ensure that the relevant assessed risks are managed in accordance with the organization's risk appetite.
Answer (B) is incorrect. CEO approval is an operational decision ordinarily delegated to a lower level manager. Answer (C) is incorrect. A policy concerning standard journal entries is an accounting control, not a risk management and insurance control. Answer (D) is incorrect. Cutoff procedures with regard to insurance expense reporting are an accounting control, not a risk management and insurance control.

23. Which of the following is an operating control for a research and development department?

A. Research and development personnel are hired by the payroll department.
B. Research and development expenditures are reviewed by an independent person.
C. All research and development costs are charged to expense in accordance with the applicable accounting principles.
D. The research and development budget is properly allocated between new products, product maintenance, and cost reduction programs.

Answer (D) is correct.
REQUIRED: The operating control for a research and development department.
DISCUSSION: Operating controls are those applicable to production and support activities. Because they may lack established criteria or standards, they should be based on management principles and methods. The appropriate allocation of R&D costs to new products, product maintenance, and cost reduction programs is an example. This is in contrast to the expensing of R&D costs, which is required by the rules of external financial reporting.
Answer (A) is incorrect. Only the human resources department should be responsible for hiring. A department responsible for recordkeeping (e.g., payroll) should not authorize transactions. Answer (B) is incorrect. Reviewing monetary amounts is a financial control. Answer (C) is incorrect. Expensing R&D costs is an accounting treatment rather than a control.

24. A recent inventory shortage at XYZ Corp., an unaffiliated supplier, contributed to production failures at OPS Corp. in the current period. To avoid future production failures because of supplier inventory shortages, the most appropriate method is for OPS to

A. Establish an inventory control framework at XYZ.
B. Increase the size of orders.
C. Produce the inventory items instead of purchasing from suppliers.
D. Inform XYZ about its risk appetite regarding supply failures.

Answer (D) is correct.
REQUIRED: The most effective method to prevent accepting excessive risk of supplier failure.
DISCUSSION: The risk appetite is the level of risk that an organization is willing to accept (The IIA Glossary). Thus, communicating about the risk appetite with external parties is an important aspect of risk management. It allows the organization to develop strategies to work with suppliers who may have different objectives.
Answer (A) is incorrect. OPS has no authority to establish an inventory control framework at XYZ. Answer (B) is incorrect. Increasing order size does not address the cause of supplier failures. Answer (C) is incorrect. Although in-house production will eliminate the external parties, it may not be the most cost-effective method. The external party may have cost advantages the organization does not.

25. A system of internal control includes physical controls over access to and use of assets and records. A departure from the purpose of such procedures is that

A. Access to the safe-deposit box requires two officers.
B. Only storeroom personnel and line supervisors have access to the raw materials storeroom.
C. The mailroom compiles a list of the checks received in the incoming mail.
D. Only salespersons and sales supervisors use sales department vehicles.

Answer (B) is correct.
REQUIRED: The departure from the purpose of control activities that limit access to assets.
DISCUSSION: Storeroom personnel have custody of assets, and supervisors are in charge of execution functions. To give supervisors access to the raw materials storeroom is a violation of the essential internal control principle of segregation of functions.
Answer (A) is incorrect. It is appropriate for two officers to be required to open the safe-deposit box. One supervises the other. Answer (C) is incorrect. The mailroom typically compiles a prelisting of cash. The list is sent to the accountant as a control for actual cash sent to the cashier. Answer (D) is incorrect. Use of sales department vehicles by only sales personnel is appropriate.

Notes

STUDY UNIT FIVE
DATA GATHERING AND DATA ANALYSIS

(14 pages of outline)

5.1	The Four Qualities of Information	113
5.2	Sources and Nature of Information	115
5.3	Establishing Engagement Objectives	117
5.4	Questionnaires	120
5.5	Interviewing	121
5.6	Other Data-Gathering Techniques	125

This study unit is the first of three covering **Section III: Conducting Internal Audit Engagements – Audit Tools and Techniques** from The IIA's CIA Exam Syllabus. This section makes up 25% to 35% of Part 1 of the CIA exam and is tested at the **proficiency level**. The relevant portion of the syllabus is highlighted below. (The complete syllabus is in Appendix B.)

III. CONDUCTING INTERNAL AUDIT ENGAGEMENTS – AUDIT TOOLS AND TECHNIQUES (25%–35%)

  A. **Data Gathering (Collect and analyze data on proposed engagements)**
   1. Review previous audit reports and other relevant documentation as part of a preliminary survey of the engagement area
   2. Develop checklists/internal control questionnaires as part of a preliminary survey of the engagement area
   3. Conduct interviews as part of a preliminary survey of the engagement area
   4. Use observation to gather data
   5. Conduct engagement to assure identification of key risks and controls
   6. Sampling (non-statistical [judgmental] sampling method, statistical sampling, discovery sampling, and statistical analyses techniques)
  B. Data Analysis and Interpretation
  C. Data Reporting
  D. Documentation / Work Papers
  E. Process Mapping, Including Flowcharting
  F. **Evaluate Relevance, Sufficiency, and Competence of Evidence**
   1. Identify potential sources of evidence

5.1 THE FOUR QUALITIES OF INFORMATION

 The practice of internal auditing is governed by professional standards. Thus, how an internal auditor performs an engagement is as important as the final product. Part 1 of the CIA exam contains numerous questions regarding (1) the procedures to be applied in a given situation and (2) the proper documentation. Working papers must be formatted and cross-referenced so that a reviewer can understand how the engagement was conducted and whether the evidence gathered supports the results reported.

Performance Standard 2310
Identifying Information
Internal auditors must identify sufficient, reliable, relevant, and useful information to achieve the engagement's objectives.

> **Interpretation of Standard 2310**
> - **Sufficient** information is factual, adequate, and convincing so that a prudent, informed person would reach the same conclusions as the auditor.
> - **Reliable** information is the best attainable information through the use of appropriate engagement techniques.
> - **Relevant** information supports engagement observations and recommendations and is consistent with the objectives for the engagement.
> - **Useful** information helps the organization meet its goals.

1. Determining whether information is adequate for the internal auditor's purposes is a matter of judgment that depends on the particular situation.
   a. Although the judgment is supposed to be objective, it inevitably varies with the internal auditor's training, experience, and other personal traits.
   b. Furthermore, the decision about the adequacy of information is not readily quantifiable.
2. **Sufficient Information**
   a. The sufficiency criterion is explicitly defined in objective terms. The conclusions reached should be those of a prudent, informed person.
      1) For example, objectivity is enhanced when samples are chosen using standard statistical methods.
   b. The basic issue is whether the information has the degree of persuasiveness needed based on the circumstances.
      1) Thus, persuasiveness must be greater in a fraud investigation of a senior manager than in an engagement involving petty cash. The difference in risk determines the quality and quantity of information.
3. **Reliable Information**
   a. Reliable information is the best information attainable using appropriate methods. Information is reliable when the internal auditor's results can be verified by others.
      1) Reliable information is valid. It accurately represents the observed facts and is free from error and bias.
   b. Information should consist of what may be collected using reasonable efforts subject to such inherent limitations as the cost-benefit constraint.
      1) Accordingly, internal auditors employ different methods, e.g., statistical sampling and analytical auditing procedures.
   c. Information is more reliable if it is
      1) Obtained from sources independent of the engagement client, such as confirmations of receivables or expert appraisals that are timely and made by a source with no connection to the auditee.
      2) Corroborated by other information.
      3) Direct, such as the internal auditor's personal observation, rather than indirect, such as hearsay.
      4) An original document, not a copy.
4. **Relevant Information**
   a. The definition of relevance emphasizes the need for work to be restricted to achieving objectives. However, information also should be gathered on all matters within the engagement's scope.

b. Relevant information has a logical relationship to what it is offered to prove.

   1) For example, vouching journal entries to the original documents does not support the completeness assertion about reported transactions. Instead, tracing transactions to the accounting records provides relevant information.

5. **Useful Information**

   a. Information is useful when it helps the organization meet its objectives.
   b. The organization's ultimate objective is to create value for its owners, other stakeholders, customers, and clients. Accordingly, this characteristic of information is consistent with the definition of internal auditing. It should add value, improve operations, and help an organization achieve its objectives.
   c. Furthermore, the identification of information that is useful to the organization is the ultimate justification for the existence of an internal audit activity.

The following is a useful memory aid for the four qualities of information:

S = **S**ufficient	**S**hould
R = **R**eliable	**R**ick
R = **R**elevant	**R**ecord
U = **U**seful	**U**niformly

Stop and review! You have completed the outline for this subunit. Study multiple-choice questions 1 through 3 beginning on page 126.

5.2 SOURCES AND NATURE OF INFORMATION

1. **Sources of Information**

   a. **Internal information** originates and remains with the engagement client.

      1) Payroll records are an example. They are initially generated by the client and then are subsequently processed and retained by the client.
      2) Lack of involvement of external parties reduces the persuasiveness of information.

         a) The reliability of information is greater when it comes from sources that are independent of the client.

   b. **Internal-external information** originates with the client but also is processed by an external party.

      1) Examples are canceled checks. These documents are created by the client but circulate through the banking system. A bank's acceptance of a check is some confirmation of its validity.
      2) Internal-external information is deemed to be more reliable than purely internal information.

   c. **External-internal information** is created by an external party but subsequently processed by the client.

      1) Such information has greater validity than information initiated by the client, but its value is impaired because of the client's opportunity to alter or destroy it.

         a) Suppliers' invoices are typical examples of external-internal information. Others include the canceled checks included in a cutoff bank statement received by the auditor directly from the bank.

d. **External information** is created by an independent party and transmitted directly to the internal auditor. External information is ordinarily regarded as the most reliable because it has not been exposed to possible alteration or destruction by the client.

   1) Common examples are confirmations of receivables sent in response to the internal auditor's requests.

e. **Outsourcing services**, such as clerical, accounting, and internal audit services, may result in information difficult to classify in this framework.

2. **Nature of Information**

   a. The following are forms of **legal evidence**:

     1) **Direct evidence** establishes a particular fact or conclusion without having to make any assumptions.

       a) Testimony by a witness to an event is a form of direct evidence.

     2) **Circumstantial evidence** establishes a fact or conclusion that can then lead by inference to another fact.

       a) The existence of a flat tire can lead to the conclusion that the tire was sabotaged. Obviously, such evidence must be used very carefully because the tire might have been damaged accidentally.

     3) **Conclusive evidence** is absolute proof, by itself.

       a) The classic example is that of a watch in the desert. The mere fact of finding the watch proves that someone put it there. It did not assemble itself spontaneously out of sand.

     4) **Corroborative evidence** serves to confirm a fact or conclusion that can be inferred from other evidence.

       a) An example is an employee who claims to have been working late on a certain night. A member of the building custodial staff can provide corroborating evidence that this employee was seen in the office.

   b. The following are forms of **audit evidence**:

     1) **Physical information** consists of the internal auditor's direct observation and inspection of people, property, or activities, e.g., of the counting of inventory.

       a) Photographs, maps, graphs, and charts may provide compelling physical information.

       b) When physical observation is the only information about a significant condition, at least two internal auditors should view it.

     2) **Testimonial information** consists of written or spoken statements of client personnel and others in response to inquiries or interview questions.

       a) Such information may give important indications about the direction of engagement work.

       b) Testimonial information may not be conclusive and should be supported by other forms of information when possible.

     3) **Documentary information** exists in some permanent form, such as checks, invoices, shipping records, receiving reports, and purchase orders.

       a) Thus, it is the most common type gathered by internal auditors.

SU 5: Data Gathering and Data Analysis

    b) Documentary information may be internal or external.

      i) Examples of external information are replies to confirmation requests, invoices from suppliers, and public information held by a governmental body, such as real estate records.

      ii) Examples of internal information include accounting records, receiving reports, purchase orders, depreciation schedules, and maintenance records.

   4) **Analytical information** is drawn from the consideration of the interrelationships among data or, in the case of internal control, the particular policies and procedures of which it is composed.

    a) Analysis produces circumstantial information in the form of inferences or conclusions based on examining the components as a whole for consistencies, inconsistencies, cause-and-effect relationships, relevant and irrelevant items, etc.

3. **Levels of Persuasiveness of Evidence**

 a. An auditor's **physical examination** provides the most persuasive form of evidence.

 b. Direct **observation** by the auditor, e.g., of performance of work by client personnel, is the next most persuasive.

 c. Information originating from a **third party** is less persuasive than information gathered by the auditor but more persuasive than information originating from the client.

 d. Information originating with the **client** can be somewhat persuasive in documentary form, especially if it is subject to effective internal control. But client oral testimony is the least persuasive of all.

4. **Other Issues**

 a. Engagement client feedback is valuable in the internal auditor's determination of whether the information supports observations, conclusions, and recommendations.

 b. If engagement observations are negative, the client has a reason to find flaws in the internal auditor's information and reasoning. Constructive feedback of this kind helps the internal auditor strengthen the evidential base of engagement communications.

  1) The client's tendency to be critical of negative observations means that agreement lends substantial credibility to the internal auditor's position.

  2) However, agreement with positive observations may represent client self-interest rather than useful feedback.

Stop and review! You have completed the outline for this subunit. Study multiple-choice questions 4 through 12 beginning on page 127.

5.3 ESTABLISHING ENGAGEMENT OBJECTIVES

> **Performance Standard 2210**
> **Engagement Objectives**
>
> Objectives must be established for each engagement.

1. **Risk**

 a. Risk is the possibility that an event will occur having an impact on the achievement of objectives. It is measured in terms of impact and likelihood (The IIA Glossary).

> **Implementation Standard 2210.A1**
> Internal auditors must conduct a preliminary assessment of the risks relevant to the activity under review. Engagement objectives must reflect the results of this assessment.

2. **Components of a Preliminary Survey**

    a. The internal auditors conduct a survey to (1) become familiar with activities, risks, and controls for the purpose of identifying areas of audit emphasis and (2) invite comments and suggestions from engagement clients. The following are components of a survey:

    1) Input from the engagement client
    2) Analytical procedures
    3) Interviews (covered in Subunit 5.5)
    4) Prior audit reports and other relevant documentation
    5) Process mapping
    6) Checklists

3. **Input from the Engagement Client**

    a. Client management may be a source of information for the formulation of engagement objectives.

    b. Onsite observations and interviews with users of the activity's output and other stakeholders may be part of the survey.

4. **Analytical Procedures**

    a. In the absence of known conditions to the contrary, certain relationships may reasonably be expected to exist and continue.

    1) The assessment is based on a comparison of the results of procedures with expectations identified or developed by the internal auditor.

    b. During engagement planning, analytical procedures assist in identifying conditions that may require additional audit procedures.

    1) Analytical procedures also are used to gather evidence.

    c. Analytical procedures may use monetary amounts, physical quantities, ratios, or percentages. Specific procedures include

    1) Ratio, trend, and regression analysis;
    2) Reasonableness tests;
    3) Period-to-period comparisons; and
    4) Comparisons with budgets, forecasts, and external economic information.

5. **Prior Audit Reports and Other Relevant Documentation**

    a. Prior audit reports may be another source of information. This is especially true of prior working papers. The issues and the process by which they were resolved may provide insights into the client's particular circumstances.

    1) However, the auditor must use such documentation for informational purposes only, not as a basis for objectives or conclusions.

6. **Process Mapping**

    a. A process map is the pictorial representation or narrative description of a client process. During the preliminary survey, reviewing the process map aids the internal auditor in assessing the efficiency of processes and controls.

    1) Narratives should be used only for simple processes.

b. Pictorial process mapping uses the three most common flowcharting symbols:

Process Mapping Symbols

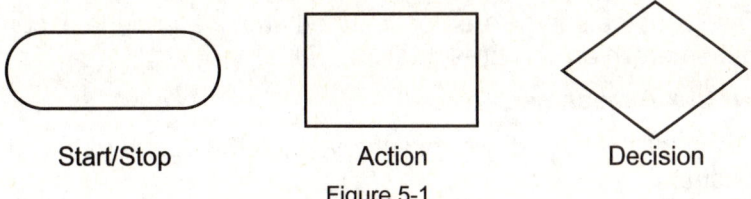

Figure 5-1

c. Below is an example of a process map prepared by the client or auditor for processing an invoice against a purchase order (P.O.). Approved invoices ultimately are forwarded to accounts payable (A.P.).

Process Map for Invoice Processing in Purchasing Department

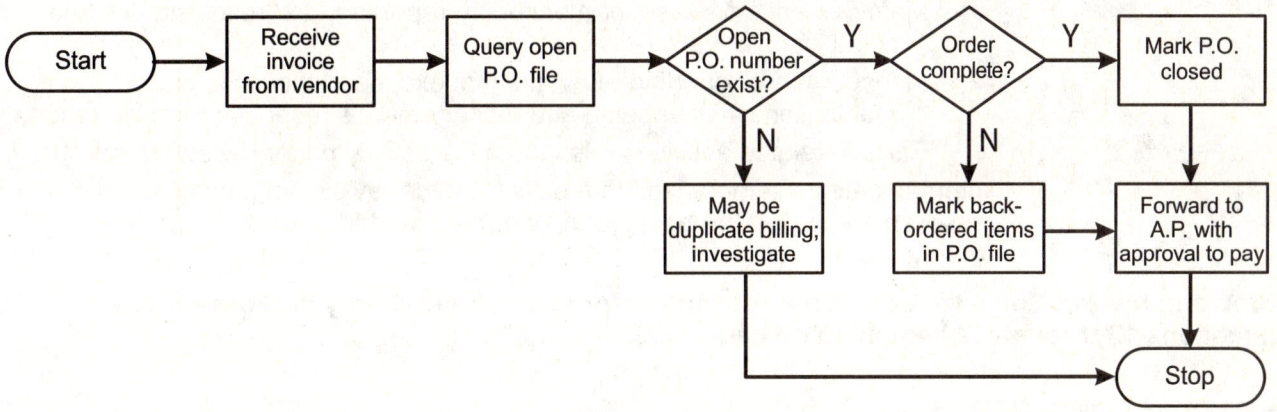

Figure 5-2

d. The auditor verifies the map by observing the process (a functional walk-through).

7. **Checklists**

   a. During the preliminary survey and throughout the engagement, checklists (reminder lists) ensure that the auditor has completed necessary tasks. For example, they include receipt of requested documentation and updates of the continuing audit file.

   ### Sample Checklist

   Add to permanent audit file:
   - ☐ Amortization schedule for new bond issues
   - ☐ Plan for disposal of assets of discontinued operation
   - ☐ Most recent forms filed with regulators
   - ☐ Most recent client-prepared process control maps

   b. Checklists increase the uniformity of data acquisition. They ensure that a standard approach is taken and minimize the possibility of omitting factors that can be anticipated.

   c. Disadvantages of checklists include the following:
   1) Providing a false sense of security that all relevant factors are addressed
   2) Inappropriately implying that equal weight is given to each item
   3) The difficulty of translating the observation represented by each item
   4) Treating a checklist as a rote exercise rather than part of a thoughtful understanding of the unique aspects of the audit

d. Checklists may be used to control administrative details involved in performing the engagement, to prepare for opening and closing conferences, etc.

8. **Documentation and Communication of Results**

   a. The results of the survey are documented and, if appropriate, communicated to management in an oral presentation.

9. **Preliminary Risk Assessment**

   a. After completing the preliminary survey, the internal auditor performs a preliminary risk assessment.

   b. Relevant guidance is in Practice Advisory 2210.A1-1, *Risk Assessment in Engagement Planning*:

   1) "Internal auditors consider management's assessment of risks relevant to the activity under review. The internal auditor also considers:

      - The reliability of management's assessment of risk.
      - Management's process for monitoring, reporting, and resolving risk and control issues.
      - Management's reporting of events that exceeded the limits of the organization's risk appetite and management's response to those reports.
      - Risks in related activities relevant to the activity under review" (para.1).

   2) "Internal auditors summarize the results from the reviews of management's assessment of risk, the background information, and any survey work" (para. 4).

Stop and review! You have completed the outline for this subunit. Study multiple-choice questions 13 through 17 beginning on page 129.

5.4 QUESTIONNAIRES

1. **Internal Control Questionnaires**

   a. One use of questionnaires is to obtain an understanding of the client's controls. An internal control questionnaire is often very structured and detailed and is drafted in a yes/no or short-answer format.

   b. Appropriate uses of an internal control questionnaire include

   1) Filling out the questionnaire while interviewing the person who has responsibility for the function or subunit being reviewed,
   2) Drafting the questionnaire so that a "no" response requires attention, and
   3) Supplementing the completed questionnaire with a narrative description or flowchart.

   c. Disadvantages of these questionnaires are that

   1) They are difficult to prepare.
   2) They are time-consuming to administer.
   3) Engagement clients may anticipate the preferred responses and therefore may lie or give insufficient consideration to the task.
   4) Not all circumstances can be addressed.
   5) They are less effective than interviewing.

SU 5: Data Gathering and Data Analysis   121

2. **Pre-Interview Questionnaires**

   a. Questionnaires are also an efficient way of preparing for an interview if they are properly designed and transmitted in advance. A formal questionnaire

      1) Involves the engagement client's supervisors and employees in the engagement and minimizes their anxiety.
      2) Provides an opportunity for engagement client self-evaluation.
      3) May result in a more economical engagement because the information it generates is prepared by those most familiar with it.

         a) The internal auditor must still ask clarifying questions and verify responses. However, only those answers that appear inappropriate should be pursued by asking for clarification or explanation.
         b) In this way, problems may be isolated and either compensating controls identified or extensions to the engagement procedures planned.

3. **Sequence and Format**

   a. The sequence and format of questions have many known effects.

      1) For example, questions should be in a logical order, and personal questions should be asked last because of possible emotional responses.

   b. One method of reducing these effects is to use questionnaire variations that cause these biases to average out across the sample.

      1) Many types of questions may be used, e.g., multiple-choice, checklists, fill-in-the-blank, essay, or options indicating levels of agreement or disagreement.
      2) Questions must be reliably worded so that they measure what was intended to be measured.
      3) The questionnaire should be short to increase the response rate.

Stop and review! You have completed the outline for this subunit. Study multiple-choice questions 18 through 20 on page 131.

5.5 INTERVIEWING

1. **Use**

   a. Interviewing and other data-gathering activities are usually performed during the preliminary survey phase of an audit engagement.

      1) Interviews obtain testimonial evidence from engagement clients, other members of the organization who have contact with them, and independent parties.

   b. An interview allows auditors to ask questions clarifying initial testimony. Thus, auditors may deepen their understanding of operations and seek reasons for unexpected results and unusual events and circumstances.

      1) An interview is a secure and personal form of communication compared with, for example, email or paper-based documents.
      2) People tend to be less careful in their responses if the interview is one-to-one.

   c. The main purpose of interviews is to gather facts related to the audit engagement.

2. **Dislike of Evaluation**

   a. One fundamental human relations problem faced by the internal auditor-interviewer is that people dislike being evaluated.

      1) Engagement clients may resent even the most constructive criticism and fear the possible adverse consequences of an audit report.

b. Consequently, the internal auditor must gain the confidence of clients by demonstrating self-assurance, persuasiveness, fairness, empathy, and competence.

1) The internal auditor may gain clients' willing cooperation by explaining how the engagement may be helpful and by emphasizing that all parties are members of a team with the same objectives.
2) Moreover, the internal auditor must avoid over-criticism.

a) An internal auditor who finds no major problems may be insecure about the result. (S)he may therefore resort to excessive criticism of minor matters, an approach that may alienate engagement clients and management and not be cost beneficial.

3. **Four Types of Interviews**

a. A preliminary interview is used to

1) Promote the value of internal auditing,
2) Understand the interviewee,
3) Gather general information, and
4) Serve as a basis for planning future interview strategies.

b. A fact-gathering interview is oriented to the specific details that can be provided by a particular interviewee.

1) Additional information can be sought in a nondirective manner, i.e., by asking open-ended questions.

c. A follow-up interview is intended to answer questions raised during the analysis of the fact-gathering interview. It also tests the interviewee's acceptance of new ideas generated by the auditor.

d. An exit interview helps to ensure the accuracy of conclusions, findings, and recommendations in the final engagement communication by discussing it with the interviewee.

4. **Planning an Interview**

a. The auditor should prepare by reading operations manuals, organizational charts, prior engagement communications, results of questionnaires, etc.

1) The auditor should understand not only the engagement client's functions, procedures, and terminology but also the psychological traits of auditee managers.

b. The auditor should design basic questions.

1) An auditor may use a directive approach emphasizing narrowly focused questions.
2) An alternative is a nondirective approach using broad questions that are more likely to provide clarification and to result in unexpected observations.
3) A combination of these approaches is often recommended.

5. **Scheduling Issues**

a. Except when surprise is needed (e.g., in a review of cash or a fraud engagement), an appointment should be made well in advance for a specific time and place.
b. The meeting should be in the engagement client's office, if feasible.
c. The interview's duration should be set in advance.
d. People tend to respond more freely if the interview is one-to-one.
e. Except in fraud engagements, the purpose should be explained to the client.
f. If possible, interviews should not be scheduled very late in the day, just before or after a vacation, or just before or after a meal.

6. **Opening the Interview**
   a. The auditor should be on time, and prompt notice should be given if delay is unavoidable.
   b. Engaging in initial, brief pleasantries may put the engagement client at ease.
   c. The purpose of the interview should be explained.
   d. The auditor should be polite, helpful, and nonthreatening.
   e. Confidentiality should be assured if feasible.
7. **Conducting the Interview**
   a. Interviewing requires an understanding of basic communications theory.
      1) A sender transmits an idea through a message.
      2) This message is encoded in a writing, in an oral statement, or in body language.
      3) The encoded message is transmitted through a channel or medium to a receiver.
         a) Barriers in the channel may interrupt or distort the message.
      4) The receiver decodes the message and interprets the message in accordance with his or her experience and knowledge.
         a) Technical jargon should be avoided so as to increase the chance that the message will be accurately decoded.
      5) The receiver may then undertake **action** or respond to the message.
      6) The words or actions of the receiver provide feedback to the sender.
         a) Feedback is vital because it tells the sender whether the message has been understood and acted upon.
      7) Nonverbal communication (body language) consists of facial expressions, vocal intonations, posture, gestures, appearance, and physical distance. Thus, by its nature, nonverbal communication is much less precise than verbal communication. However, in some cases, it may convey more information than verbal communication. But it is not necessarily more truthful.
         a) Nonverbal communication is heavily influenced by culture. For example, a nod of the head may have opposite meanings in different cultures.
   b. The interviewer should be tactful, objective, reasonable, and interested.
      1) (S)he also must avoid an accusatory tone and avoid statements not yet supported by evidence.
      2) The interviewer should not react negatively if the interviewee is uncooperative. (S)he should carefully explain the situation and provide an opportunity for the interviewee to calm down and continue the interview.
      3) The interviewee should not feel pressured or coerced during the interview.
   c. The interview should follow the agenda developed in the planning phase.
      1) Nevertheless, the interviewer should be flexible. Unexpected but worthwhile lines of inquiry may open up during the interview.
   d. Active (effective) listening includes observing interviewee behavior (body language, such as eye contact), reserving judgment about what is said, asking clarifying questions, and allowing for periods of silence.
      1) An effective listener also enhances the communication process by sending appropriate nonverbal signals to the speaker.
         a) Thus, a listener who wishes to convey a positive and encouraging message should stop other activities and focus complete attention on the speaker.

2) Reflecting what is said, that is, summarizing or rephrasing an answer, is a means of stimulating additional comments.
3) Furthermore, the interviewee should be encouraged to ask relevant questions.
   a) These questions should be respectfully heard and duly included in the record of the interview.
4) Empathy is a sensitive awareness of the speaker's feelings, thoughts, and experience. An empathic listener understands what the speaker wants to communicate rather than what the listener wants to understand.
5) Listening with intensity involves concentrating on the speaker's message and disregarding distractions.
6) Attentiveness is promoted by use of active listening techniques.
   a) For example, changing the wording of the questions and the sequence in which they are asked may eliminate some of the boredom associated with a series of interviews.
      i) The interviewer also may be able to refine the technique during the process.

e. Anticipation is one approach the interviewer can use to maintain focus during a far-ranging discussion. It assumes that the interviewer has done some preparation and is ready to listen intelligently.
   1) Active listening permits anticipation because the mind can process information more rapidly than most people speak. Thus, the listener has time to analyze the information and determine what is most important.
f. Leading questions (questions suggesting the answer) should be avoided.
g. Loaded questions (questions with self-incriminating answers) also should be avoided.
h. Questions requiring an explanatory response are usually preferable to those with binary (yes or no) responses.
i. An interviewer should be suspicious of answers that (1) are too smoothly stated, (2) fit too neatly with the interviewer's own preconceptions, (3) consist of generalizations, or (4) contain unfamiliar technical terminology.
   1) Thus, the interviewer must ask for greater specificity or other clarifications.
j. Care should be taken to differentiate statements of fact from statements of opinion.
k. The interviewer should understand what the interviewee regards as important.
l. Debate and disagreement with the interviewee should be avoided.

8. **Documentation**
   a. Good note taking during the interview is essential.
      1) Notes should be sufficiently readable and thorough to permit a full reconstruction of the information gathered. This write-up step should occur as soon as possible after the interview.
      2) The interviewee should be informed about the need for note taking.
      3) Notes should be properly dated and labeled, and the names and positions of interviewees should be included.
      4) The amount of time spent not looking at the interviewee should be minimized, and questions should not be asked while jotting notes.
      5) Interviews may be recorded only with the permission of the client.

b. The notes and the memorandum prepared with their help are part of the working papers and therefore the documentation of the engagement used to prepare communications.

1) The memorandum should include significant events during the interview, such as interruptions or emotional outbursts.
2) The internal auditor must be careful to use information in its proper context.

9. **Evaluation**

a. This step is especially important if a follow-up interview is considered, but it is useful as a means of internal auditor self-improvement.
b. The internal auditor should consider whether objectives were appropriate, whether they were attained, and, if not, why not.
c. The internal auditor also should consider whether the planning was efficient, the interviewee was cooperative, and the interviewer made errors.

Stop and review! You have completed the outline for this subunit. Study multiple-choice questions 21 through 23 on page 132.

5.6 OTHER DATA-GATHERING TECHNIQUES

1. **Observation**

a. By watching the physical activities of employees to see how they perform their duties, the auditor can determine whether written policies have been implemented.

1) Moreover, observing a phenomenon in its natural setting eliminates some experimental bias.

b. Observation is limited because employees who know they are being observed may behave differently while being observed. Accordingly, unobtrusive measures may be preferable.

1) The possibility of observing unexpected or unusual behavior makes such measures useful for exploratory investigations.

c. Observation is most persuasive for the existence or occurrence assertion (whether assets or liabilities exist and whether transactions have occurred).

1) It is less persuasive for the completeness assertion (whether all transactions that should be reported are reported).

d. Lack of experimental control and measurement precision are other weaknesses of observational research.

1) Another is that some things, such as private behavior, attitudes, feelings, and motives, cannot be observed.

2. **Internal Surveys**

a. Mail questionnaires are relatively cheap, eliminate interviewer bias, and gather large amounts of data. However, they tend to be inflexible, have a slow response time, and have nonresponse bias.

1) The sample will not be truly random if respondents as a group differ from nonrespondents. Thus, people may choose not to respond for reasons related to the purpose of the questionnaire.

b. Telephone interviews are a flexible means of obtaining data rapidly and controlling the sample. However, they introduce interviewer bias, are more costly, and gather less data than mail surveys.

c. Rating scales are used to allow people to rate such things as service. The scale represents a continuum of responses.

EXAMPLE of a Rating Scale

Rate the service you received on a scale of 1 to 10, 10 being the best. Circle the appropriate number.

1 2 3 4 5 6 7 8 9 10

---

3. **External Data Sources**

    a. Many external data sources are available that provide useful information for performing the engagement. These sources include the following:

        1) Online sources such as Lexis-Nexis or the National Automated Accounting Research System (NAARS)
        2) Authoritative and technical literature relevant to the issue being researched

Stop and review! You have completed the outline for this subunit. Study multiple-choice questions 24 and 25 on page 133.

QUESTIONS

5.1 The Four Qualities of Information

1. Engagement information is usually considered relevant when it is

A. Derived through valid statistical sampling.
B. Objective and unbiased.
C. Factual, adequate, and convincing.
D. Consistent with the engagement objectives.

Answer (D) is correct.
REQUIRED: The circumstance in which information is usually considered relevant.
DISCUSSION: Relevant information supports engagement observations and recommendations and is consistent with the objectives for the engagement (Inter. Std. 2310).
Answer (A) is incorrect. Whether sampling is appropriate and the results are valid are issues related to the determination of sufficiency and reliability rather than relevance. Answer (B) is incorrect. Objectivity and lack of bias do not ensure that information will support observations and recommendations and be consistent with the engagement objectives. Answer (C) is incorrect. Sufficient information is factual, adequate, and convincing so that a prudent, informed person would reach the same conclusions as the internal auditor.

2. In an operational audit, the internal auditors discovered an increase in absenteeism. Accordingly, the chief audit executive decided to identify information about workforce morale. To achieve this engagement objective, the internal auditors must understand that

A. Morale cannot be reliably analyzed.
B. Only outcomes that are directly quantifiable can be reliably analyzed.
C. Reliable information may be obtained about morale factors such as job satisfaction.
D. Morale is always proportional to compensation.

Answer (C) is correct.
REQUIRED: The true statement about workforce morale.
DISCUSSION: Reliable information is the best information attainable through the use of appropriate engagement techniques (Inter. Std. 2310). Such information need not consist only of quantifiable outcomes, such as rates of workforce turnover and absenteeism. Reliable information may be identified about such difficult-to-measure things as attitudes toward supervisors, other workers, and compensation. For example, surveys may produce statistically valid information about job satisfaction.
Answer (A) is incorrect. Difficulty of analysis does not preclude reliability. Answer (B) is incorrect. With proper engagement tools, even emotional responses may be measured and analyzed reliably. Answer (D) is incorrect. According to research and common human experience, the availability of, for example, intrinsic awards (e.g., personal achievement) may offset a low level of extrinsic awards (e.g., compensation).

3. Reliable information is

   A. Supportive of the engagement observations and consistent with the engagement objectives.
   B. Helpful in assisting the organization in meeting prescribed goals.
   C. Factual, adequate, and convincing so that a prudent person would reach the same conclusion as the internal auditor.
   D. Competent and the best attainable through the use of appropriate engagement techniques.

Answer (D) is correct.
REQUIRED: The definition of reliable information.
DISCUSSION: Reliable information is the best attainable information through the use of appropriate engagement techniques (Inter. Std. 2310). An original document is the prime example of such information.
Answer (A) is incorrect. Relevant information supports engagement observations and is consistent with engagement objectives. Answer (B) is incorrect. Useful information assists the organization in meeting goals. Answer (C) is incorrect. Sufficient information is factual, adequate, and convincing to a prudent person.

5.2 Sources and Nature of Information

4. To verify the proper value of costs charged to real property records for improvements to the property, the best source of information is

   A. Inspection by the internal auditor of real property improvements.
   B. A letter signed by the real property manager asserting the propriety of costs incurred.
   C. Original invoices supporting entries into the accounting records.
   D. Comparison of billed amounts with contract estimates.

Answer (C) is correct.
REQUIRED: The best source of evidence to verify costs charged to real property records for improvements.
DISCUSSION: To verify real property costs, the best method of obtaining engagement information is to examine records. Records originating outside the engagement client, such as original invoices, are much more reliable than internal documents or engagement client testimony. Also, these invoices support actual accounting record entries.
Answer (A) is incorrect. An inspection confirms that the improvements were made, not their cost. Answer (B) is incorrect. Records or documents generated internally are less reliable than those produced externally. Answer (D) is incorrect. A comparison of billed amounts with contract estimates measures the reasonableness of costs but is less persuasive than original invoices supporting entries into the accounting records.

5. The most conclusive information to support supplier account balances is obtained by

   A. Reviewing the vendor statements obtained from the accounts payable clerk.
   B. Obtaining confirmations of balances from the suppliers.
   C. Performing analytical account analysis.
   D. Interviewing the accounts payable manager to determine the internal controls maintained over accounts payable processing.

Answer (B) is correct.
REQUIRED: The most conclusive information to support supplier account balances.
DISCUSSION: Confirmation has the advantage of obtaining information from sources external to the entity. Information from external sources provides greater assurances of reliability than information from sources within the entity.
Answer (A) is incorrect. Vendor statements obtained from the accounts payable clerk may be inaccurate, purposely misstated, or prepared for nonexisting vendors. Answer (C) is incorrect. Analytical account analysis is effective for identifying circumstances that require additional consideration. Answer (D) is incorrect. Interviewing an employee provides oral, or testimonial, information, which is inherently less reliable than information obtained from independent sources.

6. A set of engagement working papers contained a copy of a document providing information that an expensive item that had been special-ordered was actually on hand on a particular date. The most likely source of this information is a printout from a computerized

   A. Purchases journal.
   B. Cash payments journal.
   C. Perpetual inventory file.
   D. Receiving report file.

Answer (C) is correct.
REQUIRED: The most likely source of evidence that an item was actually on hand on a particular date.
DISCUSSION: In a perpetual inventory system, purchases are directly recorded in the inventory account, and cost of goods sold is determined as the goods are sold. A computerized perpetual inventory file has a record of each debit or credit transaction with its date, amount, etc., and the inventory balance for any given date could therefore be determined.
Answer (A) is incorrect. The purchases journal indicates when the item was ordered but not whether it was still on hand at a specific later date. Answer (B) is incorrect. The cash payments journal indicates when the item was paid for but not whether it was still on hand at a specific later date. Answer (D) is incorrect. The receiving report indicates when the item was received but not whether it was still on hand at a specific later date.

7. The chief audit executive is reviewing the working papers produced by an internal auditor during a fraud investigation. Among the items contained in the working papers is a description of an item of physical information. Which of the following is the most probable source of this item of information?

A. Observing conditions.
B. Interviewing people.
C. Examining records.
D. Computing variances.

Answer (A) is correct.
REQUIRED: The most probable source of physical information.
DISCUSSION: Physical information results from the verification of the actual existence of things, activities, or individuals by observation, inspection, or count. It may take the form of photographs, maps, charts, or other depictions.
Answer (B) is incorrect. Interviewing produces testimonial information. Answer (C) is incorrect. The examination of records requires documentary information and produces analytical information. Answer (D) is incorrect. Computations and verifications lead to analytical information.

8. An internal auditor takes a photograph of the engagement client's workplace. The photograph is a form of what kind of information?

A. Physical.
B. Testimonial.
C. Documentary.
D. Analytical.

Answer (A) is correct.
REQUIRED: The kind of information represented by a photograph.
DISCUSSION: Physical information results from the verification of the actual existence of things, activities, or individuals by observation, inspection, or count. It may take the form of photographs, maps, charts, or other depictions.
Answer (B) is incorrect. Testimonial information consists of oral or written statements derived from inquiries or interviews. Answer (C) is incorrect. Documentary information consists of letters, memoranda, invoices, shipping and receiving reports, etc. Answer (D) is incorrect. Analytical information is derived from a study and comparison of the relationships among data.

9. The most likely source of information indicating employee theft of inventory is

A. Physical inspection of the condition of inventory items on hand.
B. A warehouse employee's verbal charge of theft.
C. Differences between an inventory count and perpetual inventory records.
D. Accounts payable transactions vouched to inventory receiving reports.

Answer (B) is correct.
REQUIRED: The most likely source of evidence indicating employee theft of inventory.
DISCUSSION: Testimonial information may not be conclusive and should be supported by other forms of information whenever possible. However, it may provide a lead not indicated by other procedures.
Answer (A) is incorrect. Physical inspection of items on hand does not disclose shortages or indicate theft. Answer (C) is incorrect. Differences between inventory counts and perpetual records are normal and, by themselves, do not indicate theft. Answer (D) is incorrect. Vouching transactions from accounts payable to receiving reports provides no information about a shortage or theft arising after receipt of the goods.

10. Which of the following are **least** valuable in predicting the amount of uncollectible accounts for an organization?

A. Published economic indices indicating a general business downturn.
B. Dollar amounts of accounts actually written off by the organization for each of the past 6 months.
C. Total monthly sales for each of the past 6 months.
D. Written forecasts from the credit manager regarding expected future cash collections.

Answer (D) is correct.
REQUIRED: The data least valuable in predicting the amount of uncollectible accounts.
DISCUSSION: Written forecasts from the credit manager may be relevant and useful, but they cannot be considered sufficient or reliable. Opinion evidence does not have as much reliability as factual evidence. In addition, the source of the evidence may have a bias, which should be considered by the internal auditor when evaluating the reliability of this data.
Answer (A) is incorrect. Although these statistics might not be quite as relevant as some of the other data, they are reliable, having been compiled and published by an independent source. Answer (B) is incorrect. The dollar amounts of write-offs are relevant and reliable, representing the actual experience of the organization. Answer (C) is incorrect. These amounts include cash as well as credit sales. Thus, the inclusion of cash sales reduces the relevance of these data. However, prior sales also represent the actual experience of the organization and therefore have a high degree of reliability.

11. Which of the following techniques is most likely to result in sufficient information with regard to an engagement to review the quantity of fixed assets on hand in a particular department?

    A. Physical observation.
    B. Analytical review of purchase requests and subsequent invoices.
    C. Interviews with department management.
    D. Examination of the account balances contained in general and subsidiary ledgers.

Answer (A) is correct.
REQUIRED: The best technique for obtaining sufficient information regarding the quantity of fixed assets.
DISCUSSION: First-hand observation by the auditor is more persuasive than analytical reviews performed, client-prepared records examined by the auditor, or interviews with client personnel.
Answer (B) is incorrect. Items purchased may no longer be present in the department being reviewed, even though they were originally purchased for that department. Answer (C) is incorrect. Interviews are useful in gaining insight into operations and understanding exceptions but are not sufficient. Answer (D) is incorrect. Ledger balances may not indicate whether assets have been moved or stolen.

12. An internal auditor at a savings and loan association concludes that a secured real estate loan is collectible. Which of the following engagement procedures provides the most persuasive information about the loan's collectibility?

    A. Confirming the loan balance with the borrower.
    B. Reviewing the loan file for proper authorization by the credit committee.
    C. Examining documentation of a recent, independent appraisal of the real estate.
    D. Examining the loan application for appropriate borrowers' signatures.

Answer (C) is correct.
REQUIRED: The most persuasive information about the loan's collectibility.
DISCUSSION: Real estate appraisals are based on estimated resale value or future cash flows. A recent, independent appraisal provides information about the borrower's ability to repay the loan. Such an appraisal tends to be reasonably reliable because it is timely and derives from an expert source independent of the engagement client.
Answer (A) is incorrect. A confirmation provides information about a loan's existence, not its collectibility. Answer (B) is incorrect. Information about the loan's authorization is not relevant to its collectibility. Answer (D) is incorrect. The validity of the loan is not relevant to the borrower's ability to repay the loan.

5.3 Establishing Engagement Objectives

13. In planning an assurance engagement, a survey could assist with all of the following **except**

    A. Obtaining engagement client comments and suggestions on control problems.
    B. Obtaining preliminary information on controls.
    C. Identifying areas for engagement emphasis.
    D. Evaluating the adequacy and effectiveness of controls.

Answer (D) is correct.
REQUIRED: The planning item not assisted by a survey.
DISCUSSION: Internal auditors conduct a survey to (1) become familiar with activities, risks, and controls to identify areas for engagement emphasis and (2) invite comments and suggestions from engagement clients (PA 2210.A1-1, para. 3). A survey is not sufficient for evaluating the adequacy and effectiveness of controls. Evaluation requires testing.

14. Which of the following best describes a preliminary survey?

    A. A standardized questionnaire used to obtain an understanding of management objectives.
    B. A statistical sample of key employee attitudes, skills, and knowledge.
    C. A "walk-through" of the financial control system to identify risks and the controls that can address those risks.
    D. A process used to become familiar with activities and risks to identify areas for engagement emphasis.

Answer (D) is correct.
REQUIRED: The best description of a preliminary survey.
DISCUSSION: If appropriate, internal auditors conduct a survey to (1) become familiar with the activities, risks, and controls to identify areas for engagement emphasis and (2) invite comments and suggestions from engagement clients (PA 2210.A1-1, para. 3).
Answer (A) is incorrect. A preliminary survey covers many areas besides management objectives. Answer (B) is incorrect. A preliminary survey would not normally include statistical sampling. Answer (C) is incorrect. A walk-through of controls is merely one possible component of a preliminary survey.

15. In advance of a preliminary survey, a chief audit executive sends a memorandum and questionnaire to the supervisors of the department to be evaluated. What is the most likely result of that procedure?

A. It creates apprehension about the engagement.
B. It involves the engagement client's supervisory personnel in the engagement.
C. It is an uneconomical approach to obtaining information.
D. It is only useful for engagements of distant locations.

Answer (B) is correct.
REQUIRED: The most likely result of sending a memorandum and questionnaire to the auditee.
DISCUSSION: Sending a memorandum and questionnaire to the engagement client is part of a participative approach. It helps involve the supervisors of the engagement client's department and thereby encourages a more collegial approach to the engagement. Obtaining the assistance of the engagement client in data gathering, evaluating operations, and solving problems should result in improved relations and in more effective and efficient engagements.
Answer (A) is incorrect. Greater knowledge of the upcoming engagement is more likely to remove some of the apprehension about the engagement. Answer (C) is incorrect. Sending a memorandum and questionnaire to the engagement client is normally more economical. Some of the basic data gathering will be done by those most competent to do it rapidly. Answer (D) is incorrect. Sending a memorandum and questionnaire is advantageous in most circumstances.

16. The audit committee has raised a few issues that the internal audit activity will examine during an operational audit for the current year. When performing the preliminary survey, which of the following is **not** an appropriate technique?

A. Performing interviews.
B. Developing questionnaires.
C. Determining the largest risk of financial statement misstatement.
D. All of the answers are appropriate techniques.

Answer (C) is correct.
REQUIRED: The appropriate preliminary investigation techniques.
DISCUSSION: Determining potential misstatements is not the objective of an operational audit. Additionally, a final risk analysis is developed at a later time in the audit, not during the preliminary survey. A preliminary risk assessment is appropriate during this stage.
Answer (A) is incorrect. Performing interviews allows the auditor to explore objectives, goals, and standards of operation, along with risks. The interview also allows the auditor to gain insights into management's style. Answer (B) is incorrect. Questionnaires can trigger appropriate preparation for the auditor's arrival as well as give the auditor insight into the organization's operations. Answer (D) is incorrect. The development and use of risk analysis to determine the largest risk of misstatement is not an appropriate preliminary survey technique.

17. Checklists used to assess risk have been criticized for all of the following reasons **except**

A. Providing a false sense of security that all relevant factors are addressed.
B. Inappropriately implying equal weight to each item on the checklist.
C. Decreasing the uniformity of data acquisition.
D. Being incapable of translating the experience or sound reasoning intended to be captured by each item on the checklist.

Answer (C) is correct.
REQUIRED: The factor not a criticism of checklists.
DISCUSSION: Checklists increase the uniformity of data acquisition. They ensure that a standard approach to assessing risk is taken and minimize the possibility of omitting consideration of factors that can be anticipated.
Answer (A) is incorrect. A checklist may omit factors the importance of which could not be foreseen. Answer (B) is incorrect. Each item will not be of equal significance. Answer (D) is incorrect. A checklist does not substitute for the sound professional judgment needed to understand the process of assessing risk.

5.4 Questionnaires

18. A well-designed internal control questionnaire should

- A. Elicit "yes" or "no" responses rather than narrative responses and be organized by department.
- B. Be a sufficient source of data for assessment of control risk.
- C. Help evaluate the effectiveness of internal control.
- D. Be independent of the objectives of the internal auditing engagement.

Answer (C) is correct.
REQUIRED: The function of an internal control questionnaire.
DISCUSSION: An internal control questionnaire consists of a series of questions about the organization's controls designed to prevent or detect errors or fraud. Answers to the questions help the internal auditor to identify specific controls relevant to specific assertions and to design tests of controls to evaluate the effectiveness of their design and operation.
Answer (A) is incorrect. Yes/no question formats and organizing question sequence by department may facilitate administering the questionnaire, but other formats and methods of question organization are possible. Answer (B) is incorrect. The questionnaire is a tool to help understand and document internal control but is not sufficient as the sole source of information to support the assessment of control risk. Answer (D) is incorrect. The internal control questionnaire must be designed to achieve the engagement objectives.

19. A questionnaire consists of a series of questions relating to controls normally required to prevent or detect errors and fraud that may occur for each type of transaction. Which of the following is **not** an advantage of a questionnaire?

- A. A questionnaire provides a framework that minimizes the possibility of overlooking aspects of internal control.
- B. A questionnaire can be easily completed.
- C. A questionnaire is flexible in design and application.
- D. The completed questionnaire provides documentation that the internal auditor become familiar with internal control.

Answer (C) is correct.
REQUIRED: The statement not an advantage of a questionnaire.
DISCUSSION: Questionnaires are designed to be inflexible in that the responses to certain questions are expected. Questionnaires are not easily adapted to unique situations. The approach that offers the most flexibility is a narrative memorandum describing internal control. The next most flexible approach is a flowchart.
Answer (A) is incorrect. A questionnaire provides a framework to assure that control concerns are not overlooked. Answer (B) is incorrect. A questionnaire is relatively easy to complete. For the most part, only yes/no responses are elicited from management and employees. Answer (D) is incorrect. The completed questionnaire can become part of the working papers to document the internal auditor's becoming familiar with the engagement client's activities, risks, and controls.

20. Which of the following is **not** an advantage of sending an internal control questionnaire prior to an audit engagement?

- A. The engagement client can use the questionnaire for self-evaluation prior to the auditor's visit.
- B. The questionnaire will help the engagement client understand the scope of the engagement.
- C. Preparing the questionnaire will help the auditor plan the scope of the engagement and organize the information to be gathered.
- D. The engagement client will respond only to the questions asked, without volunteering additional information.

Answer (D) is correct.
REQUIRED: The item not an advantage of sending an internal control questionnaire prior to an audit engagement
DISCUSSION: An internal control questionnaire consists of a series of questions about the organization's controls designed to prevent or detect errors or fraud. Answers to the questions help the internal auditor to identify specific controls relevant to specific assertions and to design tests of controls to evaluate the effectiveness of their design and operation. However, the information obtained is limited to that elicited by the questions asked.
Answer (A) is incorrect. Answering the questionnaire will help the engagement client identify areas where procedures are weak or not properly documented. Answer (B) is incorrect. The questionnaire will communicate the areas that the auditor plans to evaluate. Answer (C) is incorrect. The auditor can use the preparation of the questionnaire to organize the information to be gathered.

5.5 Interviewing

21. When conducting interviews during the early stages of an internal auditing engagement, it is more effective to

A. Ask for specific answers that can be quantified.
B. Ask people about their jobs.
C. Ask surprise questions about daily procedures.
D. Take advantage of the fact that fear is an important part of the engagement.

Answer (B) is correct.
REQUIRED: The most effective way to conduct interviews during the early stages of an engagement.
DISCUSSION: To improve internal auditor-client cooperation, the internal auditor should, to the extent feasible, humanize the engagement process. For example, individuals feel more important being asked people-type questions, such as asking people about their jobs, rather than control-type questions.
Answer (A) is incorrect. Later field work will cover information that can be quantified. Building rapport is more important in the early interviews. Answer (C) is incorrect. Unless fraud is suspected or the engagement concerns cash or negotiable securities, the more effective approach is to defuse the engagement client anxiety that results from anticipating the engagement. Answer (D) is incorrect. Although engagement client fear is a natural part of anticipating the engagement, the internal auditor should keep it from playing an important role by using good interpersonal skills to build a positive, participative relationship with the engagement client.

22. To elicit views on broad organizational risks and objectives from the board and senior management, an internal auditor should

A. List specific risk factors for consideration.
B. Develop spreadsheets with quantitative data relevant to the industry.
C. Use a nondirective approach to initiating discussion of mitigating risks.
D. Ask each member of management about specific risks listed in an industry reference.

Answer (C) is correct.
REQUIRED: The appropriate interview technique.
DISCUSSION: Effective interview planning includes formulating basic questions. An internal auditor may use a directive approach by asking narrowly focused questions. A preferable alternative given the interviewees and the subject matter is a nondirective approach using broad questions that are more likely to provide clarification and yield unexpected observations.
Answer (A) is incorrect. Although such factors may be relevant, they will not necessarily create an opportunity for management to brainstorm. Answer (B) is incorrect. Facts provide more of a teaching tool than a proper means to start relevant discussion. Answer (D) is incorrect. Although an industry reference may raise many valid points, it may not address concerns specific to the organization.

23. Tolerating silence, asking open-ended questions, and paraphrasing are three aids to more effective

A. Meetings.
B. Listening.
C. Interviews.
D. Feedback.

Answer (B) is correct.
REQUIRED: The process rendered more effective by tolerating silence, asking open-ended questions, and paraphrasing.
DISCUSSION: Listening entails decoding and understanding the first message sent. The sender then becomes a listener with respect to the feedback. Hence, listening is necessary at both ends of the communication channel. Other aids to effective listening are using body language to encourage the speaker, showing appropriate emotion to signify empathy, understanding and correcting for one's biases, avoiding making premature judgments, and briefly summarizing what has been said.
Answer (A) is incorrect. These methods may slow down a meeting. Answer (C) is incorrect. These methods may or may not help depending on the purpose of the interview. Answer (D) is incorrect. Only paraphrasing relates to feedback.

5.6 Other Data-Gathering Techniques

24. An internal auditing team developed a preliminary questionnaire with the following response choices:

1. Probably not a problem
2. Possibly a problem
3. Probably a problem

The questionnaire illustrates the use of

A. Trend analysis.
B. Ratio analysis.
C. Unobtrusive measures or observations.
D. Rating scales.

Answer (D) is correct.
REQUIRED: The technique illustrated by the questionnaire.
DISCUSSION: A rating scale may be used when a range of opinions is expected. The scale represents a continuum of responses. In this case, it reflects probability statements.
Answer (A) is incorrect. Trend analysis extrapolates past and current conditions. Answer (B) is incorrect. Ratio analysis considers the internal relationships of financial data. Answer (C) is incorrect. Use of rating scales requires the participant to participate actively. Thus, it is not unobtrusive.

25. Which of the following procedures is the **least** effective in gathering information about the nature of the processing and potential problems?

A. Interview supervisors in the claims department to find out more about the procedures used, and the rationale for the procedures, and obtain their observations about the nature and efficiency of processing.
B. Send an email message to all clerical personnel detailing the alleged problems and request them to respond.
C. Interview selected clerical employees in the claims department to find out more about the procedures used, and the rationale for the procedures, and obtain their observations about the nature and efficiency of processing.
D. Distribute a questionnaire to gain a greater understanding of the responsibilities for claims processing and the control procedures utilized.

Answer (B) is correct.
REQUIRED: The least effective procedure for gathering information about the nature of processing and potential problems.
DISCUSSION: Sending an email message to clerical staff is the least effective communication and information-gathering technique. It is impersonal and alleges inefficiencies before evidence has indicated that the problems are caused by inefficiencies in processing. This impersonal method might have been useful if the auditor wished to solicit open responses, but not enough guidance is given to encourage that kind of response.
Answer (A) is incorrect. Interviewing supervisors and employees is a good method of learning more about the nature of processing and soliciting input as to the potential causes of the problems being investigated. These individuals are intimately involved with the processing of transactions. Answer (C) is incorrect. Interviewing supervisors and employees is a good method of learning more about the nature of processing and soliciting input as to the potential causes of the problems being investigated. These individuals are intimately involved with the processing of transactions. Answer (D) is incorrect. Using a questionnaire is a procedure that is not as effective as interviewing individuals, but it is an efficient method of gathering preliminary information that would be useful in structuring the interviews.

Practice even more exam-emulating questions in **Gleim CIA Test Prep**!

STUDY UNIT SIX
CONDUCTING THE ENGAGEMENT: SAMPLING

(15 pages of outline)

6.1	Statistical Concepts	135
6.2	Sampling Concepts	138
6.3	Attribute Sampling	141
6.4	Variables Sampling	143
6.5	Process Control Techniques	146

This study unit is the second of three covering **Section III: Conducting Internal Audit Engagements – Audit Tools and Techniques** from The IIA's CIA Exam Syllabus. This section makes up 25% to 35% of Part 1 of the CIA exam and is tested at the **proficiency level**. The relevant portion of the syllabus is highlighted below. (The complete syllabus is in Appendix B.)

III. **CONDUCTING INTERNAL AUDIT ENGAGEMENTS – AUDIT TOOLS AND TECHNIQUES (25%–35%)**
  A. **Data Gathering (Collect and analyze data on proposed engagements)**
    1. Review previous audit reports and other relevant documentation as part of a preliminary survey of the engagement area
    2. Develop checklists/internal control questionnaires as part of a preliminary survey of the engagement area
    3. Conduct interviews as part of a preliminary survey of the engagement area
    4. Use observation to gather data
    5. Conduct engagement to assure identification of key risks and controls
    6. Sampling (non-statistical [judgmental] sampling method, statistical sampling, discovery sampling, and statistical analyses techniques)
  B. **Data Analysis and Interpretation**
  C. **Data Reporting**
  D. **Documentation / Work Papers**
  E. **Process Mapping, Including Flowcharting**
  F. **Evaluate Relevance, Sufficiency, and Competence of Evidence**

6.1 STATISTICAL CONCEPTS

1. **Populations and Samples**

    a. Sampling involves selecting representative items from a population (an entire group of items), examining those selected items, and drawing a conclusion about the population based on the results derived from the examination of the selected items.

    b. Auditors must draw conclusions about populations (invoices, accounts receivable, etc.) that are too numerous for every item to be tested.

      1) By applying the principles of statistics, auditors can test relatively small samples that allow them to draw conclusions about a population with measurable reliability.

      2) The main issue in sampling is choosing a sample that is representative of the population. Valid conclusions then may be stated about the population.

2. **Population Distributions**

    a. For audit purposes, each item in a population is associated with a variable of interest to the auditor.

      1) Discrete variables, such as the yes/no decision whether to authorize payments of invoices, are tested using attribute sampling (this is discussed in further detail in Subunit 6.3).

2) Continuous variables, such as the monetary amounts of accounts receivable, are tested using variables sampling (this is discussed in further detail in Subunit 6.4).

b. An important characteristic of a population is the distribution of the values of the variable of interest.

1) Of the many types of distributions, the most important is the normal distribution (the bell curve), depicted in Figure 6-1 below. Its values form a symmetrical, bell-shaped curve centered around the mean.

3. **Measures of Central Tendency**

a. The shape, height, and width of a population's distribution curve are quantified through its measures of central tendency.

1) The **mean** is the arithmetic average of a set of numbers.
2) The **median** is the middle value if data are arranged in numerical order. Thus, half the values are smaller than the median, and half are larger. It is the 50th percentile.
3) The **mode** is the most frequently occurring value. If all values are unique, no mode exists.

EXAMPLE of Mean, Median, and Mode

An investor has eight investments and calculates the measures of central tendency for returns on the portfolio.

Mean = Arithmetic average of population values
= (US $43,500 + $52,100 + $19,800 + $41,600 + $52,100 + $66,700 + $33,900 + $54,900) ÷ 8
= US $364,600 ÷ 8
= US $45,575

Median = Midpoint between two central-most population values
Values ranked: US $19,800; $33,900; $41,600; $43,500; $52,100; $52,100; $54,900; $66,700
= (US $43,500 + $52,100) ÷ 2
= US $95,600 ÷ 2
= US $47,800

Mode = Most frequent value in population
= US $52,100

---

b. In a **normal distribution**, the mean, median, and mode are the same, and the tails are identical. See Figure 6-1.

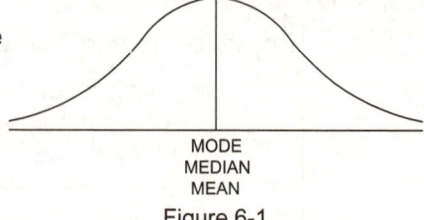

Figure 6-1

c. In some asymmetrical frequency distributions, the mean is greater than the mode. The right tail is longer, and the distribution is positively skewed (to the right).

1) Accounting distributions tend to be skewed to the right. For instance, accounts receivable generally include many medium- and low-value items and a few high-value items. See Figure 6-2.

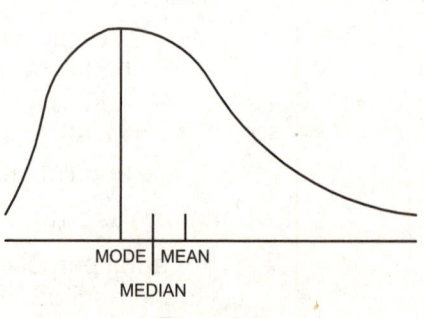

Figure 6-2

d. In some asymmetrical frequency distributions, the median is greater than the mean. The left tail is longer, and the distribution is negatively skewed (to the left). See Figure 6-3.

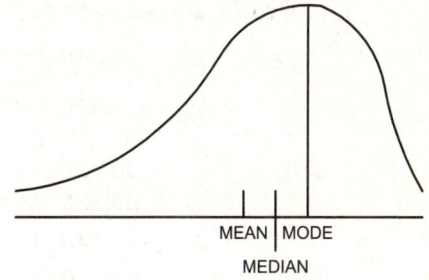

Figure 6-3

e. The median is the best estimate of central tendency for many asymmetrical distributions because the median is not biased by extremes.

4. **Standard Deviation and Confidence Level for Normal Distributions**

a. A population's variability is the extent to which the values of items are spread about the mean (dispersion). It is measured by the **standard deviation**.

1) The standard deviation is a measure of the dispersion of a set of data from its mean.

a) When the items have little dispersion, the standard deviation is small.
b) When the items are highly dispersed, the bell curve is relatively flat and the standard deviation is large.

2) Normal distributions may have the following fixed relationships between the area under the curve and the distance from the mean.

Distance (±) in Standard Deviations (Confidence Coefficient)	Area under the Curve (Confidence Level)
1.0	68%
1.64	90%
1.96	95%
2.0	95.5%
2.57	99%
3.0	99.7%

3) For example, 68% of the items are within one standard deviation of the mean in either direction.

a) Approximately 95% of the items are within 2 standard deviations of the mean.

EXAMPLE of a Normal Distribution

A certain species of pine tree has an average adult height of 20 feet, with each standard deviation representing 1 foot. The conclusion from the distribution below is that 68% of all trees of this species will reach a height between 19 and 21 feet (1 standard deviation), 95.5% will be between 18 and 22 feet (2 standard deviations), and 99.7% will be between 17 and 23 feet (3 standard deviations).

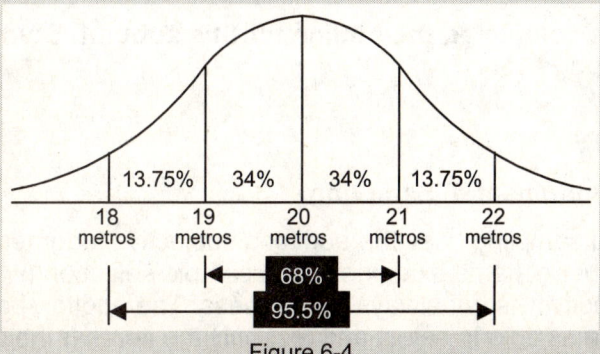

Figure 6-4

5. **Confidence Level and Confidence Interval**
    a. The area under the curve is the confidence level.
        1) A person selecting an item at random from a normally distributed population can be, for example, 95% confident that the value of the item is within 1.96 standard deviations of the mean and 99% confident that it will fall within 2.57 standard deviations of the mean.
        2) The **confidence level** is the percentage of times that a sample is expected to be representative of the population; i.e., a confidence level of 95% should result in representative samples 95% of the time.
    b. A **confidence interval** for a given confidence level is the range around a sample value that is expected to contain the true population value. It is constructed using the confidence coefficient for the number of standard deviations (based on the normal distribution) for the confidence level chosen.
        1) If repeated random samples are drawn from a normally distributed population, and the auditor specifies a 95% confidence level, the probability is that 95% of the confidence intervals constructed around the sample results will contain the population value.

EXAMPLE

An auditor took a random sample of sales authorizations. Based on the sample, the sales department authorized a sale after checking the credit score of the customer 88% of the time.

- If the confidence interval is 5%, the auditor can be confident that between 83% (88% − 5%) and 93% (88% + 5%) of all the company's sales were authorized after checking credit scores.
- The confidence level is the auditor's desired reliability of the sample. If the specified confidence level is 95% and the precision is 5%, the auditor can be 95% confident that the percentage of all the company's sales that were authorized after checking credit scores is between 83% and 93%.

---

        2) For a given confidence level, the size of the confidence interval depends on the sample size.
            a) The larger the sample size, the smaller the confidence interval can be.
            b) A smaller confidence interval means that the precision of the sample is greater, and the true population value is expected to be in the narrower range around the sample value.

6. **Pilot Sampling and Standard Error**
    a. The auditor can estimate the standard deviation of a population using a pilot sample.
    b. The **standard error of the mean** is the standard deviation of the distribution of sample means. The standard error is used to compute precision (the confidence interval). The larger the standard error, the wider the interval.
    c. The **coefficient of variability** measures the relative variability within the data and is calculated by dividing the standard deviation of the sample by the mean.

Stop and review! You have completed the outline for this subunit. Study multiple-choice questions 1 through 4 on page 150.

6.2 SAMPLING CONCEPTS

1. **Nonstatistical (Judgmental) Sampling**
    a. Judgmental sampling uses the auditor's subjective judgment to determine the sample size (number of items examined) and sample selection (which items to examine). This subjectivity is not always a weakness. The auditor, based on his or her experience, is able to select and test only the items (s)he considers to be the most important.

b. The following are the advantages of judgmental sampling:
 1) The process can be less expensive and less time consuming. No special knowledge of statistics and no special statistics software are required.
 2) The auditor has greater discretion to use his or her judgment and expertise. Thus, if the auditor has substantial experience, no time is wasted on testing immaterial items.
c. The following are the disadvantages of judgmental sampling:
 1) It does not provide a quantitative measure of sampling risk.
 2) It does not provide a quantitative expression of sample results.
 3) If the auditor is not proficient, the sample may not be effective.

2. **Statistical Sampling**
 a. Statistical sampling provides an objective method of determining sample size and selecting the items to be examined. Unlike judgmental sampling, it also provides a means of **quantitatively** assessing **precision** (how closely the sample represents the population) and **confidence level** (the percentage of time the sample will adequately represent the population).
 b. Statistical sampling helps the auditor design an efficient sample, measure the sufficiency of evidence obtained, and evaluate the sample results based on quantified data.
 c. The following are the advantages of statistical sampling:
  1) It provides a quantitative measure of sampling risk, confidence level, and precision.
  2) It provides a quantitative expression of sample results.
  3) It helps the auditor to design an efficient sample.
 d. The following are the disadvantages of statistical sampling:
  1) It can be more expensive and time consuming than nonstatistical sampling.
  2) It requires special statistical knowledge and training.
  3) It requires statistical software.

3. **Nonsampling vs. Sampling Risk**
 a. Nonsampling risk is audit risk not related to sampling. A common audit risk is the auditor's failure to detect an error in a sample.
  1) Nondetection of an error in a sample can be caused by auditor inattention or fatigue. It also can be caused by application of an inappropriate audit procedure, such as looking for the wrong approvals in a sample of documents.
 b. Sampling risk is the risk that a sample is not representative of the population. An unrepresentative sample may result in an incorrect conclusion.
  1) Statistical sampling allows the auditor to quantify sampling risk. An auditor should never attempt to quantify the sampling risk of a nonstatistically drawn sample.
  2) Sampling risk is **inversely related** to sample size. As the sample increases, sampling risk decreases.

4. **Selecting the Sampling Approach**
 a. In a **random sample**, every item in the population has an equal and nonzero chance of being selected.
  1) If enough large random samples are drawn, the mean of their means will approximate the population mean closely enough that they are considered to be representative of the population.
  2) For very large populations, the absolute size of the sample affects the precision of its results more than its size relative to the population. Thus, above a certain population size, the sample size generally does not increase.

3) The traditional means of ensuring randomness is to assign a random number to each item in the population. Random number tables are often used for this purpose.

    a) Random number tables contain collections of digits grouped randomly into columns and clusters. After assigning numbers to the members of the population, the tables can be used to select the sample items.

b. An **interval (systematic) sampling** plan assumes that items are arranged randomly in the population. If they are not, a random selection method should be used.

    1) Interval sampling divides the population by the sample size and selects every *n*th item after a random start in the first interval. For example, if the population has 1,000 items and the sample size is 35, every 28th item (1,000 ÷ 35 = 28.57) is selected.

        a) Interval sampling is appropriate when, for instance, an auditor wants to test whether controls were operating throughout an entire year. (A random sample might result in all items being selected from a single month.)
        b) Because interval sampling requires only counting in the population, no correspondence between random numbers and the items in the population is necessary as in random number sampling.

EXAMPLE

If the population contains 8,200 items and a sample of 50 is required, every 164th item is selected (8,200 ÷ 50). After a random start in the first interval (1 to 164), every additional 164th item is selected. For example, if the 35th item is the first selected randomly, the next is the 199th (35 + 164). The third item is the 363rd (199 + 164). The process is continued until the 50 items are identified.

---

c. **Block (cluster) sampling** randomly selects groups of items as the sampling units rather than individual items. An example is the inclusion in the sample of all cash payments for May and September.

    1) One possible disadvantage is that the variability of items within the clusters may not be representative of the variability within the population.

5. **Basic Steps in a Statistical Plan**

    a. **Determine the objectives of the plan.**

        1) For a test of controls, an example is to conclude that control is reasonably effective.
        2) For a test of details, an example is to conclude that a balance is not misstated by more than an immaterial amount.

    b. **Define the population.** This step includes defining the sampling unit (an individual item in the population) and considering the completeness of the population.

        1) For tests of controls, the period covered is defined.
        2) For tests of details, individually significant items may be defined.

    c. **Determine acceptable levels of sampling risk** (e.g., 5% or 10%).
    d. **Calculate the sample size** using tables or sample-size formulas.

        1) In some cases, it is efficient to divide the population into subpopulations or strata. The primary objective of **stratification** is to minimize variability.
        2) Stratification also allows the auditor to apply more audit effort to larger elements or more risky parts of the population.
        3) For example, when auditing sales revenue, an auditor could divide the population into strata of dollar increments. The auditor could test transactions under US $500, between US $501 and US $2,000, and US $2,001 and above.

- e. **Select the sampling approach**, e.g., random, interval, or block.
- f. **Take the sample.** The auditor selects the items to be evaluated.
- g. **Evaluate the sample results.** The auditor draws conclusions about the population.
- h. **Document the sampling procedures.** The auditor prepares appropriate working papers.

Stop and review! You have completed the outline for this subunit. Study multiple-choice questions 5 through 9 beginning on page 151.

6.3 ATTRIBUTE SAMPLING

1. **Uses**
   a. In attribute sampling, each item in the population has an attribute of interest to the auditor, e.g., evidence of proper authorization. Thus, attribute sampling is appropriate for discrete variables.
      1) Attribute sampling is used for tests of controls, i.e., when two outcomes are possible (compliance or noncompliance).

2. **Sample Size**
   a. The sample size for an attribute test depends on the following four factors:
      1) The **confidence level** is the percentage of times that a sample is expected to be representative of the population. The **greater** the desired confidence level, the **larger** the sample size should be.
         a) For a test of the controls, the confidence level is the complement of the allowable risk of **overreliance** on the control. For example, if this risk is 5%, the confidence level is 95% (100% – 5%).
      2) The **population size** is the sum of the items to be considered for testing. The larger the population size, the larger the sample size should be.
         a) However, for a very large population, the population size has a small effect on the sample size. Above a certain population size, the sample size generally does not increase.
      3) The **expected deviation rate** (expected rate of occurrence) is an estimate of the deviation rate in the current population.
         a) The **greater** the population deviation (variability in the population), the **larger** the sample size should be.
      4) The **tolerable deviation rate** (desired precision) is the highest allowable percentage of the population that can be in error (noncompliance rate) and still allow the auditor to rely on the tested control.
         a) The **lower** the tolerable deviation rate, the **larger** the sample size should be.

Factors Affecting Attribute Sample Size			
As the confidence level	increases,	the sample size must	increase.
As the expected deviation rate	increases,	the sample size must	increase.
As the tolerable deviation rate	increases,	the sample size can	decrease.
As the confidence level	decreases,	the sample size must	decrease.
As the expected deviation rate	decreases,	the sample size must	decrease.
As the tolerable deviation rate	decreases,	the sample size can	increase.

3. **Evaluation of Sample Results**
    a. The evaluation includes calculating the sample deviation rate and the achieved upper deviation limit.
    b. The **sample deviation rate** is the number of deviations observed divided by the sample size.
        1) This rate is the best estimate of the population deviation rate.
    c. The **achieved upper deviation limit (UDL)** is based on the sample size and the number of deviations discovered. Auditors use standard tables to calculate the UDL. In Table 1 below (adapted from an Audit Practice Release of the AICPA), the intersection of the sample size and the number of deviations indicates the achieved upper deviation limit.

EXAMPLE
Assume the risk of overreliance is 5%, the tolerable rate is 6%, the expected population deviation rate is 2.5%, and the population size is over 5,000. Given these data, the sample size is 150.

Table 1 -- Results Evaluation for Tests of Controls -- Upper % Limits at 5% Risk of Overreliance

Sample Size	Actual Number of Deviations Found										
	0	1	2	3	4	5	6	7	8	9	10
100	3.0	4.7	6.2	7.6	9.0	10.3	11.5	12.8	14.0	15.2	16.4
125	2.4	3.8	5.0	6.1	7.2	8.3	9.3	10.3	11.3	12.3	13.2
150	2.0	3.2	4.2	5.1	6.0	6.9	7.8	8.6	9.5	10.3	11.1
200	1.5	2.4	3.2	3.9	4.6	5.2	5.9	6.5	7.2	7.8	8.4

1) Accordingly, if the auditor discovers 3 deviations in a sample of 150, (s)he can state at a 95% confidence level (the complement of a 5% risk of overreliance) that the true occurrence rate is not greater than 5.1%.
2) The difference between the achieved UDL determined from a standard table and the sample rate (3 ÷ 150 = 2%) is the allowance for sampling risk (achieved precision). In the example, it is 3.1% (5.1% – 2%).
3) When the sample deviation rate exceeds the expected population deviation rate, the achieved UDL exceeds the tolerable rate at the given risk of overreliance. In that case, the sample does not support the planned reliance on the control. For example, if the sample rate is 4% (6 deviations), the UDL is 7.8, which exceeds the 6% tolerable rate.
4) When the sample deviation rate does not exceed the expected population deviation rate, the achieved UDL does not exceed the tolerable rate at the given risk level. Thus, the sample supports the planned reliance on the control. In the example, the sample deviation rate (2%) does not exceed the expected population rate (2.5%). Therefore, the achieved UDL (5.1%) does not exceed the tolerable rate (6%).

d. Each deviation should be analyzed to determine its nature, importance, and probable cause. Obviously, some are much more significant than others. Sampling provides a means of forming a conclusion about the overall population but should not be used as a substitute for good judgment.

1) The table below is based on a method for testing sampling concepts related to tests of controls. It is used to explain how to analyze the information. Many questions can be answered based on the analysis. The table depicts the possible combinations of the sample results and the true state of the population.

Auditor's Estimate Based on Sample Results	True State of Population	
	Deviation rate is less than tolerable rate.	Deviation rate exceeds tolerable rate.
Deviation rate is less than tolerable rate.	I. Correct	III. Incorrect
Deviation rate exceeds tolerable rate.	II. Incorrect	IV. Correct

    a) Cell II represents potential underreliance on internal control. It affects the efficiency but not the effectiveness of the audit.

    b) Cell III represents potential overreliance on internal control. It may result in audit failure.

4. **Other Attribute Sampling Methods**

　a. **Discovery sampling** is appropriate when even a single deviation (noncompliance) is critical.

　　1) The occurrence rate is assumed to be at or near 0%, and the method cannot be used to evaluate results statistically if deviations are found in the sample.

　　2) The sample size is calculated so that it will include **at least one** instance of a deviation if deviations occur in the population at a given rate.

　b. The objective of **stop-or-go sampling**, sometimes called sequential sampling, is to reduce the sample size when the auditor believes the deviation rate in the population is low.

　　1) The auditor examines only enough sample items to be able to state that the deviation rate is below a specified rate at a specified level of confidence. If the auditor needs to expand the sample to obtain the desired level of confidence, (s)he can do so in stages.

　　2) Because the sample size is not fixed, the internal auditor can achieve the desired result, even if deviations are found, by enlarging the sample sufficiently. In contrast, discovery sampling uses a fixed sample size.

Stop and review! You have completed the outline for this subunit. Study multiple-choice questions 10 through 13 beginning on page 152.

6.4 VARIABLES SAMPLING

1. **Uses**

　a. Variables sampling is used for continuous variables, such as weights or monetary amounts. Variables sampling provides information about whether a stated amount (e.g., the balance of accounts receivable) is materially misstated.

　　1) Thus, variables sampling is useful for substantive tests. The auditor can determine, at a specified confidence level, a range that includes the true value.

　b. In variables sampling, both the upper and lower limits are relevant (a balance, such as accounts receivable, can be either under- or overstated).

c. Auditors may employ the following variables sampling techniques:
1) Unstratified mean-per-unit
2) Stratified mean-per-unit
3) Difference estimation
4) Ratio estimation
5) Monetary unit sampling

NOTE: Each method is covered in this subunit, following a discussion of sample selection and interpretation.

2. **Sample Size**

   a. The sample size for a variables test depends on the following four factors:

   1) **Confidence level.** The **greater** the desired confidence level, the **greater** the sample size should be.

      a) If the auditor needs a more precise estimate of the tested amount, (s)he must increase the confidence level and the sample size.
      b) The confidence coefficient serves the same function as in attribute sampling. But, in variables sampling, it corresponds to a range around the calculated amount rather than an estimate of the maximum error rate.

   2) **Population size.** The **larger** the population, the **larger** the sample. However, for a very large population, the population size has a small effect on sample size. Above a certain population size, the sample size generally does not increase.

   3) **Tolerable misstatement** (precision) is an interval around the sample statistic that is expected to include the true balance of the population at the specific confidence level.

      a) For example, an auditor has tested a variables sample with precision of ±4% and a confidence level of 90%. The conclusion is that the true balance of the account is US $1,000,000. The precision of ±4% gives the boundaries of the computed range. Thus, 4% of US $1,000,000 equals US $40,000, resulting in a range of US $960,000 to US $1,040,000. The auditor can conclude that the probability is only 10% that the true balance lies outside this range.
      b) The **narrower** the precision, the **larger** the sample should be.

   4) **Standard deviation** (variability) of the population is a measure of the variability of the amounts in the population. An **increase** in the estimated standard deviation **increases** the sample size. The estimate can be based on pilot sample.

Factors Affecting Variables Sample Size			
As the confidence level	increases,	the sample size must	increase.
As the estimated standard deviation	increases,	the sample size must	increase.
As the population size	increases,	the sample size must	increase.
As the tolerable misstatement	increases,	the sample size can	decrease.
As the confidence level	decreases,	the sample size must	decrease.
As the estimated standard deviation	decreases,	the sample size must	decrease.
As the population size	decreases,	the sample size must	decrease.
As the tolerable misstatement	decreases,	the sample size can	increase.

3. **Primary Methods of Variables Sampling**

   a. **Mean-per-unit (MPU) estimation** averages the audited amounts of the sample items. It multiplies the average by the number of items in the population to estimate the population amount. An achieved precision at the desired level of confidence is then calculated.

      1) **Stratified** MPU is a means of increasing audit efficiency by separating the population into logical groups, usually by various ranges of the tested amounts. By creating multiple populations, the variability within each is reduced, allowing for a smaller overall sample size.

   b. **Difference estimation** estimates the misstatement of an amount by calculating the difference between the observed and recorded amounts for items in the sample. This method is appropriate only when per-item recorded amounts and their total are known. Difference estimation

      1) Determines differences between the audited and recorded amounts of items in the sample,
      2) Adds the differences,
      3) Calculates the mean difference,
      4) Multiplies the means by the number of items in the population, and
      5) Calculates an achieved precision at the desired level of confidence.

   c. **Ratio estimation** is similar to difference estimation. However, it estimates the population misstatement by multiplying the recorded amount of the population by the ratio of the total audited amount of the sample items to their total recorded amount.

      1) Ratio estimation is preferable to MPU estimation when the standard deviation of the distribution of ratios is less than the standard deviation of the sample item amounts.
      2) Ratio estimation is preferable to difference estimation when differences are relatively uniform.

EXAMPLE

An auditor examines a sample of 150 accounts receivable with a total recorded amount of US $172,500. The total population of 3,400 accounts receivable has a total recorded amount of US $3,500,000. Based on the audit, the total amount of the 150 sampled accounts is US $168,000.

MPU Estimation

- The average amount per sampled item is US $1,120 ($168,000 ÷ 150).
- The estimated correct balance of the population (accounts receivable) is **US $3,808,000** ($1,120 mean per unit value × 3,400 number of items in the population).

Difference Estimation

- The difference between the audited and recorded amounts of items in the sample is US $4,500 ($172,500 − $168,000).
- The mean difference is US $30 ($4,500 ÷ 150 number sample items).
- The estimated total population error is determined by multiplying the mean by the number of items in the population. It equals US $102,000 (3,400 × $30).
- The estimated correct balance of the population (accounts receivable) is **US $3,398,000** ($3,500,000 recorded amount of the population − $102,000 estimated error).

Ratio Estimation

- The ratio of the total audited amount of the sample items to their total recorded amount is US $0.974 ($168,000 audited amount ÷ $172,500 recorded amount).
- The estimated correct balance of the population (accounts receivable) is **US $3,409,000** ($3,500,000 recorded amount of the population × $0.974 ratio).

NOTE: An achieved precision at the desired level of confidence is then calculated. For example, assume the sample of 150 accounts with a total amount of US $168,000 was based on precision of ±3% and a confidence level of 95%. Using ratio estimation, the precision interval equals ±US $102,270 ($3,409,000 × 3%). The auditor can conclude that the probability is only 5% that the true balance lies outside the range of US $3,306,730 to US $3,511,270.

d. **Monetary-unit sampling (MUS)**, also known as probability-proportional-to-size (PPS) sampling, uses a monetary unit as the sampling unit. It applies **attribute sampling** methods to reach a conclusion about the probability of overstating monetary amounts.

1) Under MUS, the sampling unit is a unit of money rather than, for example, an invoice or an account balance. The item (invoice, account, etc.) containing the sampled monetary unit is selected for testing.
2) MUS is appropriate for testing account balances for overstatement when some items may be far larger than others in the population. In effect, it stratifies the population because the larger account balances have a greater chance of being selected.
3) MUS is most useful if few misstatements are expected.
4) MUS does not require the use of a measure of variability (e.g., standard deviation) to determine the sample size or interpret the results.
5) Thus, in the example on the previous page, the objective of MUS may be to determine that the total recorded amount of accounts receivable (US $3,500,000) is not overstated by more than 3%, with a confidence level of 95%.

Stop and review! You have completed the outline for this subunit. Study multiple-choice questions 14 through 20 beginning on page 153.

6.5 PROCESS CONTROL TECHNIQUES

1. **Uses**

    a. Statistical quality control determines whether a shipment or production run of units lies within acceptable limits. Items are either good or bad, i.e., inside or outside of control limits. It is also used to determine whether production processes are out of control.

2. **Acceptance Sampling**

    a. This method determines the probability that the rate of defective items in a batch is less than a specified level.

EXAMPLE

Assume a sample is taken from a population of 500. According to standard acceptance sampling tables, if the sample consists of 25 items and not one is defective, the probability is 93% that the population deviation rate is less than 10%. If 60 items are examined and no defects are found, the probability is 99% that the deviation rate is less than 10%. If two defects in 60 units are observed, the probability is 96% that the deviation rate is less than 10%.

---

3. **Statistical Control Charts**

    a. Statistical control charts are graphic aids for monitoring the status of any process subject to acceptable or unacceptable variations during repeated operations.

    1) They also have applications of direct interest to auditors and accountants, for example, (a) unit cost of production, (b) direct labor hours used, (c) ratio of actual expenses to budgeted expenses, (d) number of calls by sales personnel, or (e) total accounts receivable.

    b. A control chart consists of three lines plotted on a horizontal time scale.

    1) The center line represents the overall mean or average range for the process being controlled. The other two lines are the upper control limit (UCL) and the lower control limit (LCL).

2) The processes are measured periodically, and the values (Ẋ) are plotted on the chart.
    a) If the value falls within the control limits, no action is taken.
    b) If the value falls outside the limits, the result is abnormal, the process is considered out of control, and an investigation is made for possible corrective action.
c. Another advantage of the chart is that it makes trends and cycles visible.
    1) A disadvantage of the chart is that it does not indicate the cause of the variation.

EXAMPLE

The chart below depicts 2 weeks of production by a manufacturer who produces a single precision part each day. To be salable, the part can vary from the standard by no more than ± 0.1 millimeter.

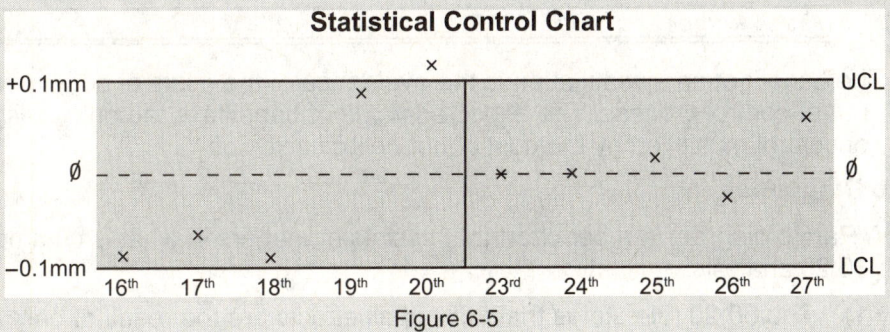

Figure 6-5

The part produced on the 20th had to be scrapped, and changes were made to the equipment to return the process to the controlled state for the following week's production.

---

d. Other Chart Types
    1) P charts show the percentage of defects in a sample. They are based on an attribute (acceptable/not acceptable) rather than a measure of a variable.
    2) C charts also are attribute control charts. They show defects per item.
    3) An R chart shows the range of dispersion of a variable, such as size or weight. The center line is the overall mean.
    4) An X-bar chart shows the sample mean for a variable. The center line is the average range.

4. **Variations**
    a. Variations in a process parameter may have several causes.
        1) Random variations occur by chance. Present in virtually all processes, they are not correctable because they will not repeat themselves in the same manner. Excessively narrow control limits will result in many investigations of what are simply random fluctuations.
        2) Implementation deviations occur because of human or mechanical failure to achieve target results.
        3) Measurement variations result from errors in the measurements of actual results.
        4) Model fluctuations can be caused by errors in the formulation of a decision model.
        5) Prediction variances result from errors in forecasting data used in a decision model.

5. **Benchmarks**

    a. Establishing control limits based on benchmarks is a common method. A more objective method is to use the concept of expected value. The limits are important because they are the decision criteria for determining whether a deviation will be investigated.

6. **Cost-Benefit Analysis**

    a. An analysis using expected value provides a more objective basis for setting control limits. The limits of controls should be set so that the cost of an investigation is less than or equal to the benefits derived.

    1) The expected costs include investigation cost and the cost of corrective action.

    ```
      (Probability of being out of control × Cost of corrective action)
    + (Probability of being in control × Investigation cost)
      Total expected cost
    ```

    b. The benefit of an investigation is the avoidance of the costs of continuing to operate an out-of-control process. The expected value of benefits is the probability of being out of control multiplied by the cost of not being corrected.

7. **Pareto Diagrams**

    a. A Pareto diagram is a bar chart that assists managers in what is commonly called 80:20 analysis.

    1) The 80:20 rule states that 80% of all effects are the result of only 20% of all causes. In the context of quality control, managers optimize their time by focusing their effort on the sources of most problems.

    b. The independent variable, plotted on the x axis, is the factor selected by the manager as the area of interest: department, time period, geographical location, etc. The frequency of occurrence of the defect (dependent variable) is plotted on the y axis.

    1) The occurrences of the independent variable are ranked from highest to lowest, allowing the manager to see at a glance which areas are of most concern.

EXAMPLE

A chief administrative officer uses a Pareto diagram to view which departments are generating the most travel vouchers that have been rejected because of incomplete documentation.

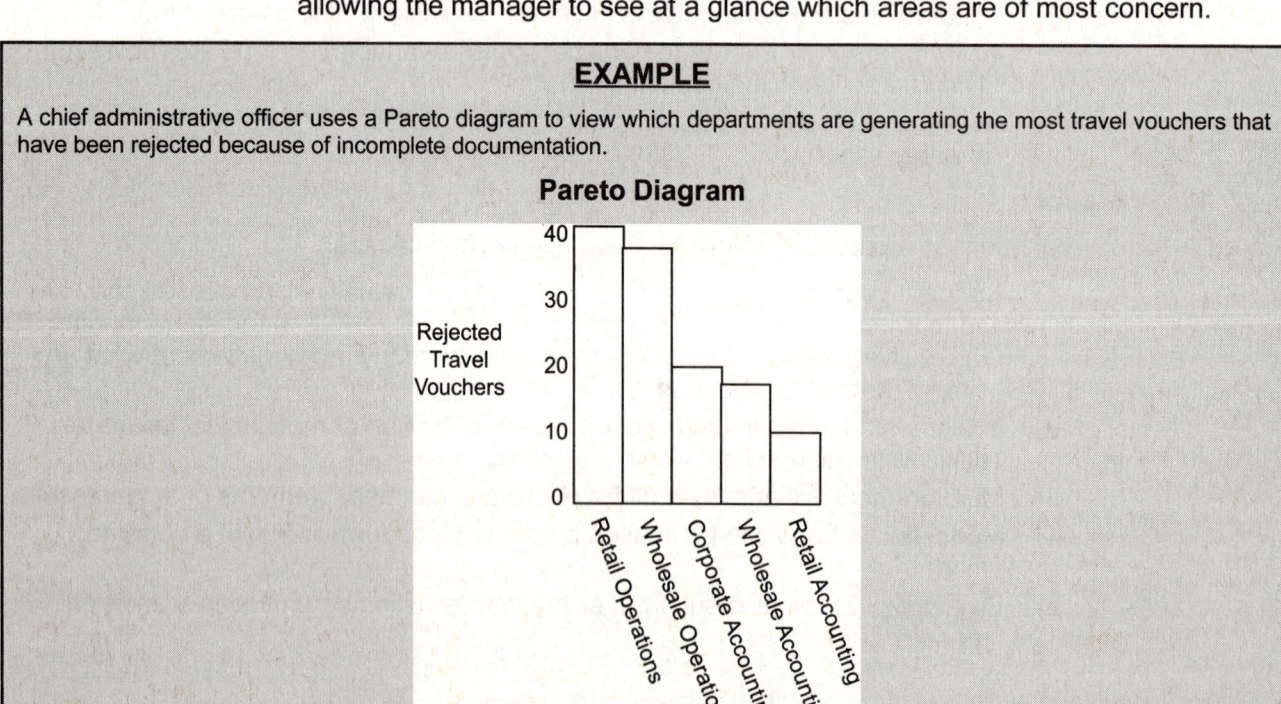

Figure 6-6

8. **Histograms**

   a. A histogram displays a continuous frequency distribution of the independent variable.

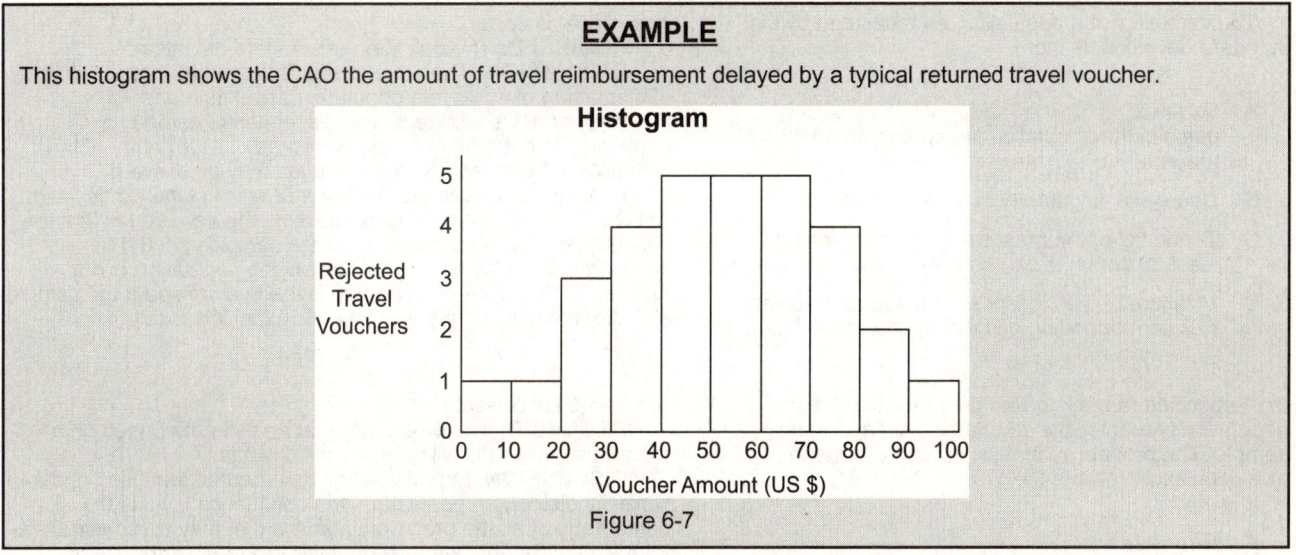

Figure 6-7

9. **Fishbone Diagrams**

   a. A fishbone (Ishikawa) diagram (also called a cause-and-effect diagram) is a total quality management process improvement technique.

      1) Fishbone diagrams are useful in studying causation (why the actual and desired situations differ).

   b. This format organizes the analysis of causation and helps to identify possible interactions among causes.

      1) The head of the skeleton contains the statement of the problem.
      2) The principal classifications of causes are represented by lines (bones) drawn diagonally from the heavy horizontal line (the spine).
      3) Smaller horizontal lines are added in their order of probability in each classification.

   c. Below is a generic fishbone diagram.

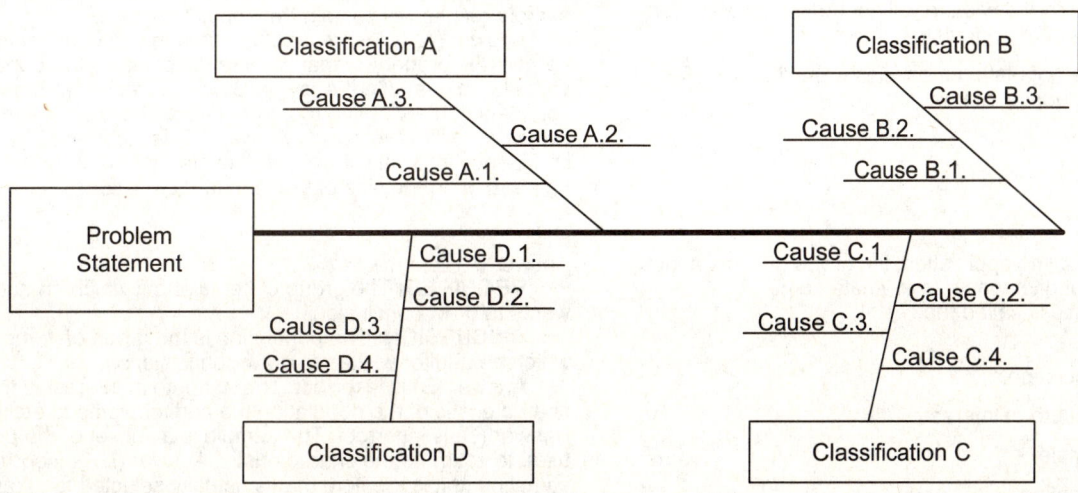

Figure 6-8

Stop and review! You have completed the outline for this subunit. Study multiple-choice questions 21 through 25 beginning on page 155.

QUESTIONS

6.1 Statistical Concepts

1. The variability of a population, as measured by the standard deviation, is the

A. Extent to which the individual values of the items in the population are spread about the mean.
B. Degree of asymmetry of a distribution.
C. Tendency of the means of large samples (at least 30 items) to be normally distributed.
D. Measure of the closeness of a sample estimate to a corresponding population characteristic.

Answer (A) is correct.
REQUIRED: The definition of standard deviation.
DISCUSSION: The standard deviation measures the degree of dispersion of items in a population about its mean.
Answer (B) is incorrect. The dispersion of items in a population is not a function of the degree of asymmetry of the distribution. For example, a distribution may be skewed (positively or negatively) with a large or small standard deviation. Answer (C) is incorrect. The central limit theorem states that the distribution of sample means for large samples should be normally distributed even if the underlying population is not. Answer (D) is incorrect. Precision is the interval about the sample statistic within which the true value is expected to fall.

2. A specified range is based on an estimate of a population characteristic calculated from a random sample. The probability that the range contains the true population value is the

A. Error rate.
B. Lower precision limit.
C. Confidence level.
D. Standard error of the mean.

Answer (C) is correct.
REQUIRED: The probability that an estimate based on a random sample falls within a specified range.
DISCUSSION: In principle, given repeated sampling and a normally distributed population, the confidence level is the percentage of all the precision intervals that may be constructed from simple random samples that will include the population value. In practice, the confidence level is regarded as the probability that a precision interval calculated from a simple random sample drawn from a normally distributed population will contain the population value.
Answer (A) is incorrect. The error rate in an attribute sampling application is the proportion of incorrect items in a population. Answer (B) is incorrect. The lower precision limit is the lower bound of the interval constructed from the sample result at a specified confidence level. Answer (D) is incorrect. The standard error of the mean is the standard deviation of the distribution of sample means.

3. A 90% confidence interval for the mean of a population based on the information in a sample always implies that there is a 90% chance that the

A. Estimate is equal to the true population mean.
B. True population mean is no larger than the largest endpoint of the interval.
C. Standard deviation will not be any greater than 10% of the population mean.
D. True population mean lies within the specified confidence interval.

Answer (D) is correct.
REQUIRED: The meaning of a confidence interval.
DISCUSSION: The confidence level, e.g., 90%, is specified by the auditor. A confidence interval based on the specified confidence level, also called precision, is the range around a sample value that is expected to contain the true population value. In this situation, if the population is normally distributed and repeated simple random samples are taken, the probability is that 90% of the confidence intervals constructed around the sample results will contain the population value.
Answer (A) is incorrect. Computation of a confidence interval permits the probability that the interval contains the population value to be quantified. Answer (B) is incorrect. Two-sided confidence intervals are more common. The area in each tail of a two-sided 90% level is 5%. Answer (C) is incorrect. The confidence interval is based on the standard deviation, but it has no bearing on the size of the standard deviation.

4. In a sampling application, the group of items about which the auditor wants to estimate some characteristic is called the

A. Population.
B. Attribute of interest.
C. Sample.
D. Sampling unit.

Answer (A) is correct.
REQUIRED: The group of items about which an auditor wants to draw conclusions.
DISCUSSION: The population is the group of items about which an auditor wishes to draw conclusions.
Answer (B) is incorrect. The attribute of interest is the characteristic of the population the auditor wants to estimate. Answer (C) is incorrect. The sample is a subset of the population used to estimate the characteristic. Answer (D) is incorrect. A sampling unit is the item that is actually selected for examination. It is a subset of the population.

6.2 Sampling Concepts

5. In preparing a sampling plan for an inventory pricing test, which of the following describes an advantage of statistical sampling over nonstatistical sampling?

A. Requires nonquantitative expression of sample results.
B. Provides a quantitative measure of sampling risk.
C. Minimizes nonsampling risk.
D. Reduces the level of tolerable error.

Answer (B) is correct.
REQUIRED: The statement describing an advantage of statistical sampling over nonstatistical sampling.
DISCUSSION: Statistical and nonstatistical sampling are both used to project the characteristics of a population. However, statistical sampling permits the internal auditor to make a quantitative assessment of how closely the sample represents the population for a given level of reliability.
Answer (A) is incorrect. Statistical sampling provides quantified results. Answer (C) is incorrect. Nonsampling risk exists in both statistical and nonstatistical sampling. Answer (D) is incorrect. Tolerable error is related to materiality and auditor judgment.

6. To project the frequency of shipments to wrong addresses, an internal auditor chose a random sample from the busiest month of each of the four quarters of the most recent year. What underlying concept of statistical sampling did the auditor violate?

A. Attempting to project a rate of occurrence rather than an error rate.
B. Failing to give each item in the population an equal chance of selection.
C. Failing to adequately describe the population.
D. Using multistage sampling in conjunction with attributes.

Answer (B) is correct.
REQUIRED: The concept of statistical sampling violated by sampling from the busiest month.
DISCUSSION: A random sample is one in which every item in the population has an equal and nonzero chance of being selected for the sample. Here, the auditor deliberately excluded shipments from the slower months.
Answer (A) is incorrect. Randomness is not associated with a rate of occurrence (often referred to as an error rate). Answer (C) is incorrect. The population is adequately described as the four quarters of the most recent year. Answer (D) is incorrect. Multistage sampling is appropriate when homogeneous subpopulations can be identified and sampled from; sample items are then selected from the randomly selected subpopulations.

7. Which one of the following statements about sampling is true?

A. A larger sample is always more representative of the underlying population than a smaller sample.
B. For very large populations, the absolute size of the sample has more impact on the precision of its results than does its size relative to its population.
C. For a given sample size, a simple random sample always produces the most representative sample.
D. The limitations of an incomplete sample frame can almost always be overcome by careful sampling techniques.

Answer (B) is correct.
REQUIRED: The true statement about sampling.
DISCUSSION: When the size of the population is very large, the absolute size of the sample may vary considerably even though its size relative to the population does not.
Answer (A) is incorrect. A large sample selected in a biased way is often less representative than a smaller but more carefully selected sample. Answer (C) is incorrect. Simple random sampling does not eliminate sampling risk. Proper execution of a simple random sample increases the probability of drawing a representative sample. Answer (D) is incorrect. Items excluded from the sampling frame cannot be included by an appropriate sampling technique.

8. Random numbers can be used to select a sample only when each item in the population

A. Can be assigned to a specific stratum.
B. Is independent of outside influence.
C. Can be identified with a unique number.
D. Is expected to be within plus or minus three standard deviations of the population mean.

Answer (C) is correct.
REQUIRED: The requirement for use of random numbers in sample selection.
DISCUSSION: A random sample is one in which every item in the population has an equal and nonzero chance of being selected and that selection is not influenced by whether any other item is selected.
Answer (A) is incorrect. Random-number sampling applies to both simple and stratified sampling. Answer (B) is incorrect. No such requirement exists. Answer (D) is incorrect. By definition, there are a few population items outside plus or minus three standard deviations from the population mean.

9. Systematic selection can be expected to produce a representative sample when

A. Random number tables are used to determine the items included in the sample.
B. The population is arranged randomly with respect to the audit objective.
C. The sample is determined using multiple random starts and includes more items than required.
D. Judgmental sampling is used by the auditor to offset any sampling bias.

Answer (B) is correct.
REQUIRED: The condition under which systematic selection produces a representative sample.
DISCUSSION: A sample selected using a systematic sampling procedure and a random start will behave as if it were a random sample when the population is randomly ordered with respect to the audit objective. Sampling bias due to systematic selection will be small when the population items are not arranged in a pattern.
Answer (A) is incorrect. Systematic selection is random only with respect to the start. Answer (C) is incorrect. The number of items in a sample is not relevant to the procedures used to select the specific items in the sample. The use of multiple random starts might increase the chance that a sample will behave randomly, but only if the population is arranged randomly. Answer (D) is incorrect. Judgmental sampling will not increase the randomness of a sample but will introduce sampling bias into the sample.

6.3 Attribute Sampling

10. When planning an attribute sampling application, the difference between the expected error rate and the maximum tolerable error rate is the planned

A. Precision.
B. Reliability.
C. Dispersion.
D. Skewness.

Answer (A) is correct.
REQUIRED: The difference between the expected error rate and the maximum tolerable error rate.
DISCUSSION: The precision of an attribute sample (also called the confidence interval or allowance for sampling risk) is an interval around the sample statistic that the auditor expects to contain the true value of the population. In attribute sampling (used for tests of controls), the achieved precision is the difference between the sample deviation rate and the achieved upper deviation limit (customarily determined from a standard table given the sample deviation rate and the sample size).
Answer (B) is incorrect. Reliability is the confidence level. It is the percentage of times that repeated samples will be representative of the population from which they are taken. Answer (C) is incorrect. Dispersion is the degree of variation in a set of values. Answer (D) is incorrect. Skewness is the lack of symmetry in a frequency distribution.

11. If all other sample size planning factors were exactly the same in attribute sampling, changing the confidence level from 95% to 90% and changing the desired precision from 2% to 5% would result in a revised sample size that would be

A. Larger.
B. Smaller.
C. Unchanged.
D. Indeterminate.

Answer (B) is correct.
REQUIRED: The sample size effect of decreasing the confidence level and widening the desired precision interval.
DISCUSSION: In an attribute test, the confidence level is directly related, and the precision is inversely related, to sample size. Thus, if the confidence level is reduced and precision is widened, sample size will be smaller.
Answer (A) is incorrect. Increasing the confidence level while narrowing the precision interval would result in a larger sample size. Answer (C) is incorrect. Decreasing the confidence level while widening the precision interval would allow the sample size to be decreased. Answer (D) is incorrect. The revised sample size is determinable.

SU 6: Conducting the Engagement: Sampling

12. The size of a given sample is jointly a result of characteristics of the population of interest and decisions made by the internal auditor. Everything else being equal, sample size will

A. Increase if the internal auditor decides to accept more risk of incorrectly concluding that controls are effective when they are in fact ineffective.

B. Double if the internal auditor finds that the variance of the population is twice as large as was indicated in the pilot sample.

C. Decrease if the internal auditor increases the tolerable rate of deviation.

D. Increase as sampling risk increases.

Answer (C) is correct.
REQUIRED: The true statement about the effect on the sample size resulting from a change in a relevant variable.
DISCUSSION: In an attribute test, the tolerable deviation rate is inversely related to sample size. If it is increased, sample size will decrease.
Answer (A) is incorrect. An increase in allowable risk decreases sample size. Answer (B) is incorrect. Doubling the variability of the population will cause the sample size to more than double. Answer (D) is incorrect. Sampling risk increases as the sample size decreases.

13. An internal auditor is planning to use attribute sampling to test the effectiveness of a specific internal control related to approvals for cash disbursements. In attribute sampling, decreasing the estimated occurrence rate from 5% to 4% while keeping all other sample size planning factors exactly the same would result in a revised sample size that would be

A. Larger.
B. Smaller.
C. Unchanged.
D. Indeterminate.

Answer (B) is correct.
REQUIRED: The sample size effect of decreasing the estimated occurrence rate.
DISCUSSION: In an attribute test, the expected deviation rate is directly related to sample size. If it is decreased, sample size will decrease.
Answer (A) is incorrect. Increasing the expected error rate increases the sample size. Answer (C) is incorrect. Changing one variable while holding all other factors constant changes the sample size. Answer (D) is incorrect. Decreasing the expected error rate while holding all other factors constant decreases the sample size.

6.4 Variables Sampling

14. In a variables sampling application, which of the following will result when confidence level is changed from 90% to 95%?

A. Standard error of the mean will not be affected.
B. Nonsampling error will decrease.
C. Sample size will increase.
D. Point estimate of the arithmetic mean will increase.

Answer (C) is correct.
REQUIRED: The effect of raising the confidence level.
DISCUSSION: In any sampling application (attribute or variables), an increase in the confidence level requires a larger sample.
Answer (A) is incorrect. The standard error of the mean is the standard deviation of the distribution of sample means. The larger the sample, the lower the degree of variability in the sample. An increase in confidence level from 90% to 95% requires a larger sample. Thus, the standard error of the mean will be affected. Answer (B) is incorrect. By definition, nonsampling error is unaffected by changes in sampling criteria. Answer (D) is incorrect. The estimate of the mean may increase or decrease if sample size changes.

15. An auditor for the state highway and safety department needs to estimate the average highway weight of tractor-trailer trucks using the state's highway system. Which estimation method must be used?

A. Mean-per-unit.
B. Difference.
C. Ratio.
D. Probability-proportional-to-size.

Answer (A) is correct.
REQUIRED: The best sampling estimation method to estimate an average weight.
DISCUSSION: Mean-per-unit sampling estimates the average value of population items, in this case, truck weight.
Answer (B) is incorrect. Difference estimation compares recorded and audit amounts. Recorded amounts are not relevant to the current procedure. Answer (C) is incorrect. Ratio estimation compares recorded and audit amounts. Recorded amounts are not relevant to the current procedure. Answer (D) is incorrect. Probability-proportional-to-size estimation compares recorded and audit amounts. Recorded amounts are not relevant to the current procedure.

16. An auditor is using the mean-per-unit method of variables sampling to estimate the correct total value of a group of inventory items. Based on the sample, the auditor estimates, with precision of ±4% and confidence of 90%, that the correct total is US $800,000. Accordingly,

A. There is a 4% chance that the actual correct total is less than US $720,000 or more than US $880,000.
B. The chance that the actual correct total is less than US $768,000 or more than US $832,000 is 10%.
C. The probability that the inventory is not significantly overstated is between 6% and 14%.
D. The inventory is not likely to be overstated by more than 4.4% (US $35,200) or understated by more than 3.6% (US $28,800).

Answer (B) is correct.
REQUIRED: The proper interpretation of the sample results.
DISCUSSION: A 90% confidence level implies that 10% of the time the true population total will be outside the computed range. Precision of ±4% gives the boundaries of the computed range: US $800,000 × 4% = US $32,000. Hence, the range is US $768,000 to US $832,000.
Answer (A) is incorrect. The precision, not the confidence level, is ±4%. Answer (C) is incorrect. Precision is a range of values, not the probability (confidence level) that the true value will be included within that range. Answer (D) is incorrect. The precision percentage is not multiplied by the confidence percentage.

17. When relatively few items of high monetary value constitute a large proportion of an account balance, stratified sampling techniques and complete testing of the high monetary-value items will generally result in a

A. Simplified evaluation of sample results.
B. Smaller nonsampling error.
C. Larger estimate of population variability.
D. Reduction in sample size.

Answer (D) is correct.
REQUIRED: The effect of using stratified selection in statistical sampling.
DISCUSSION: Stratifying a population means dividing it into subpopulations, thereby reducing sample size. Stratifying allows for greater emphasis on larger or more important items.
Answer (A) is incorrect. While stratifying reduces sample size, stratification requires a combination of sample results from more than one sample, in contrast to simple random sampling. Answer (B) is incorrect. A nonsampling error is an error in "performing" audit procedures, which is independent of sample selection. Answer (C) is incorrect. Stratified sampling, when properly used, will result in a smaller estimate of population variability.

18. Difference estimation sampling would be appropriate to use to project the monetary error in a population if

A. Subsidiary ledger book balances for some individual inventory items are unknown.
B. Virtually no differences between the individual carrying amounts and the audited amounts exist.
C. A number of nonproportional differences between carrying amounts and audited amounts exist.
D. Observed differences between carrying amounts and audited amounts are proportional to carrying amounts.

Answer (C) is correct.
REQUIRED: The condition for use of difference estimation sampling.
DISCUSSION: Difference estimation of population error entails determining the differences between the audit and carrying amounts for items in the sample, calculating the mean difference, and multiplying the mean by the number of items in the population. This method is used when the population contains sufficient misstatements to provide a reliable sample and when differences between carrying and audit amounts are not proportional. If differences are proportional, ratio estimation is used. A sufficient number of nonproportional errors must exist to generate a reliable sample estimate.
Answer (A) is incorrect. Individual carrying amounts must be known to use difference estimation. Answer (B) is incorrect. Sufficient misstatements must exist to generate a reliable sample. Answer (D) is incorrect. Ratio estimation is appropriate for proportional differences.

SU 6: Conducting the Engagement: Sampling   155

19. The auditor wishes to sample the perpetual inventory records to develop an estimate of the monetary amount of misstatement, if any, in the account balance. The account balance is made up of a large number of small-value items and a small number of large-value items. The auditor has decided to audit all items over US $50,000 plus a random selection of others. This audit decision is made because the auditor expects to find a large amount of errors in the perpetual inventory records but is not sure that it will be enough to justify taking a complete physical inventory. The auditor expects the errors to vary directly with the value recorded in the perpetual records. The most efficient sampling procedure to accomplish the auditor's objectives is

    A. Monetary-unit sampling.

    B. Ratio estimation.

    C. Attribute sampling.

    D. Stratified mean-per-unit sampling.

Answer (B) is correct.
    REQUIRED: The most efficient sampling procedure.
    DISCUSSION: Ratio estimation estimates the population misstatement by multiplying the recorded amount of the population by the ratio of the total audit amount of the sample to its total recorded amount. It is reliable and efficient when small errors predominate and are not skewed. Thus, ratio estimation should be used in this situation because the auditor is not sampling the very large items and the errors are not skewed (they vary directly with the size of the recorded values).
    Answer (A) is incorrect. Monetary-unit (probability-proportional-to-size) sampling becomes less accurate when many errors are expected. Answer (C) is incorrect. Attribute sampling is not used to estimate a monetary amount. Answer (D) is incorrect. Mean-per-unit (MPU) variables sampling averages audit values in the sample and multiplies by the number of items in the population to estimate the population value. When many errors are expected, MPU and stratified MPU are not as efficient as ratio estimation.

20. When an internal auditor uses monetary-unit statistical sampling to examine the total value of invoices, each invoice

    A. Has an equal probability of being selected.

    B. Can be represented by no more than one monetary unit.

    C. Has an unknown probability of being selected.

    D. Has a probability proportional to its monetary value of being selected.

Answer (D) is correct.
    REQUIRED: The effect of using monetary-unit sampling to examine invoices.
    DISCUSSION: Monetary-unit sampling, also called probability-proportional-to-size sampling, results in the selection of every *n*th monetary unit. Thus, a US $1,000 item is 1,000 times more likely to be selected than a US $1 monetary unit item. The probability of selection of a sampled item is directly proportional to the size of the item.
    Answer (A) is incorrect. Each monetary unit, not each invoice, has an equal probability of being selected (unless all invoices are for the same amount). Answer (B) is incorrect. It is possible for two or more monetary units to be selected from the same item; e.g., a US $4,500 item will be represented by four monetary units if every 1,000th dollar is selected. Answer (C) is incorrect. The probability of selection can be calculated using the monetary value of the item and the monetary value of the population.

6.5 Process Control Techniques

21. A manufacturer mass produces nuts and bolts on its assembly line. The line supervisors sample every *n*th unit for conformance with specifications. Once a nonconforming part is detected, the machinery is shut down and adjusted. The most appropriate tool for this process is a

    A. Fishbone (Ishikawa) diagram.

    B. Cost of quality report.

    C. ISO 9000 audit.

    D. Statistical quality control chart.

Answer (D) is correct.
    REQUIRED: The most appropriate tool used to verify that runs of units are within acceptable limits.
    DISCUSSION: Statistical quality control is a method of determining whether the shipment or production run of units lies within acceptable limits. It is also used to determine whether production processes are out of control. Statistical control charts are graphic aids for monitoring the status of any process subject to random variations.
    Answer (A) is incorrect. A fishbone diagram is useful for determining the unknown causes of problems, not routine mechanical adjustments. Answer (B) is incorrect. The contents of a cost of quality report are stated in monetary terms. This tool is not helpful for determining when to adjust machinery. Answer (C) is incorrect. An ISO 9000 audit focuses on the quality of the organization's total process, not the routine adjustment of machinery.

Questions 22 and 23 are based on the following information. An organization has collected data on the complaints made by personal computer users and has categorized the complaints.

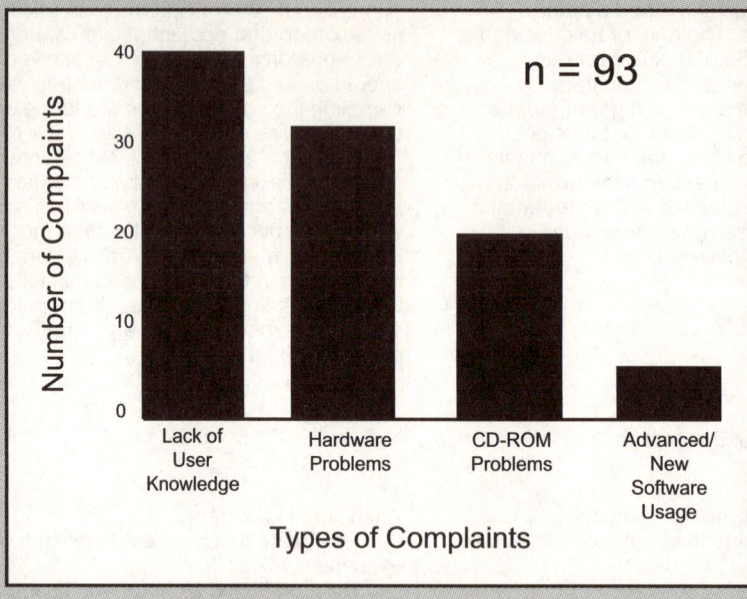

22. Using the information collected, the organization should focus on

A. The total number of personal computer complaints that occurred.
B. The number of computer complaints associated with CD-ROM problems and new software usage.
C. The number of computer complaints associated with the lack of user knowledge and hardware problems.
D. The cost to alleviate all computer complaints.

Answer (C) is correct.
REQUIRED: The organization's focus based on the data.
DISCUSSION: Complaints based on lack of user knowledge and hardware problems are by far the most frequent according to this chart. Consequently, the company should devote its resources primarily to these issues.
Answer (A) is incorrect. The organization should focus its scarce resources on those areas generating the highest levels of dissatisfaction. Pareto diagrams such as this one are tools for facilitating this kind of analysis. Answer (B) is incorrect. Complaints about CD-ROMs and software are infrequent. Answer (D) is incorrect. Cost information is not provided.

23. The chart displays the

A. Arithmetic mean of each computer complaint.
B. Relative frequency of each computer complaint.
C. Median of each computer complaint.
D. Absolute frequency of each computer complaint.

Answer (D) is correct.
REQUIRED: The information displayed.
DISCUSSION: This Pareto diagram depicts the frequencies of complaints in absolute terms. It displays the actual number of each type of complaint. The chart does not display arithmetic means, relative frequencies, or medians of each type of complaint.

24. The director of sales asks for a count of customers grouped in descending numerical rank by (1) the number of orders they place during a single year and (2) the dollar amounts of the average order. The visual format of these two pieces of information is most likely to be a

A. Fishbone (Ishikawa) diagram.
B. Cost of quality report.
C. Kaizen diagram.
D. Pareto diagram.

Answer (D) is correct.
REQUIRED: The best visual format used to display the values of two independent variables.
DISCUSSION: A Pareto diagram (also known as 80:20 analysis) displays the values of an independent variable such that managers can quickly identify the areas most in need of attention.
Answer (A) is incorrect. A fishbone diagram is useful for determining the unknown causes of problems, not for stratifying quantifiable variables. Answer (B) is incorrect. The contents of a cost of quality report are stated in monetary terms. This report is not helpful for stratifying quantifiable variables. Answer (C) is incorrect. Kaizen diagram is not a meaningful term in this context.

SU 6: Conducting the Engagement: Sampling

25. A health insurer uses a computer application to monitor physician bill amounts for various surgical procedures. This program allows the organization to better control reimbursement rates. The X-bar chart below is an example of the output from this application.

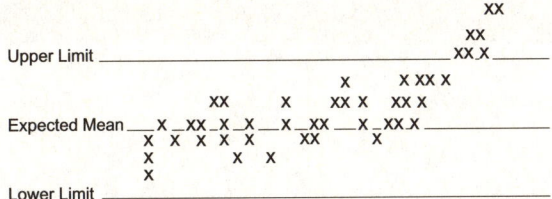

Select the interpretation that best explains the data plotted on the chart.

- A. Random variation.
- B. Abnormal variation.
- C. Normal variation.
- D. Cyclic variation.

Answer (B) is correct.
REQUIRED: The interpretation that best explains the data plotted on the chart.
DISCUSSION: Statistical quality control charts are graphic aids for monitoring the status of any process subject to random variations. The X-bar chart presented here depicts the sample means for a variable. If the values fall within the upper and lower control limits, no action is taken. Accordingly, values outside these limits are abnormal and should be investigated for possible corrective action.
Answer (A) is incorrect. Random variations should fall within realistically determined control limits. Answer (C) is incorrect. Normal variations should fall within realistically determined control limits. Answer (D) is incorrect. In time series analysis, cyclic variation is the fluctuation in the value of a variable caused by change in the level of general business activity.

Practice even more exam-emulating questions in **Gleim CIA Test Prep**!

Notes

STUDY UNIT SEVEN
PROCEDURES, ANALYSIS, CONCLUSIONS, AND DOCUMENTATION

(17 pages of outline)

7.1	Analytical Review Techniques	159
7.2	Benchmarking	162
7.3	Performing Audit Procedures	164
7.4	Drawing Conclusions	165
7.5	Working Papers -- Functions and Preparation	168
7.6	Working Papers -- Control and Retention	170
7.7	Computerized Audit Tools and Techniques	172

This study unit is the third of three covering **Section III: Conducting Internal Audit Engagements – Audit Tools and Techniques** from The IIA's CIA Exam Syllabus. This section makes up 25% to 35% of Part 1 of the CIA exam and is tested at the **proficiency level**. The relevant portion of the syllabus is highlighted below. (The complete syllabus is in Appendix B.)

III. **CONDUCTING INTERNAL AUDIT ENGAGEMENTS – AUDIT TOOLS AND TECHNIQUES (25%–35%)**
   A. Data Gathering (Collect and analyze data on proposed engagements)
   B. **Data Analysis and Interpretation**
      1. Use computerized audit tools and techniques (e.g., data mining and extraction, continuous monitoring, automated work papers, embedded audit modules)
      2. Conduct spreadsheet analysis
      3. Use analytical review techniques (e.g., ratio estimation, variance analysis, budget vs. actual, trend analysis, other reasonableness tests)
      4. Conduct benchmarking
      5. Draw conclusions
   C. **Data Reporting**
      1. Report test results to auditor in charge
      2. Develop preliminary conclusions regarding controls
   D. **Documentation / Work Papers**
      1. Develop work papers
   E. Process Mapping, Including Flowcharting
   F. Evaluate Relevance, Sufficiency, and Competence of Evidence

7.1 ANALYTICAL REVIEW TECHNIQUES

> **Performance Standard 2320**
> **Analysis and Evaluation**
>
> Internal auditors must base conclusions and engagement results on appropriate analyses and evaluations.

1. **Analytical Procedures in Auditing**

    a. Specific guidance is found in Practice Advisory 2320-1, *Analytical Procedures*:

    1) "Internal auditors may use analytical procedures to obtain audit evidence. Analytical procedures involve studying and comparing relationships among both financial and nonfinancial information. The application of analytical procedures is based on the premise that, in the absence of known conditions to the contrary, relationships among information may reasonably be expected to exist and continue. Examples of contrary conditions include unusual or nonrecurring transactions or events; accounting, organizational, operational, environmental, and technological changes; inefficiencies; ineffectiveness; errors; fraud; or illegal acts" (para. 1).

    2) "Analytical procedures often provide the internal auditor with an efficient and effective means of obtaining evidence. The assessment results from comparing information with expectations identified or developed by the internal auditor. Analytical procedures are useful in identifying:

        a) Unexpected differences.
        b) The absence of differences when they are expected.
        c) Potential errors.
        d) Potential fraud or illegal acts.
        e) Other unusual or nonrecurring transactions or events" (para. 2).

    3) "Analytical procedures include:

        a) Comparing current period information with expectations based on similar information for prior periods as well as budgets or forecasts.
        b) Studying relationships between financial and appropriate nonfinancial information (e.g., recorded payroll expense compared to changes in average number of employees).
        c) Studying relationships among elements of information (e.g., fluctuation in recorded interest expense compared to changes in related debt balances).
        d) Comparing information with expectations based on similar information for other organizational units as well as for the industry in which the organization operates" (para. 3).

    4) "Internal auditors may perform analytical procedures using monetary amounts, physical quantities, ratios, or percentages. Specific analytical procedures include ratio, trend, and regression analysis; reasonableness tests; period-to-period comparisons; comparisons with budgets; forecasts; and external economic information" (para. 4).

    5) "Internal auditors may use analytical procedures to generate evidence during the audit engagement. When determining the extent of analytical procedures, the internal auditor considers the:

        a) Significance of the area being audited.
        b) Assessment of risk management in the area being audited.
        c) Adequacy of the internal control system.
        d) Availability and reliability of financial and nonfinancial information.
        e) Precision with which the results of analytical audit procedures can be predicted.
        f) Availability and comparability of information regarding the industry in which the organization operates.
        g) Extent to which other procedures provide evidence" (para. 5).

2. **Ratio Analysis**

   a. One of the most common analytical procedures is ratio analysis, the comparison of one financial statement element with another. Ratios are used frequently to assess an organization's liquidity and profitability.

   b. **Liquidity** is the ability to meet current obligations as they come due and continue operating in the short run. The following ratios are measures of an organization's relative liquidity (the higher the ratio, the higher the liquidity) based on balance sheet amounts:

   1) The **current ratio** equals the balance of current assets divided by the balance of current liabilities.

   $$\frac{Current\ assets}{Current\ liabilities}$$

   2) The **accounts receivable turnover ratio** measures the number of times the organization's average balance in receivables is converted to cash during a fiscal year (or financial statement cycle).

   $$\frac{Net\ credit\ sales}{Average\ balance\ in\ receivables}$$

   3) The **inventory turnover ratio** measures the number of times the organization's average balance in inventory is converted to cash in the space of a year (or financial statement cycle).

   $$\frac{Cost\ of\ goods\ sold}{Average\ balance\ in\ inventory}$$

   c. **Profitability** is measured by three common percentages based on income statement amounts:

   1) **Gross profit margin** is the ratio of gross margin to sales. The key issue is the relationship of gross profit to the increase or decrease in sales. For example, a 10% increase in sales should be accompanied by at least a 10% increase in the gross profit.

   $$\frac{Gross\ profit}{Sales}$$

   2) **Operating profit margin** is the ratio of operating profit to sales.

   $$\frac{Operating\ profit}{Sales}$$

   3) **Net profit margin** is the ratio of net profit to sales. This percentage is particularly important because it measures the proportion of the organization's revenues that it can pass on to its owners.

   $$\frac{Net\ profit}{Sales}$$

   d. Sometimes ratio analysis is used to relate a financial statement item to nonfinancial data. An example is average sales per retail location.

3. **Ratio Comparisons**

   a. Ratios by themselves reveal little about the organization.

   1) **Trend** analysis tracks the changes in a ratio over time, e.g., the last 3 fiscal years. It helps assess the effects of changes in the overall economy or the relative success of a marketing campaign.

2) **Period-to-period** analysis compares performance for similar time periods, e.g., the third quarter of the current year and the third quarter of the prior year. This approach is especially informative in seasonal industries, such as retailing and agriculture.

3) **Industry** analysis compares the organization's ratios with those of competitors or with the published averages for the entire industry. These must be used with caution because different organizations in the same industry may have different cost structures.

4. **Other Analytical Procedures**

   a. **Regression analysis** determines the degree of relationship, if any, between two variables, such as that between sales and cost of goods sold. The degree of relationship can be used as a benchmark to test for reasonableness.

   b. **Variance analysis** studies the difference (favorable or unfavorable) between an amount based on an actual result and the corresponding budgeted amount. It is a method of planning and control that focuses attention on the causes of significant deviations from expectations.

      1) Variance analysis is a form of **reasonableness test** used in accounting applications.

EXAMPLE

An internal auditor reviews the accounts receivables system and determines that credit requirements for new customers have been loosened. The result is an increase in sales and accounts receivable. To determine (1) whether further investigation is justified and (2) what should be investigated, the auditor should review the reasonableness of the accounts receivables balance and the effects of the new credit requirements on the accounts receivable turnover ratio. Amounts can be compared with those for prior periods and for similar organizations in the same industry.

Internal auditors have many resources for analyzing and interpreting data. Analytical procedures often provide the internal auditor with an efficient and effective means of obtaining evidence. The assessment results from comparing information with expectations identified or developed by the internal auditor.

Stop and review! You have completed the outline for this subunit. Study multiple-choice questions 1 through 3 beginning on page 175.

7.2 BENCHMARKING

1. **Overview**

   a. Benchmarking compares some aspect of an organization's performance with best-in-class performance. Thus, it may be used to develop expectations for analytical procedures.

      1) The process should be continuous, and what is best-in-class should be evaluated frequently.

   b. Benchmarking is a continuous evaluation of the practices of the best organizations in their class and the adaptation of processes to reflect the best of these practices. It involves (1) analyzing and measuring key outputs against those of the best organizations and (2) identifying the underlying key actions and causes that contribute to the performance difference.

      1) **Best practices** are recognized by authorities in the field and by customers for generating outstanding results. They are generally innovative technically or in their management of human resources.

      2) Benchmarking is an ongoing process that involves quantitative and qualitative measurement of the difference between the organization's performance of an activity and the performance by the benchmark organization.

c. The following are kinds of benchmarking:

1) **Competitive benchmarking** studies an organization in the same industry.
2) **Process (function) benchmarking** studies operations of organizations with similar processes regardless of industry. Thus, the benchmark need not be a competitor or even a similar organization.

   a) This method may introduce new ideas that provide a significant competitive advantage.

3) **Strategic benchmarking** is a search for successful competitive strategies.
4) **Internal benchmarking** is the application of best practices in one part of the organization to its other parts.

d. Benchmarking may be either **internal** (comparison with the performance of another unit within the organization) or **external** (comparison with the performance of another organization). It also may be either **financial** or **nonfinancial**.

e. The following are examples of benchmarks:

1) Internal financial -- Return on investment for most successful division
2) Internal nonfinancial -- Average time from initiation of customer service request to final resolution of problem for division that reports highest overall customer satisfaction
3) External financial -- Return on investment for biggest competitor
4) External nonfinancial -- Number of unique website hits for biggest competitor

f. The first phase in the benchmarking process is to select and prioritize benchmarking projects.

1) An organization must understand its critical success factors and business environment to identify key business processes and drivers and to develop parameters defining what processes to benchmark. The criteria for selecting what to benchmark are based mostly on satisfaction of customer needs.

g. The next phase is to organize benchmarking teams. A team organization is appropriate because it permits (1) a fair division of labor, (2) participation by those responsible for implementing changes, and (3) inclusion of a variety of functional expertise and work experience.

1) The benchmarking team must thoroughly investigate and document the organization's internal processes.

   a) The team must develop a family of measures that are true indicators of process performance.
   b) The development of key indicators for performance measurement in a benchmarking context is an extension of the basic evaluative function of internal auditors.

h. Researching and identifying best-in-class performance is often the most difficult phase. The critical steps are

1) Setting up databases,
2) Choosing information-gathering methods (internal sources, external public domain sources, and original research),
3) Formatting questionnaires (lists of questions prepared in advance), and
4) Selecting benchmarking partners.

i. Data analysis involves (1) identifying performance gaps, (2) understanding the reasons, and (3) prioritizing the key activities that will facilitate the behavioral and process changes needed to implement recommendations.

j. Leadership is most important in the implementation phase because the team must justify its recommendations. Moreover, the process improvement teams must manage the implementation of approved changes.

Stop and review! You have completed the outline for this subunit. Study multiple-choice questions 4 through 6 on page 176.

7.3 PERFORMING AUDIT PROCEDURES

1. **Preliminary Conclusions about Controls**

    a. Internal auditors obtain an understanding of the design of the engagement client's internal controls. The auditors then draw conclusions about whether internal controls are designed adequately to achieve management's control objectives.

    1) These preliminary conclusions are used to determine whether (a) the system of internal control is so poorly designed that testing it would serve no purpose, or (b) the auditors should test internal controls to determine whether they are operating as intended.

2. **Interpreting Results**

    a. Guidance for proceeding with the results of analytical procedures is also provided in Practice Advisory 2320-1, *Analytical Procedures*:

    1) "When analytical audit procedures identify unexpected results or relationships, the internal auditor evaluates such results or relationships. This evaluation includes determining whether the difference from expectations could be a result of fraud, error, or a change in conditions. The auditor may ask management about the reasons for the difference and would corroborate management's explanation, for example, by modifying expectations and recalculating the difference or by applying other audit procedures. In particular, the internal auditor needs to be satisfied that the explanation considers both the direction of the change (e.g., sales decreased) and the amount of the difference (e.g., sales decreased by 10 percent). Unexplained results or relationships from applying analytical procedures may be indicative of a significant problem (e.g., a potential error, fraud, or illegal act). Results or relationships that are not adequately explained may indicate a situation to be communicated to senior management and the board in accordance with Standard 2060. Depending on the circumstances, the internal auditor may recommend appropriate action" (para. 6).

3. **Audit Procedures**

    a. **Risk assessment procedures** are performed to obtain an understanding of the entity and its environment, including internal control.

    b. **Further audit procedures** include tests of controls and substantive procedures.

    1) **Tests of controls** test the operating effectiveness of controls in preventing, or detecting and correcting, instances of noncompliance, whether they take the form of a material misstatement in the financial statements, failure to comply with a law or regulation, or some other undesired outcome. They are required when

        a) The auditor's risk assessment is based on an expectation of the operating effectiveness of controls or

        b) Substantive procedures alone do not provide sufficient appropriate evidence.

2) **Substantive procedures** are used to detect material misstatements at the relevant assertion level. They include (a) tests of details and (b) substantive analytical procedures.

   a) They should be performed for **all** relevant assertions about each material (1) transaction class, (2) account balance, and (3) disclosure.

c. A **management's specialist** is an individual or organization having expertise in a field other than accounting or auditing that assists in preparing the financial statements. The client may rely on a management's specialist to prepare information used as audit evidence. An example is estimation of the fair value of securities.

   1) The auditor should (a) evaluate the competence, capabilities, and objectivity of such specialists; (b) obtain an understanding of their work relevant to the audit; and (c) evaluate its appropriateness.

4. **Types of Audit Procedures**

   a. The auditor should use the following, singly or in combination, as risk assessment procedures, tests of controls, or substantive procedures:

      1) **Inspection of records or documents** is the examination of records or documents, whether internal or external, in paper, electronic, or other media.
      2) **Inspection of tangible assets** is the physical examination of assets to test existence. For example, it is combined with observation of inventory counts.
      3) **Observation** is looking at a process or procedure being performed.
      4) **Inquiry** seeks financial or nonfinancial information from knowledgeable persons within the entity or outside the entity.
      5) **External confirmation** obtains audit evidence as a direct, written response to the auditor from a third party, e.g., confirmation of account balances or the terms of agreements.
      6) **Recalculation** is checking mathematical accuracy.
      7) **Reperformance** is the independent execution of procedures or controls.
      8) **Analytical procedures** are evaluations of data made by a study of plausible relationships among both financial and nonfinancial data.

         a) **Scanning** is a type of analytical procedure used to review accounting data to identify significant or unusual items for testing.

Stop and review! You have completed the outline for this subunit. Study multiple-choice questions 7 through 10 beginning on page 177.

7.4 DRAWING CONCLUSIONS

1. **Guidance**

   a. The internal auditor draws conclusions about the data (s)he has gathered in the course of engagement work.

      1) Practice Advisory 2410-1 states, "Conclusions and opinions are the internal auditor's evaluations of the effects of the observations and recommendations on the activities reviewed. They usually put the observations and recommendations in perspective based upon their overall implications and clearly identify any engagement conclusions in the engagement report" (para. 8).

         a) The terms "conclusion" and "opinion" are interchangeable.

2) Practice Advisory 2410-1 also states, "Conclusions may encompass the entire scope of an engagement or specific aspects" (para. 8). In other words, the internal auditor may draw conclusions based on the results of a single procedure, of a group of procedures, or for the engagement as a whole.

   a) The internal auditor performs engagement procedures and drafts findings (observations) based on the results. The auditor then draws conclusions.

2. **Root Cause Analysis**

   a. When reporting a condition or observation, internal auditors might be tempted to accept a description of the immediate problem rather than to search for the underlying problem. The IIA issued Practice Advisory 2320-2, *Root Cause Analysis*, to encourage auditors to probe more deeply for the fundamental causes of identified problems.

      1) "Root cause analysis is defined as the identification of why an issue occurred (versus only identifying or reporting on the issue itself). In this context, an issue is defined as a problem, error, instance of noncompliance, or missed opportunity" (para. 1).

      2) "Auditors whose reporting only recommends that management fix the issue — and not the underlying reason that caused the issue — are failing to add insights that improve the longer-term effectiveness and efficiency of business processes and thus, the overall governance, risk, and control environment" (para. 2).

      3) "Internal audit can be the ideal group to analyze issues and identify the root cause(s) given their independence and objectivity. This perspective helps ensure biases are minimized, assumptions are challenged, and evidence is fully evaluated" (para. 3).

      4) "Root cause analysis benefits the organization by identifying the underlying cause(s) of an issue. This approach provides a long-term perspective for the improvement of business processes. Without the performance of an effective root cause analysis and the appropriate remediation activities, an issue may have a higher probability to reoccur" (para. 4).

      5) "The resources spent on root cause analysis should be commensurate with the impact of the issue or potential future issues and risks. In certain circumstances, root cause analysis may be as simple as asking 'five whys.' For example:

         The worker fell. *Why?* Because of oil on the floor. *Why?* Because of a broken part. *Why?* Because the part keeps failing. *Why?* Because of changes in procurement practices.

         By the fifth 'why,' the internal auditor should have identified or be close to identifying the root cause. More complex issues, however, may require a greater investment of resources and more rigorous analysis" (para. 5).

      6) "Prior to performing root cause analysis, internal auditors should anticipate potential barriers that could impede the effort and proactively develop an approach for handling those circumstances.

         a) "Business management may be reluctant to support internal audit's role in root cause analysis. The CAE and auditors may need to work with management to explain and demonstrate the audit activity's role and capabilities.

SU 7: Procedures, Analysis, Conclusions, and Documentation

b) "Business management may resist conducting a root cause analysis due to the necessary time and resource commitment from their staff. Management may be focused on a short-term fix to immediately maintain compliance or return the business process or transaction to its corrected state.

c) "Determining true root cause may be difficult and subjective — even when significant quantitative and qualitative data is available. Auditors should strongly consider including the input from multiple stakeholders of the business process in the design, analysis, and evaluation of data. Multiple errors with varying degrees of influence may be the root cause of an issue" (para. 6).

7) "Root cause analysis that stops at the identification of physical and process components as the root cause (e.g., technology systems, policies, components, training) may not be complete. A true root cause analysis will seek to understand why good people make bad or inadequate decisions (e.g., Why did the person who made the decision think it was the right thing to do at the time?). In these cases, auditors are searching for situational awareness and trying to understand all the circumstances those executing the process faced that led them to make their decisions" (para. 7).

3. **Examples**

a. Below is an example of the process of moving from a finding to a conclusion for a specific engagement objective:

1) The engagement work program called for the auditor to examine all purchase orders exceeding $100,000 to determine whether they were approved by the appropriate division vice president. The results of the procedure are stated as a finding:

Of 38 purchase orders over $100,000 examined, 3 lacked required vice presidential approval, an exception rate of 7.9%.

a) The finding is an objective statement of fact about the results of audit work without interpretation or commentary.

2) From the finding, the internal auditor can draw a conclusion that informs the reader of the implications of the finding for one or more engagement objectives:

The system of internal controls over purchases of material dollar amounts in the Eastern Division is not functioning as designed.

3) The relationship of a finding and a conclusion need not be one-to-one. If the auditor finds it useful, multiple findings can be used to support a single conclusion:

Of 38 purchase orders over $100,000 examined, 3 lacked required vice presidential approval, an exception rate of 7.9%. Of 115 purchase orders less than $100,000 randomly selected and examined, 12 lacked required approvals, an exception rate of 10.4%. Given these findings, the system of internal controls over all purchases in the Eastern Division is not functioning as designed.

b. Auditor judgment is the essential element in moving from a finding to a conclusion. No formula can tell an auditor whether a certain exception rate is indicative of a working or failing control.

1) Depending on context, decisions about materiality, and knowledge of the auditee, the findings in the example above could have resulted in positive, not negative, conclusions.

4. **Report Test Results to Auditor in Charge**

   a. The auditor in charge of the engagement is responsible for coordinating the results of audit work and ensuring that work performed supports conclusions and opinions.

      1) For this reason, internal audit staff must report the results of audit work to the auditor in charge.

Stop and review! You have completed the outline for this subunit. Study multiple-choice questions 11 through 14 beginning on page 178.

7.5 WORKING PAPERS -- FUNCTIONS AND PREPARATION

> **Performance Standard 2330**
> **Documenting Information**
>
> Internal auditors must document relevant information to support the conclusions and engagement results.

1. **Functions**

   a. The functions of engagement working papers are described in Practice Advisory 2330-1, *Documenting Information*:

      1) "Internal auditors prepare working papers. Working papers document the information obtained, the analyses made, and the support for the conclusions and engagement results. Internal audit management reviews the prepared working papers" (para. 1).

      2) "Engagement working papers generally:

         a) Aid in the planning, performance, and review of engagements.
         b) Provide the principal support for engagement results.
         c) Document whether engagement objectives were achieved.
         d) Support the accuracy and completeness of the work performed.
         e) Provide a basis for the internal audit activity's quality assurance and improvement program.
         f) Facilitate third-party reviews" (para. 2).

      3) "The organization, design, and content of engagement working papers depend on the engagement's nature and objectives and the organization's needs. Engagement working papers document all aspects of the engagement process from planning to communicating results. The internal audit activity determines the media used to document and store working papers" (para. 3).

      4) "The chief audit executive establishes working paper policies for the various types of engagements performed. Standardized engagement working papers, such as questionnaires and audit programs, may improve the engagement's efficiency and facilitate the delegation of engagement work. Engagement working papers may be categorized as permanent or carry-forward engagement files that contain information of continuing importance" (para. 4).

2. **Best Practices**

   a. Each working paper must, at a minimum, identify the engagement and describe the contents or purpose of the working paper, for example, in the heading.

      1) Also, each working paper should be signed (initialed) and dated by the internal auditor and contain an index or reference number.

b. Working papers should be consistently and efficiently prepared to facilitate review. They should be

1) Neat, not crowded, and written on only one side (if written at all).
2) Uniform in size and appearance.
3) Economical, avoiding unnecessary copying, listing, or scheduling.
   a) They should use copies of engagement clients' records if applicable.
4) Arranged in a logical and uniform style.
   a) The best organization is that of the work program. Each section should have statements of purpose and scope followed by observations, conclusions, recommendations, and corrective action.
5) Clear, concise, and complete.
6) Restricted to matters that are relevant and significant.
7) Written in a simple style.

c. While clarity, concision, and accuracy are desirable qualities of working papers, completeness and support for conclusions are the most important considerations.

3. **Other Content**

   a. Working papers should document such matters as how sampling populations were defined and how statistical samples were selected.
   b. Furthermore, verification symbols (tick marks) are likely to appear on most working papers and should be explained.

4. **Indexing**

   a. Indexing permits cross-referencing. It is important because it simplifies supervisory review either during the engagement or subsequently by creating a trail of related items through the working papers.

   1) Indexing facilitates preparation of final engagement communications, later engagements for the same client, and internal and external assessments of the internal audit activity.

5. **Summaries**

   a. Internal auditors summarize information in working papers. Summaries help to coordinate working papers related to a subject by providing concise statements of the most important information. Thus, they provide for an orderly and logical flow of information and facilitate supervisory review.

6. **Permanent Files**

   a. The following are typical items contained in the permanent or carry-forward files:

   1) Previous engagement communications, responses, and results of follow-up
   2) Engagement communications provided by other organizational subunits
   3) Reviews of the long-term engagement work schedule by senior management
   4) Results of post-engagement reviews
   5) Auditor observations during past engagements that may have future relevance
   6) The chart of accounts with items referenced to engagement projects
   7) Management's operating reports
   8) Applicable engagement work programs and questionnaires
   9) Long-term contracts
   10) Flowcharts of operations
   11) Historical financial information
   12) Project control information
   13) Correspondence about the engagement project
   14) Updated organizational charter, bylaws, minutes, etc.

7. **Computerized Working Papers**

   a. Electronic working papers have the following advantages:

      1) Uniformity of format
      2) Ease of storage
      3) Searchability and automated cross-indexing
      4) Backup and recovery functions
      5) Built-in audit methodologies, such as sampling routines

   b. However, the use of electronic media involves security issues that do not arise when working papers exist only on paper.

      1) Electronic working papers and reviewer comments should be protected from unauthorized access and change.

      2) Information recorded by scanning working papers should be adequately controlled to ensure its continued integrity.

      3) Working paper retention policies should consider changes made in the original operating system, other software, and hardware to ensure the continued retrievability of electronic working papers throughout the retention cycle.

   c. Software packages have moved beyond the simple storage and retrieval of working papers.

Stop and review! You have completed the outline for this subunit. Study multiple-choice questions 15 through 18 beginning on page 179.

7.6 WORKING PAPERS -- CONTROL AND RETENTION

> **Implementation Standard 2330.A1**
>
> The chief audit executive must control access to engagement records. The chief audit executive must obtain the approval of senior management and/or legal counsel prior to releasing such records to external parties, as appropriate.

1. **Control**

   a. The primary objective of maintaining security over working papers is to prevent unauthorized changes or removal of information.

      1) The working papers are essential to the proper functioning of the internal audit activity. Among many other purposes, they document the information obtained, the analyses made, and the support for the conclusions and engagement results.

      2) Unauthorized changes or removal of information would seriously compromise the integrity of the internal audit activity's work. For this reason, the chief audit executive must ensure that working papers are kept secure.

   b. Working papers contain sensitive information, but they are generally not protected from disclosure in civil and criminal legal matters. Thus, auditors do not have the equivalent of the attorney-client privilege.

      1) The responsibility for the safety and security of the working papers is set out in the Implementation Standard above. The IIA has issued two Practice Advisories to provide guidance on this topic, one on control of working papers and one on access.

SU 7: Procedures, Analysis, Conclusions, and Documentation 171

c. Practice Advisory 2330.A1-1, *Control of Engagement Records*, emphasizes the ownership aspect of working papers.

1) "Internal audit engagement records include reports, supporting documentation, review notes, and correspondence, regardless of storage media. Engagement records or working papers are the property of the organization. The internal audit activity controls engagement working papers and provides access to authorized personnel only" (para. 1).

2. **Access**

a. When engagement objectives will not be compromised, the internal auditor may show all or part of the working papers to the client.

1) For instance, the results of certain engagement procedures may be shared with the client to encourage corrective action.

b. One potential use of engagement working papers is to provide support in the organization's pursuit of insurance claims, fraud cases, or lawsuits.

1) In such cases, management and other members of the organization may request access to engagement working papers. This access may be necessary to substantiate or explain engagement observations and recommendations or to use engagement documentation for other business purposes.

c. Practice Advisory 2330.A1-2, *Granting Access to Engagement Records*, begins with a cautionary note to the auditor:

"Caution: Internal auditors are encouraged to consult legal counsel in matters involving legal issues as requirements may vary significantly in different jurisdictions. The guidance contained in this practice advisory is based primarily on the legal systems that protect information and work performed for, or communicated to, an engaged attorney (i.e., attorney-client privilege), such as the legal system in the United States of America. PA 2400-1 discusses attorney-client privilege."

1) "Internal audit engagement records include reports, supporting documentation, review notes, and correspondence, regardless of storage media.

a) Engagement records are generally produced under the presumption that their contents are confidential and may contain a mix of facts and opinions. However, those who are not familiar with the organization or its internal audit process may misunderstand those facts and opinions. Outside parties may seek access to engagement records in different types of proceedings, including criminal prosecutions, civil litigation, tax audits, regulatory reviews, government contract reviews, and reviews by self-regulatory organizations.

b) Most of an organization's records that are not protected by the attorney-client privilege may be accessible in criminal proceedings. In noncriminal proceedings, the issue of access is less clear and may vary according to the jurisdiction of the organization" (para. 1).

3. **Retention**

> **Implementation Standard 2330.A2**
>
> The chief audit executive must develop retention requirements for engagement records, regardless of the medium in which each record is stored. These retention requirements must be consistent with the organization's guidelines and any pertinent regulatory or other requirements.

a. The IIA does not prescribe the length of time that an internal audit activity should retain its working papers after conclusion of the engagement. This can only be established by the CAE's professional judgment in consultation with the organization's legal counsel.

b. Guidance is provided in Practice Advisory 2330.A2-1, *Retention of Records*:

1) "Engagement record retention requirements vary among jurisdictions and legal environments" (para. 1).
2) "The chief audit executive develops a written retention policy that meets organizational needs and legal requirements of the jurisdictions within which the organization operates" (para. 2).
3) "The record retention policy needs to include appropriate arrangements for the retention of records related to engagements performed by external service providers" (para. 3).

c. Working papers should be destroyed after they have served their purpose. Any parts having continuing value should be brought forward to current working papers or to the permanent file.

Stop and review! You have completed the outline for this subunit. Study multiple-choice questions 19 through 22 beginning on page 180.

7.7 COMPUTERIZED AUDIT TOOLS AND TECHNIQUES

1. **Overview**

    a. Auditors increasingly rely on software tools to perform virtually all auditing activities.
    b. Computer-assisted audit techniques (CAATs) may be systems- or transaction-based or may provide automated methods for extracting and analyzing data.

2. **Generalized Audit Software (GAS)**

    a. Using GAS, the auditor loads a copy of the client's production data onto the auditor's own computer to perform various analytical procedures.

    1) For example, the auditor can search for duplicate records, gaps in numerically sequenced records, high-monetary-amount transactions, and suspect vendor numbers. Also, control totals can be calculated, and balances can be stratified for receivables testing.
    2) Two GAS packages are ACL (Audit Command Language) and IDEA (Interactive Data Extraction and Analysis).

3. **Test Data**

    a. Test data allow the auditor to assess the controls embedded in an application by observing (1) whether the good data are correctly processed and (2) how well the system handles bad data.

    1) Test data, sometimes called a test deck, consist of a set of dummy inputs containing both good and bad data elements. This approach subjects auditor-created data to the client's programs.
    2) Test data must never be mingled with real data, and test data must not be allowed to interfere with production processing. Monitoring by IT personnel is crucial when the auditor uses test data.

4. **Parallel Simulation**

    a. Parallel simulation allows an auditor to determine whether the data are subjected to the processes that the client claims the application performs.

    1) Parallel simulation subjects client data to auditor-created programs.
    2) Parallel simulation requires the auditor to have considerable technical knowledge. The auditor also must have extensive communications with client personnel to learn the designed functions of the application being imitated.

5. **Data Mining and Extraction Techniques**
    a. The oldest form of data extraction is the manual copying of client records. Until the widespread use of photocopy machines, it was the only method.
        1) With the easy availability of computing, especially networking technology, data extraction can be performed quickly in very large volumes.
        2) The problem is to ensure that the data extracted are those required for the audit procedure being performed. Control totals and other methods are used for this purpose.
6. **Integrated Test Facility (ITF)**
    a. In this approach, the auditor creates a fictitious entity (a department, vendor, employee, or product) on the client's live production system.
        1) All transactions associated with the dummy entity are processed by the live system, and the auditor can observe the results.
    b. Relevant guidance is provided by Practice Advisory 23 2014, *Continuous Assistance*:
        1) Use of an ITF requires great care to ensure that no transactions associated with the dummy entity are included in production reports and output files.
7. **Embedded Audit Module**
    a. An embedded audit module is an integral part of an application system. It is designed to identify and report actual transactions and other information that meet criteria having audit significance.
        1) An advantage is that it permits **continuous monitoring** of online, real-time systems.
        2) A disadvantage is that audit hooks must be programmed into the operating system and application programs to permit insertion of audit modules.
    b. Relevant guidance is provided by Practice Advisory 2320-4, *Continuous Assistance*:
        1) "Internal audit should consider evaluating control effectiveness continuously, if warranted by the risk profile, rather than using more traditional periodic historic testing of selected internal controls and risks in an organization" (para. 1).
        2) "Continuous monitoring monitors whether internal controls are operating effectively on an ongoing basis. High risk events can be observed and flagged for additional attention or testing. Continuous auditing routines developed by internal auditors, when appropriate, may be applied by management, in which case they become continuous monitoring procedures performed by management" (para. 3).
        3) "The key to continuous monitoring is that the process should be owned and performed by management as part of its responsibility to implement and maintain an effective control environment. Because management is responsible for internal controls, it should have a means to determine, on an ongoing basis, whether the controls are operating as designed" (para. 4).
        4) "The annual audit plan should identify areas potentially subject to continuous auditing. Internal audit should use the organization's risk management framework (if one has been developed) as well as its own risk assessment, to identify these areas. The frequency of coverage should be based on the risk factors in an area or business process. Continuous auditing helps internal auditors identify and assess risk and establish thresholds that respond to changes in the enterprise. It also contributes to risk identification and assessment" (para. 5).

5) "Successful implementation of continuous auditing requires the support of key stakeholders. The following steps should be considered when developing and sustaining continuous auditing activities:

   a) Prioritize areas for coverage and select a continuous auditing approach.
   b) Define output requirements.
   c) Select analysis tools, which could be either in-house or vendor-provided software.
   d) Determine scope of continuous auditing routines.
   e) Assess data integrity and prepare data.
   f) Understand management's continuous monitoring approach.
   g) Develop continuous audit routines to assess controls and identify deficiencies" (para. 6).

6) "Once the objectives of continuous auditing have been defined, senior management support should be obtained for the continuous auditing coverage" (para. 7).

7) "Data files, such as detailed transaction files, often are only retained for a short time. Therefore, the internal auditor should make arrangements for retaining appropriate data. Access to programs/system and data should be arranged well in advance. The internal auditor should obtain reasonable assurance of the integrity, reliability, usefulness, and security of the continuous auditing routines through appropriate planning, design, testing, processing, and review of documentation" (para. 8).

8) "The internal auditor should examine the adequacy of management's continuous monitoring activities" (para. 9).

9) "The internal auditor should consider the objectives of continuous auditing, the risk appetite of the enterprise, and the level and nature of management's continuous monitoring, when setting the timing, scope, and coverage of continuous auditing tests" (para. 10).

10) "The frequency of continuous auditing activities will range from real-time to periodic analysis of detailed transactions, snapshots, or summarized data. Critical systems with key controls may be subject to real-time analysis of transactional data. The internal auditor should consider the regulatory requirements and the degree to which management is addressing the risk exposures and potential effects. When management has implemented continuous monitoring systems for controls, internal and external auditors should determining to what extent they can rely on the continuous monitoring processes to reduce detailed control testing" (para 11).

11) "When continuous auditing routines are changed, the internal auditor should conduct a review of the changes for integrity, reliability, usefulness, and security" (para. 12).

12) "Once the continuous auditing routines have been executed, the internal auditor should review the results to identify transactions that fail the control tests. Increased risk levels can be identified by comparative analysis. When a continuous auditing or monitoring system is implemented, it is common for a large number of exceptions to be identified that, upon investigation, prove not to be a concern. The continuous auditing system needs to allow the test parameters to be adjusted so that such exceptions do not result in alerts or notifications" (para. 13).

13) "If a control breakdown and/or risk concern is identified through continuous auditing, it should be reported to management. Once the appropriate action has been taken, the internal auditor may consider using the continuous auditing program again to verify that the remediation addressed the control weakness and reduced the level of risk" (para. 14).

14) "The internal auditor should review the efficiency and effectiveness of the continuous auditing programs periodically. Additional control points or risk exposures may need to be added and others may be deleted based on more current risk assessments. Thresholds, control tests, and parameters for various analytics may need to be tightened or relaxed" (para. 15).

15) "The continuous auditing process should be documented sufficiently to provide adequate audit evidence" (para. 16).

8. **Application Tracing and System Mapping**

   a. Application tracing uses a feature of the programming language in which the application was written.

      1) Tracing aids computer programmers in following the step-by-step operation of a computer program's source code. It can be used by auditors for the same purpose.

   b. System mapping is similar to application tracing. But mapping is performed by another computer program instead of by the auditor.

9. **Spreadsheet Analysis**

   a. Electronic spreadsheets, such as Microsoft Excel, organize information into intersecting rows and columns. This organization permits easy analysis of large amounts of client data.

   b. Internal auditors can use spreadsheets to (1) evaluate "what if" scenarios, (2) create graphs, (3) analyze variances between actual and budgeted amounts, and (4) perform other analytical procedures.

Stop and review! You have completed the outline for this subunit. Study multiple-choice questions 23 through 25 beginning on page 181.

QUESTIONS
7.1 Analytical Review Techniques

1. Accounts payable schedule verification may include the use of analytical information. Which of the following is analytical information?

A. Comparing the schedule with the accounts payable ledger or unpaid voucher file.
B. Comparing the balance on the schedule with the balances of prior years.
C. Comparing confirmations received from selected creditors with the accounts payable ledger.
D. Examining vendors' invoices in support of selected items on the schedule.

Answer (B) is correct.
 REQUIRED: The analytical information.
 DISCUSSION: Analytical procedures are useful in identifying (1) unexpected differences, (2) the absence of differences when they are expected, (3) potential errors, (4) potential fraud or illegal acts, or (5) other unusual or nonrecurring transactions or events (PA 2320-1, para. 2). Thus, they may include comparison of current-period information with budgets, forecasts, or similar information for prior periods.
 Answer (A) is incorrect. Comparing the schedule with the accounts payable ledger or unpaid voucher file is a test of details. Answer (C) is incorrect. Comparing confirmations received from selected creditors with the accounts payable ledger is a test of details. Answer (D) is incorrect. Examining vendors' invoices in support of selected items on the schedule is a test of details.

2. During an operational audit engagement, an auditor compared the inventory turnover rate of a subsidiary with established industry standards in order to

A. Evaluate the accuracy of internal financial reports.
B. Test controls designed to safeguard assets.
C. Determine compliance with corporate procedures regarding inventory levels.
D. Assess performance and indicate where additional audit work may be needed.

Answer (D) is correct.
 REQUIRED: The reason to compare the inventory turnover rate of a subsidiary with established industry standards.
 DISCUSSION: Inventory turnover provides analytical information. It equals cost of sales divided by average inventory. A low turnover ratio implies that inventory is excessive, for example, because the goods are obsolete or because the organization has overestimated demand. Accordingly, such an analytical procedure will provide an indication of the efficiency and effectiveness of the subsidiary's management of the inventory.

3. Analytical procedures enable the internal auditor to predict the balance or quantity of an item. Information to develop this estimate can be obtained by all of the following **except**

   A. Tracing transactions through the system to determine whether procedures are being applied as prescribed.
   B. Comparing financial data with data for comparable prior periods, anticipated results (e.g., budgets and forecasts), and similar data for the industry in which the entity operates.
   C. Studying the relationships of elements of financial data that would be expected to conform to a predictable pattern based upon the entity's experience.
   D. Studying the relationships of financial data with relevant nonfinancial data.

Answer (A) is correct.
REQUIRED: The procedure not a source of information for analytical procedures.
DISCUSSION: Tracing transactions through the system is a test of controls directed toward the operating effectiveness of internal control, not an analytical procedure.
Answer (B) is incorrect. The basic premise of analytical procedures is that plausible relationships among data may be reasonably expected to exist and continue in the absence of known conditions to the contrary. Well-drafted budgets and forecasts prepared at the beginning of the year should therefore be compared with actual results, and engagement client information should be compared with data for the industry in which the engagement client operates. Answer (C) is incorrect. The internal auditor should expect financial ratios and relationships to exist and to remain relatively stable in the absence of reasons for variation. Answer (D) is incorrect. Financial information is related to nonfinancial information; e.g., salary expense should be related to the number of hours worked.

7.2 Benchmarking

4. What is the first phase in the benchmarking process?

   A. Organize benchmarking teams.
   B. Select and prioritize benchmarking projects.
   C. Researching and identifying best-in-class performance.
   D. Data analysis.

Answer (B) is correct.
REQUIRED: The first phase in the benchmarking process.
DISCUSSION: The first phase in the benchmarking process is to select and prioritize benchmarking projects. The next phase is to organize benchmarking teams. Researching and identifying best-in-class is the third phase in the benchmarking process. The fourth phase is data analysis, and the final phase is the implementation phase.
Answer (A) is incorrect. Organizing benchmarking teams is a subsequent phase. Answer (C) is incorrect. Researching and identifying best-in-class performance is a subsequent phase. Answer (D) is incorrect. Data analysis is a subsequent phase.

5. The phase of the benchmarking process in which the team must be able to justify its recommendations is the

   A. Prioritize benchmarking projects phase.
   B. Implementation phase.
   C. Data analysis phase.
   D. Researching and identifying best in class performance phase.

Answer (B) is correct.
REQUIRED: The phase involving teams and their recommendations.
DISCUSSION: Leadership is most important in the implementation phase of the benchmarking process because the team must be able to justify its recommendations. Also, the process improvement teams must manage the implementation of approved changes.
Answer (A) is incorrect. This is the stage where businesses must understand key business processes and drivers. Answer (C) is incorrect. The data analysis phase entails identifying performance gaps and understanding the reasons they exist. Answer (D) is incorrect. This stage involves the setting up of databases and information-gathering methods.

6. Researching and identifying best-in-class performance is often the most difficult phase. Which of the following is **not** a critical step?

   A. Setting up databases.
   B. Choosing information-gathering methods.
   C. Formatting questionnaires.
   D. Employee training and empowerment.

Answer (D) is correct.
REQUIRED: The steps in the researching and identifying best-in-class performance phase.
DISCUSSION: The critical steps in the researching and identifying phase are setting up databases, choosing information-gathering methods, formatting questionnaires, and selecting benchmarking partners. Employee training and empowerment is part of total quality management (TQM).
Answer (A) is incorrect. Setting up databases is a critical step in the researching and identifying phase. Answer (B) is incorrect. Choosing information-gathering methods is a critical step in the researching and identifying phase. Answer (C) is incorrect. Formatting questionnaires is a critical step in the researching and identifying phase.

7.3 Performing Audit Procedures

7. The internal auditor has gained an understanding of the design of an engagement client's internal controls. The most appropriate next step is to

A. Test controls to determine whether they are functioning as designed.
B. Halt the engagement and issue a report about inadequate controls.
C. Draw preliminary conclusions about internal control.
D. Contact the engagement client's direct supervisor to recommend that the head of the department or function under audit is transferred or terminated.

Answer (C) is correct.
REQUIRED: The most appropriate next step after determining that auditee internal controls are inadequate.
DISCUSSION: Internal auditors gain an understanding of the design of the engagement client's internal controls. The auditors then draw conclusions about whether internal controls are designed adequately to achieve management's control objectives.
Answer (A) is incorrect. If controls are poorly designed, testing their operation is most likely a poor use of audit resources. Answer (B) is incorrect. A determination that internal controls are inadequate is not sufficient grounds for halting a scheduled engagement. Answer (D) is incorrect. Advising on such personnel matters is not an appropriate internal audit function.

8. While testing the effectiveness of inventory controls, the internal auditor makes a note in the working papers that most of the cycle count adjustments for the facility involved transactions of the machining department. The machining department also had generated an extraordinary number of cycle count adjustments in comparison with other departments last year. The internal auditor should

A. Interview management and apply other engagement procedures to determine whether transaction controls and procedures within the machining department are adequate.
B. Do no further work because the concern was not identified by the analytical procedures included in the engagement work program.
C. Notify internal auditing management that fraud is suspected.
D. Place a note in the working papers to review this matter in detail during the next engagement.

Answer (A) is correct.
REQUIRED: The internal auditor action when tests of controls reveal that most inventory count adjustments involve one department.
DISCUSSION: When analytical audit procedures identify unexpected results or relationships, the internal auditor evaluates such results or relationships. The auditor may ask management about the reasons for the difference and would corroborate management's explanation (PA 2320-1, para. 6).
Answer (B) is incorrect. The engagement work program is a guide that does not restrict the auditor from pursuing information unknown at the time that the program was written. Answer (C) is incorrect. The facts do not yet support a conclusion that fraud has occurred. Answer (D) is incorrect. The risk of a material misstatement of inventory should be addressed promptly.

9. An internal auditor performs an analytical review by comparing the gross margins of various divisional operations with those of other divisions and with the individual division's performance in previous years. The internal auditor notes a significant increase in the gross margin at one division. The internal auditor does some preliminary investigation and also notes that no changes occurred in products, production methods, or divisional management during the year. The most likely cause of the increase in gross margin is a(n)

A. Increase in the number of competitors selling similar products.
B. Decrease in the number of suppliers of the material used in manufacturing the product.
C. Overstatement of year-end inventory.
D. Understatement of year-end accounts receivable.

Answer (C) is correct.
REQUIRED: The most likely cause of a division's increased gross margin.
DISCUSSION: An overstatement of year-end inventory results in an increase in the gross margin (sales − cost of sales). Overstating ending inventory understates cost of sales.
Answer (A) is incorrect. An increase in the number of competitors most likely results in price competition and a decrease in sales revenue and gross margin. Answer (B) is incorrect. A decrease in the number of suppliers most likely results in less price competition on the supply side, with a consequent increase in costs and decrease in gross margin. Answer (D) is incorrect. An understatement of accounts receivable understates sales and the gross margin.

10. Which result of an analytical procedure suggests the existence of obsolete merchandise?

A. Decrease in the inventory turnover rate.
B. Decrease in the ratio of gross profit to sales.
C. Decrease in the ratio of inventory to accounts payable.
D. Decrease in the ratio of inventory to accounts receivable.

Answer (A) is correct.
REQUIRED: The analytical procedure that might uncover obsolete merchandise.
DISCUSSION: Inventory turnover is equal to cost of sales divided by average inventory. If inventory is increasing at a faster rate than sales, the turnover rate decreases and suggests a buildup of unsalable inventory. The ratios of gross profit to sales, inventory to accounts payable, and inventory to accounts receivable do not necessarily change when obsolete merchandise is on hand.

7.4 Drawing Conclusions

11. "Except for the missing documentation noted above, the system of internal controls over petty cash is functioning as intended." The preceding statement is an example of a(n)

A. Observation.
B. Objective.
C. Conclusion.
D. Finding.

Answer (C) is correct.
REQUIRED: The appropriate description of the statement.
DISCUSSION: A conclusion/opinion is the auditor's interpretation of the results of testwork. The conclusion/opinion allows the reader to understand the meaning of what the auditor discovered during the course of testwork.

12. The single most important factor in drawing a useful conclusion or stating a useful opinion in an engagement report is

A. Use of statistical sampling techniques.
B. Senior management interest in the engagement outcome.
C. Auditee management assurances.
D. Auditor judgment.

Answer (D) is correct.
REQUIRED: The single most important factor in drawing a useful conclusion or stating a useful opinion in an engagement report.
DISCUSSION: Auditor judgment is the essential element in moving from a finding/observation to a conclusion/opinion. No formula can tell an auditor whether a certain exception rate is indicative of a working or failing control.
Answer (A) is incorrect. Statistical sampling allows the auditor to state the results of testwork with a certain level of confidence, but it is not a substitute for auditor judgment. Answer (B) is incorrect. The level of interest of senior management in the engagement must not affect the auditor's judgment in drawing conclusions and stating opinions. Answer (C) is incorrect. Assurances provided by auditee management are among many factors used by internal auditors as input into forming findings/observations and the resulting conclusions/opinions.

13. An internal auditor interviewed client personnel and obtained an understanding of the auditee department's operations. The auditor then performed testwork. The auditor's presentation of the results of the testwork will usually take the form of a

A. Finding.
B. Conclusion.
C. Recommendation.
D. Meeting with senior management.

Answer (A) is correct.
REQUIRED: The audit step following the performance of testwork.
DISCUSSION: A finding (observation) is an objective statement of fact about the results of audit testwork without interpretation or commentary.
Answer (B) is incorrect. A conclusion/opinion can only be drawn once the results of testwork have taken the form of a finding/observation. Answer (C) is incorrect. A recommendation can only be prepared once a finding/observation has been formulated and a conclusion/opinion has been stated. Answer (D) is incorrect. Unless the auditor has found evidence of fraud or a control deficiency that requires immediate correction, meeting with senior management is not the appropriate next step.

14. An internal audit staffer has just completed an assessment of the engagement client's operating and financial controls. The auditor's preliminary conclusion is that controls are adequately designed to achieve management's operating and financial objectives. The auditor's next step is to

A. Present his or her findings to the chief audit executive.
B. Prepare a preliminary report on internal controls for presentation to the board.
C. Report his or her results to the auditor in charge.
D. Prepare a plan for testing internal controls.

Answer (C) is correct.
REQUIRED: The step an internal auditor performs after forming a preliminary conclusion about internal control.
DISCUSSION: The auditor in charge of the engagement is responsible for coordinating the results of audit work and ensuring that work performed supports conclusions and opinions. For this reason, internal audit staff must report the results of audit work to the auditor in charge.
Answer (A) is incorrect. The internal audit staffer presents his or her results to the auditor in charge of the engagement, not to the chief audit executive. Answer (B) is incorrect. Preliminary results are not sufficient for the preparation of a report. Also, the internal audit staffer presents his or her results to the auditor in charge of the engagement, not to the board. Answer (D) is incorrect. The auditor in charge must determine whether it is appropriate to proceed with testing controls after reviewing the internal audit staffer's results.

7.5 Working Papers -- Functions and Preparation

15. An internal auditor's working papers should support the observations, conclusions, and recommendations to be communicated. One of the purposes of this requirement is to

A. Provide support for the internal audit activity's financial budget.
B. Facilitate quality assurance reviews.
C. Provide control over working papers.
D. Permit the audit committee to review observations, conclusions, and recommendations.

Answer (B) is correct.
REQUIRED: The purpose of the requirement that working papers support the observations, conclusions, and recommendations to be communicated.
DISCUSSION: Engagement working papers, among other things, provide a basis for the internal audit activity's quality assurance and improvement program (PA 2330-1, para. 2).
Answer (A) is incorrect. Financial budgets are based on the planned scope of internal audit work. Answer (C) is incorrect. Control over working papers is obtained by other means. Answer (D) is incorrect. Audit committees rarely review the full draft of a final engagement communication, much less the supporting working papers.

16. The internal auditor prepares working papers primarily for the benefit of

A. The external auditor.
B. The internal audit activity.
C. The engagement client.
D. Senior management.

Answer (B) is correct.
REQUIRED: The primary beneficiary of the internal auditor's working papers.
DISCUSSION: Engagement working papers generally (1) aid in planning, performance, and review of engagements; (2) provide the principal support for engagement results; (3) document whether engagement objectives were achieved; (4) support the accuracy and completeness of the work performed; (5) provide a basis for the internal audit activity's quality assurance and improvement program; and (6) facilitate third-party review (PA 2330-1, para. 2). Hence, they primarily benefit internal auditors.

17. Engagement working papers are indexed by means of reference numbers. The primary purpose of indexing is to

A. Permit cross-referencing and simplify supervisory review.
B. Support the final engagement communication.
C. Eliminate the need for follow-up reviews.
D. Determine that working papers adequately support observations, conclusions, and recommendations.

Answer (A) is correct.
REQUIRED: The primary purpose of indexing.
DISCUSSION: Indexing permits cross-referencing. It is important because it simplifies supervisory review either during the engagement or subsequently by creating a trail of related items through the working papers. It thus facilitates preparation of final engagement communications, later engagements for the same engagement client, and internal and external assessments of the internal audit activity.
Answer (B) is incorrect. The working papers as a whole should support the final engagement communication. Answer (C) is incorrect. Follow-up is necessitated by engagement client conditions, not the state of working papers. Answer (D) is incorrect. The purpose of supervisory review of working papers is to determine that working papers adequately support observations, conclusions, and recommendations.

18. Which of the following conditions constitutes inappropriate working-paper preparation?

A. All forms and directives used by the engagement client are included in the working papers.
B. Flowcharts are included in the working papers.
C. Engagement observations are cross-referenced to supporting documentation.
D. Tick marks are explained in notes.

Answer (A) is correct.
REQUIRED: The wrong working-paper preparation method.
DISCUSSION: Performance Standard 2330 states that internal auditors must document relevant information to support the conclusions and engagement results. Thus, working papers should be confined to information that is material and relevant to the engagement and the observations, conclusions, and recommendations. Hence, forms and directives used by the engagement client should be included only to the extent they support the observations, conclusions, and recommendations and are consistent with engagement objectives.
Answer (B) is incorrect. A graphic representation of the engagement client's controls, document flows, and other activities is often vital for understanding operations and is therefore a necessary part of the documentation. Answer (C) is incorrect. Cross-referencing is essential to the orderly arrangement and understanding of working papers and reduces duplication. Answer (D) is incorrect. Tick marks are verification symbols that should be standard throughout the engagement. They should be described in a note.

7.6 Working Papers -- Control and Retention

19. Which of the following actions constitutes a violation of the confidentiality concept regarding working papers? An internal auditor

A. Takes working papers to his or her hotel room overnight.
B. Shows working papers on occasion to engagement clients.
C. Allows the external auditor to copy working papers.
D. Misplaces working papers occasionally.

Answer (D) is correct.
REQUIRED: The action violating the confidentiality concept regarding working papers.
DISCUSSION: The internal audit activity controls engagement working papers and provides access to authorized personnel only (PA 2330.A1-1, para. 1). By misplacing working papers occasionally, the internal auditor is thus violating the confidentiality concept.
Answer (A) is incorrect. Continuous physical control of working papers during fieldwork may be appropriate. Answer (B) is incorrect. Engagement clients may be shown working papers with the CAE's approval. Answer (C) is incorrect. Internal and external auditors commonly grant access to each others' work programs and working papers.

20. Working papers contain a record of engagement work performed and much confidential information. They are the property of the organization and remain under control of the internal audit activity, which is responsible for their security. Which of the following is the most important control requirement for working papers?

A. Allow access to working papers only to internal audit activity personnel.
B. Provide for the protection of working papers at all times and to the extent appropriate.
C. Make the administrative section of the internal audit activity responsible for the security of working papers.
D. Purge working papers periodically of materials that are considered confidential.

Answer (B) is correct.
REQUIRED: The most important control requirement for working papers.
DISCUSSION: Working papers should always be properly protected. During the field work, they should be in the internal auditor's physical possession or control or otherwise protected against fire, theft, or other disaster. For example, the internal auditor may use the engagement client's safe or other security facilities. In the internal auditing office, they should be kept in locked files and should be formally signed out when removed from the files. When others (government auditors, the external audit firm, etc.) review the working papers, the reviews should take place in the internal auditing office. Secure files should be provided for long-term storage, and itemized records of their location should be maintained. When electronic working papers are placed online, computer system security measures should be similar to those used for other highly sensitive information of the organization.
Answer (A) is incorrect. Working papers may be shown to engagement clients or others if engagement objectives will not be compromised. Answer (C) is incorrect. This arrangement is awkward for working papers needed at the engagement site. Answer (D) is incorrect. Lack of relevance to future needs, not confidentiality, is the criterion for destruction of working papers.

21. Working papers should be disposed of when they are of no further use. Retention policies must

    A. Specify a minimum retention period of 3 years.
    B. Be prepared by the audit committee.
    C. Be approved by legal counsel.
    D. Be approved by the external auditor.

Answer (C) is correct.
REQUIRED: The true statement about retention of working papers.
DISCUSSION: The chief audit executive must develop retention requirements for engagement records, regardless of the medium in which each record is stored. These retention requirements must be consistent with the organization's guidelines and any pertinent regulatory or other requirements (Impl. Std. 2330.A2). Thus, approval by the organization's legal counsel is appropriate.
Answer (A) is incorrect. Working papers should not be retained for an arbitrary period. The duration of retention is a function of usefulness, including legal considerations. Answer (B) is incorrect. The CAE must develop retention policies. Answer (D) is incorrect. Retention policies need not be approved by the external auditor.

22. When current-file working papers are no longer of use to the internal audit activity, they should be

    A. Destroyed.
    B. Placed in the custody of the organizational legal department for safekeeping.
    C. Transferred to the permanent file.
    D. Transferred to the custody of the engagement client for ease of future records.

Answer (A) is correct.
REQUIRED: The proper disposition of working papers that are no longer useful.
DISCUSSION: Working papers should be destroyed after they have served their purpose. Any parts having continuing value should be brought forward to current working papers or to the permanent file.
Answer (B) is incorrect. If working papers are useful, they should be controlled by the internal auditors. Answer (C) is incorrect. Useless working papers should be destroyed. Answer (D) is incorrect. Engagement clients should not have custody of confidential papers.

7.7 Computerized Audit Tools and Techniques

23. An auditor is **least** likely to use computer software to

    A. Construct parallel simulations.
    B. Access client data files.
    C. Prepare spreadsheets.
    D. Assess computer control risk.

Answer (D) is correct.
REQUIRED: The task least likely to be done with computer software.
DISCUSSION: The auditor is required to evaluate the adequacy and effectiveness of the system of internal control and to assess risk to plan the audit. This assessment is a matter of professional judgment that cannot be accomplished with a computer alone.
Answer (A) is incorrect. Parallel simulation involves using an auditor's program to reproduce the logic of management's program. Answer (B) is incorrect. Computer software makes accessing company files much faster and easier. Answer (C) is incorrect. Many audit spreadsheet programs are available.

24. Which of the following **cannot** be performed by an auditor using generalized audit software (GAS)?

    A. Identifying missing check numbers.
    B. Correcting erroneous data elements, making them suitable for audit testwork.
    C. Matching identical product information in separate data files.
    D. Aging accounts receivable.

Answer (B) is correct.
REQUIRED: The task that generalized audit software cannot perform.
DISCUSSION: GAS can help an auditor identify erroneous data, but correcting them before performing testwork is inappropriate.
Answer (A) is incorrect. Identifying gaps is a function of major GAS packages. Answer (C) is incorrect. Merging files is a function of GAS packages. Answer (D) is incorrect. Aging is a function of GAS packages.

25. Which of the following is the primary reason that many auditors hesitate to use embedded audit modules?

A. Embedded audit modules cannot be protected from computer viruses.
B. Auditors are required to monitor embedded audit modules continuously to obtain valid results.
C. Embedded audit modules can easily be modified through management tampering.
D. Auditors are required to be involved in the system design of the application to be monitored.

Answer (D) is correct.
REQUIRED: The primary reason many auditors hesitate to use embedded audit modules.
DISCUSSION: Continuous monitoring and analysis of transaction processing can be achieved with an embedded audit module. To be successful, the internal auditor may need to be involved in the design of the application. Designing the system may impair independence unless the client makes all management decisions.
Answer (A) is incorrect. Embedded audit modules are no more vulnerable to computer viruses than any other software. Answer (B) is incorrect. The advantage of embedded audit modules is that auditors are not required to monitor them continuously to obtain valid results. Answer (C) is incorrect. Embedded audit modules cannot be easily modified through management tampering.

Practice even more exam-emulating questions in **Gleim CIA Test Prep**!

APPENDIX A
THE IIA GLOSSARY

This appendix contains the Glossary appended by The IIA to the *Standards*.

Add Value – The internal audit activity adds value to the organization (and its stakeholders) when it provides objective and relevant assurance, and contributes to the effectiveness and efficiency of governance, risk management, and control processes.

Adequate Control – Present if management has planned and organized (designed) in a manner that provides reasonable assurance that the organization's risks have been managed effectively and that the organization's goals and objectives will be achieved efficiently and economically.

Assurance Services – An objective examination of evidence for the purpose of providing an independent assessment on governance, risk management, and control processes for the organization. Examples may include financial, performance, compliance, system security, and due diligence engagements.

Board – The highest level of governing body charged with the responsibility to direct and/or oversee the activities and management of the organization. Typically, this includes an independent group of directors (e.g., a board of directors, a supervisory board, or a board of governors or trustees). If such a group does not exist, the "board" may refer to the head of the organization. "Board" may refer to an audit committee to which the governing body has delegated certain functions.

Charter – The internal audit charter is a formal document that defines the internal audit activity's purpose, authority, and responsibility. The internal audit charter establishes the internal audit activity's position within the organization; authorizes access to records, personnel, and physical properties relevant to the performance of engagements; and defines the scope of internal audit activities.

Chief Audit Executive – Chief audit executive describes a person in a senior position responsible for effectively managing the internal audit activity in accordance with the internal audit charter and the Definition of Internal Auditing, the Code of Ethics, and the *Standards*. The chief audit executive or others reporting to the chief audit executive will have appropriate professional certifications and qualifications. The specific job title of the chief audit executive may vary across organizations.

Code of Ethics – The Code of Ethics of The Institute of Internal Auditors (IIA) are principles relevant to the profession and practice of internal auditing, and Rules of Conduct that describe behavior expected of internal auditors. The Code of Ethics applies to both parties and entities that provide internal audit services. The purpose of the Code of Ethics is to promote an ethical culture in the global profession of internal auditing.

Compliance – Adherence to policies, plans, procedures, laws, regulations, contracts, or other requirements.

Conflict of Interest – Any relationship that is, or appears to be, not in the best interest of the organization. A conflict of interest would prejudice an individual's ability to perform his or her duties and responsibilities objectively.

Consulting Services – Advisory and related client service activities, the nature and scope of which are agreed with the client, are intended to add value and improve an organization's governance, risk management, and control processes without the internal auditor assuming management responsibility. Examples include counsel, advice, facilitation, and training.

Control – Any action taken by management, the board, and other parties to manage risk and increase the likelihood that established objectives and goals will be achieved. Management plans, organizes, and directs the performance of sufficient actions to provide reasonable assurance that objectives and goals will be achieved.

Control Environment – The attitude and actions of the board and management regarding the importance of control within the organization. The control environment provides the discipline and structure for the achievement of the primary objectives of the system of internal control. The control environment includes the following elements:

- Integrity and ethical values.
- Management's philosophy and operating style.
- Organizational structure.
- Assignment of authority and responsibility.
- Human resource policies and practices.
- Competence of personnel.

Control Processes – The policies, procedures (both manual and automated), and activities that are part of a control framework, designed and operated to ensure that risks are contained within the level that an organization is willing to accept.

Engagement – A specific internal audit assignment, task, or review activity, such as an internal audit, control self-assessment review, fraud examination, or consultancy. An engagement may include multiple tasks or activities designed to accomplish a specific set of related objectives.

Engagement Objectives – Broad statements developed by internal auditors that define intended engagement accomplishments.

Engagement Opinion – The rating, conclusion, and/or other description of results of an individual internal audit engagement, relating to those aspects within the objectives and scope of the engagement.

Engagement Work Program – A document that lists the procedures to be followed during an engagement, designed to achieve the engagement plan.

External Service Provider – A person or firm outside of the organization that has special knowledge, skill, and experience in a particular discipline.

Fraud – Any illegal act characterized by deceit, concealment, or violation of trust. These acts are not dependent upon the threat of violence or physical force. Frauds are perpetrated by parties and organizations to obtain money, property, or services; to avoid payment or loss of services; or to secure personal or business advantage.

Governance – The combination of processes and structures implemented by the board to inform, direct, manage, and monitor the activities of the organization toward the achievement of its objectives.

Impairment – Impairment to organizational independence and individual objectivity may include personal conflict of interest, scope limitations, restrictions on access to records, personnel, and properties, and resource limitations (funding).

Independence – The freedom from conditions that threaten the ability of the internal audit activity to carry out internal audit responsibilities in an unbiased manner.

Information Technology Controls – Controls that support business management and governance as well as provide general and technical controls over information technology infrastructures such as applications, information, infrastructure, and people.

Information Technology Governance – Consists of the leadership, organizational structures, and processes that ensure that the enterprise's information technology supports the organization's strategies and objectives.

Internal Audit Activity – A department, division, team of consultants, or other practitioner(s) that provides independent, objective assurance and consulting services designed to add value and improve an organization's operations. The internal audit activity helps an organization accomplish its objectives by bringing a systematic, disciplined approach to evaluate and improve the effectiveness of governance, risk management and control processes.

International Professional Practices Framework – The conceptual framework that organizes the authoritative guidance promulgated by The IIA. Authoritative Guidance is comprised of two categories – (1) mandatory and (2) strongly recommended.

Must – The *Standards* use the word "must" to specify an unconditional requirement.

Objectivity – An unbiased mental attitude that allows internal auditors to perform engagements in such a manner that they believe in their work product and that no quality compromises are made. Objectivity requires that internal auditors do not subordinate their judgment on audit matters to others.

Overall Opinion – The rating, conclusion, and/or other description of results provided by the chief audit executive addressing, at a broad level, governance, risk management, and/or control processes of the organization. An overall opinion is the professional judgment of the chief audit executive based on the results of a number of individual engagements and other activities for a specific time interval.

Risk – The possibility of an event occurring that will have an impact on the achievement of objectives. Risk is measured in terms of impact and likelihood.

Risk Appetite – The level of risk that an organization is willing to accept.

Risk Management – A process to identify, assess, manage, and control potential events or situations to provide reasonable assurance regarding the achievement of the organization's objectives.

Should – The *Standards* use the word "should" where conformance is expected unless, when applying professional judgment, circumstances justify deviation.

Significance – The relative importance of a matter within the context in which it is being considered, including quantitative and qualitative factors, such as magnitude, nature, effect, relevance, and impact. Professional judgment assists internal auditors when evaluating the significance of matters within the context of the relevant objectives.

Standard – A professional pronouncement promulgated by the Internal Audit Standards Board that delineates the requirements for performing a broad range of internal audit activities, and for evaluating internal audit performance.

Technology-based Audit Techniques – Any automated audit tool, such as generalized audit software, test data generators, computerized audit programs, specialized audit utilities, and computer-assisted audit techniques (CAATs).

APPENDIX B
THE IIA CIA EXAM SYLLABUS AND CROSS-REFERENCES

For your convenience, we have reproduced verbatim The IIA's CIA Exam Syllabus for this CIA exam part (global.theiia.org/certification/cia-certification/pages/cia-2013-exam-syllabus.aspx). Note that "proficiency level" means the candidate should have a thorough understanding and the ability to apply concepts in the topics listed. Those levels labeled "awareness level" mean the candidate must have a grasp of the terminology and fundamentals of the concepts listed. We also have provided cross-references to the study units and subunits in this book that correspond to The IIA's more detailed coverage. If one entry appears above a list, it applies to all items. Please visit The IIA's website for updates and more information about the exam. Rely on the Gleim materials to help you pass each part of the exam. We have researched and studied The IIA's CIA Exam Syllabus as well as questions from prior exams to provide you with an excellent review program.

PART 1 – INTERNAL AUDIT BASICS

I. **Mandatory Guidance (35-45%)** (proficiency level)
    A.   Definition of Internal Auditing (1.1)
        1.   Define purpose, authority, and responsibility of the internal audit activity
    B.   Code of Ethics (1.3-1.7)
        1.   Abide by and promote compliance with The IIA Code of Ethics
    C.   International Standards
        1.   Comply with The IIA's Attribute Standards (1.8)
            a.   Determine if the purpose, authority, and responsibility of the internal audit activity are documented in audit charter, approved by the Board and communicated to the engagement clients
            b.   Demonstrate an understanding of the purpose, authority, and responsibility of the internal audit activity
        2.   Maintain independence and objectivity (2.1-2.3)
            a.   Foster independence
                1.   Understand organizational independence
                2.   Recognize the importance of organizational independence
                3.   Determine if the internal audit activity is properly aligned to achieve organizational independence
            b.   Foster objectivity
                1.   Establish policies to promote objectivity
                2.   Assess individual objectivity
                3.   Maintain individual objectivity
                4.   Recognize and mitigate impairments to independence and objectivity
        3.   Determine if the required knowledge, skills, and competencies are available (2.4-2.6)
            a.   Understand the knowledge, skills, and competencies that an internal auditor needs to possess
            b.   Identify the knowledge, skills, and competencies required to fulfill the responsibilities of the internal audit activity
        4.   Develop and/or procure necessary knowledge, skills, and competencies collectively required by the internal audit activity (2.5-2.6)
        5.   Exercise due professional care (2.4, 2.6)
        6.   Promote continuing professional development (2.6)
            a.   Develop and implement a plan for continuing professional development for internal audit staff
            b.   Enhance individual competency through continuing professional development

7. Promote quality assurance and improvement of the internal audit activity (2.7-2.9)
   a. Monitor the effectiveness of the quality assurance and improvement program
   b. Report the results of the quality assurance and improvement program to the board or other governing body
   c. Conduct quality assurance procedures and recommend improvements to the performance of the internal audit activity

II. **Internal Control / Risk (25-35%)** (awareness level)
   A. Types of Controls (e.g., preventive, detective, input, output, etc.) (4.1-4.2)
   B. Management Control Techniques (4.3-4.5)
   C. Internal Control Framework Characteristics and Use (e.g., COSO, Cadbury) (3.1-3.5)
      1. Develop and implement an organization-wide risk and control framework
   D. Alternative Control Frameworks (3.1-3.3)
   E. Risk Vocabulary and Concepts (3.1-3.3)
   F. Fraud Risk Awareness (3.4-3.5)
      1. Types of fraud
      2. Fraud red flags

III. **Conducting Internal Audit Engagements – Audit Tools and Techniques (25-35%)** (proficiency level)
   A. Data Gathering (Collect and analyze data on proposed engagements)
      1. Review previous audit reports and other relevant documentation as part of a preliminary survey of the engagement area (5.3)
      2. Develop checklists/internal control questionnaires as part of a preliminary survey of the engagement area (5.4)
      3. Conduct interviews as part of a preliminary survey of the engagement area (5.3)
      4. Use observation to gather data (5.6)
      5. Conduct engagement to assure identification of key risks and controls (5.3)
      6. Sampling (non-statistical [judgmental] sampling method, statistical sampling, discovery sampling, and statistical analyses techniques) (SU 6)
   B. Data Analysis and Interpretation (7.1-7.4, 7.7)
      1. Use computerized audit tools and techniques (e.g., data mining and extraction, continuous monitoring, automated work papers, embedded audit modules)
      2. Conduct spreadsheet analysis
      3. Use analytical review techniques (e.g., ratio estimation, variance analysis, budget vs. actual, trend analysis, other reasonableness tests)
      4. Conduct benchmarking
      5. Draw conclusions
   C. Data Reporting (7.3)
      1. Report test results to auditor in charge
      2. Develop preliminary conclusions regarding controls
   D. Documentation / Work Papers (7.5-7.6)
      1. Develop work papers
   E. Process Mapping, Including Flowcharting (4.3)
   F. Evaluate Relevance, Sufficiency, and Competence of Evidence (5.1-5.2)
      1. Identify potential sources of evidence

APPENDIX C
THE IIA STANDARDS AND PRACTICE ADVISORIES DISCUSSED IN PART 1

Gleim Subunit	Attribute Standard
1.8	1000 - Purpose, Authority, and Responsibility
1.8	1010 - Recognition of the Definition of Internal Auditing, the Code of Ethics, and the *Standards* in the Internal Audit Charter
2.1	1100 - Independence and Objectivity
2.1	1110 - Organizational Independence
2.1	1111 - Direct Interaction With the Board
2.2	1120 - Individual Objectivity
2.3	1130 - Impairment to Independence or Objectivity
2.4	1200 - Proficiency and Due Professional Care
2.4	1210 - Proficiency
2.6	1220 - Due Professional Care
2.6	1230 - Continuing Professional Development
2.7	1300 - Quality Assurance and Improvement Program
2.7	1310 - Requirements of the Quality Assurance and Improvement Program
2.9	1311 - Internal Assessments
2.9	1312 - External Assessments
2.8	1320 - Reporting on the Quality Assurance and Improvement Program
2.8	1321 - Use of "Conforms with the *International Standards for the Professional Practice of Internal Auditing*"
2.8	1322 - Disclosure of Nonconformance

Gleim Subunit	Performance Standard
3.3	2120 - Risk Management
5.3	2210 - Engagement Objectives
5.1	2310 - Identifying Information
7.1	2320 - Analysis and Evaluation
7.5	2330 - Documenting Information

Gleim Subunit	Practice Advisory
1.8	PA 1000-1: Internal Audit Charter
2.1	PA 1110-1: Organizational Independence
2.1	PA 1111-1: Board Interaction
2.2	PA 1120-1: Individual Objectivity
2.3	PA 1130-1: Impairment to Independence or Objectivity
2.3	PA 1130.A1-1: Assessing Operations for Which Internal Auditors Were Previously Responsible
2.3	PA 1130.A2-1: Internal Audit's Responsibility for Other (Non-Audit) Functions
2.4	PA 1200-1: Proficiency and Due Professional Care
2.4	PA 1210-1: Proficiency
2.5	PA 1210.A1-1: Obtaining External Service Providers to Support or Complement the Internal Audit Activity
2.6	PA 1220-1: Due Professional Care
2.6	PA 1230-1: Continuing Professional Development
2.7	PA 1300-1: Quality Assurance and Improvement Program
2.7	PA 1310-1: Requirements of the Quality Assurance and Improvement Program
2.9	PA 1311-1: Internal Assessments
2.9	PA 1312-1: External Assessments
3.3	PA 2120-1: Assessing the Adequacy of Risk Management Processes
5.3	PA 2210.A1-1: Risk Assessment in Engagement Planning
7.1, 7.3	PA 2320-1: Analytical Procedures
7.4	PA 2320-2: Root Cause Analysis
7.5	PA 2330-1: Documenting Information
7.6	PA 2330.A1-1: Control of Engagement Records
7.6	PA 2330.A1-2: Granting Access to Engagement Records
7.6	PA 2330.A2-1: Retention of Records
7.6	PA 2400-1: Legal Considerations in Communicating Results
7.4	PA 2410-1: Communication Criteria

APPENDIX D
THE IIA EXAMINATION BIBLIOGRAPHY

The Institute has prepared a listing of references for the CIA exam as of May 2013, reproduced below.* Thus, we have updated the bibliography for this Appendix. These publications have been chosen by the Professional Certifications Department as reasonably representative of the common body of knowledge for internal auditors. However, all of the information in these texts will not be tested. When possible, questions will be written based on the information contained in the suggested reference list. This bibliography for Part 1 is listed to give you an overview of the scope of the exam. The IIA also indicates that the examination scope includes

1. Articles from *Internal Auditor* (The IIA periodical)
2. IIA research reports
3. IIA pronouncements, e.g., The IIA's Code of Ethics and *Standards*
4. Past published CIA examinations

The IIA bibliography is reproduced for your information only. The texts you will need to prepare for the CIA exam will depend on many factors, including

1. Innate ability
2. Length of time out of school
3. Thoroughness of your undergraduate education
4. Familiarity with internal auditing due to relevant experience

SUGGESTED REFERENCES FOR PART 1 OF THE CIA EXAM

Part 1: Internal Audit Basics

Enterprise Risk Management - Integrated Framework, 2004, Committee of Sponsoring Organizations of the Treadway Commission,
www.theiia.org/bookstore/product/enterprise-risk-management-integrated-framework-1178.cfm.

Internal Auditing: Assurance & Advisory Services, 3rd Ed., Kurt F. Reding, Paul J. Sobel, Urton L. Anderson, Michael J. Head, Sridhar Ramamoorti, Mark Salamasick, Cris Riddle, 2013, The Institute of Internal Auditors Research Foundation,
www.theiia.org/bookstore/product/internal-auditing-assurance-advisory-services-1668.cfm.

Internal Control - Integrated Framework, 2013, The American Institute of Certified Public Accountants,
www.theiia.org/bookstore/product/coso-internal-control-integrated-framework-2013-framework-1684.cfm.

International Financial Reporting Standards (IFRS), 2015, International Accounting Standards Board (IASB). www.iasb.org.

International Professional Practices Framework (IPPF), 2013, The Institute of Internal Auditors, Inc.,
www.theiia.org/bookstore/product/international-professional-practice-framework-2011-1533.cfm.

Practice Guides of International Professional Practices Framework (IPPF), including *Global Technology Audit Guide (GTAG)* and *Guides to the Assessment of IT Risk (GAIT)* series, 2013, The Institute of Internal Auditors, Inc.,
global.theiia.org/standards-guidance/recommended-guidance/practice-guides/pages/practice-guides.aspx.

Sawyer's Guide for Internal Auditors, 6th Ed., L.B. Sawyer, et al., 2012, The Institute of Internal Auditors, Inc., www.theiia.org/bookstore/product/sawyers-internal-auditing-6th-edition-1597.cfm.

---

* At time of print, The IIA had not yet updated the bibliography to reflect current editions. We are confident that they are testing (and therefore candidates should be studying) the information in the most recent editions. Thus, we have updated the bibliography for this Appendix.

AVAILABILITY OF PUBLICATIONS

The listing on the previous page presents only some of the current technical literature available, and The IIA does not carry all of the reference books. Quantity discounts are provided by The IIA. Request a current catalog by phone or mail, or visit global.theiia.org/knowledge/pages/bookstore.aspx.

> The IIARF Bookstore
> 1650 Bluegrass Lakes Pkwy
> Alpharetta, GA 30004-7714
> iiapubs@pbd.com
> (877) 867-4957 (toll-free in U.S. and Canada) or (770) 280-4183

Contact the publisher directly if you cannot obtain the desired texts from The IIA or your local bookstore. Begin your study program with the Gleim CIA Review, which most candidates find sufficient. If you need additional reference material, borrow books mentioned in The IIA's bibliography from colleagues, professors, or a library.

APPENDIX E
GLOSSARY OF ACCOUNTING TERMS
U.S. TO BRITISH VS. BRITISH TO U.S.

U.S. TO BRITISH

U.S.	British
Accounts payable	Trade creditors
Accounts receivable	Trade debtors
Accrual	Provision (for liability or charge)
Accumulated depreciation	Aggregate depreciation
Additional paid-in capital	Share premium account
Allowance	Provision (for diminution in value)
Allowance for doubtful accounts	Provision for bad debt
Annual Stockholders' Meeting	Annual General Meeting
Authorized capital stock	Authorized share capital
Bellweather stock	Barometer stock
Bylaws	Articles of Association
Bond	Loan finance
Capital lease	Finance lease
Certificate of Incorporation	Memorandum of Association
Checking account	Current account
Common stock	Ordinary shares
Consumer price index	Retail price index
Corporation	Company
Cost of goods sold	Cost of sales
Credit Memorandum	Credit note
Equity	Reserves
Equity interest	Ownership interest
Financial statements	Accounts
Income statement	Profit and loss account
Income taxes	Taxation
Inventories	Stocks
Investment bank	Merchant bank
Labor union	Trade union
Land	Freehold
Lease with bargain purchase option	Hire purchase contract
Liabilities	Creditors
Listed company	Quoted company
Long-term investments	Fixed asset investments
Long-term lease	Long leasehold
Merchandise trade	Visible trade
Mutual funds	Unit trusts
Net income	Net profit
Note payable	Bill payable
Note receivable	Bill receivable
Paid-in surplus	Share premium
Par value	Nominal value
Pooling of interests method	Merger accounting
Preferred stock	Preference share
Prime rate	Base rate
Property, plant, and equipment	Tangible fixed assets
Provision for bad debts	Charge
Purchase method	Acquisition accounting
Purchase on account	Purchase on credit
Retained earnings	Profit and loss account
Real estate	Property
Revenue	Income
Reversal of accrual	Release of provision
Sales on account	Sales on credit
Sales/revenue	Turnover
Savings and loan association	Building society
Shareholders' equity	Shareholders' funds
Stock	Inventory
Stockholder	Shareholder
Stock dividend	Bonus share
Stockholders' equity	Share capital and reserves or Shareholders' funds
Taxable income	Taxable profit
Treasury bonds	Gilt-edged stock (gilts)

BRITISH TO U.S.

British	U.S.
Accounts	Financial statements
Acquisition accounting	Purchase method
Aggregate depreciation	Accumulated depreciation
Annual General Meeting	Annual Stockholders' Meeting
Articles of Association	Bylaws
Authorized share capital	Authorized capital stock
Barometer stock	Bellwether stock
Base rate	Prime rate
Bill payable	Note payable
Bill receivable	Note receivable
Bonus share	Stock dividend
Building society	Savings and loan association
Charge	Provision for bad debts
Company	Corporation
Cost of sales	Cost of goods sold
Credit note	Credit Memorandum
Creditors	Liabilities
Current account	Checking account
Finance lease	Capital lease
Fixed asset investments	Long-term investments
Freehold	Land
Gilt-edged stock (gilts)	Treasury bonds
Hire purchase contract	Lease with bargain purchase option
Income	Revenue
Inventory	Stock
Loan finance	Bond
Long leasehold	Long-term lease
Memorandum of Association	Certificate of Incorporation
Merchant bank	Investment bank
Merger accounting	Pooling of interests method
Net profit	Net income
Nominal value	Par value
Ordinary shares	Common stock
Ownership interest	Equity interest
Preference share	Preferred stock
Profit and loss account	Income statement
Profit and loss account	Retained earnings
Property	Real estate
Provision for bad debt	Allowance for doubtful accounts
Provision (for diminution in value)	Allowance
Provision (for liability or charge)	Accrual
Purchase on credit	Purchase on account
Quoted company	Listed company
Release of provision	Reversal of accrual
Reserves	Equity
Retail price index	Consumer price index
Sales on credit	Sales on account
Share capital and reserves or Shareholders' funds	Stockholders' equity
Shareholder	Stockholder
Shareholders' funds	Shareholders' equity
Share premium	Paid-in surplus
Share premium account	Additional paid-in capital
Stocks	Inventories
Tangible fixed assets	Property, plant, and equipment
Taxable profit	Taxable income
Taxation	Income taxes
Trade creditors	Accounts payable
Trade debtors	Accounts receivable
Trade union	Labor union
Turnover	Sales/revenue
Unit trusts	Mutual funds
Visible trade	Merchandise trade

INDEX

Acceptance sampling 146
Accounting
    Controls. 103
    Cycles 90
    Distributions 136
Accounts receivable turnover ratio 161
Active listening 123
Add value 183
Adequate control 183
Administrative reporting 31
Analytical
    Information 117
    Procedures 73, 160, 165
Application tracing 175
Appreciation 38
Arithmetic average 136
Assessments, risk 118
Assurance services 183
Attribute
    Sampling 141
    Standards 10
Audit
    Evidence 116
    Procedures 164

Benchmarking 148, 162
Best practices 162
Bill of lading 92
Block (cluster) sampling 140
Board 20, 183
Budgeting controls 104

C charts 147
Causation 149
Charter, internal audit 19, 183
Check register 98
Checklists 119
Chief
    Audit executive (CAE) 20
    Risk officer (CRO) 66
Chief audit executive (CAE) 183
CIA exam 7
    Syllabus 2, 187
Circumstantial evidence 116
Clock cards 100
COBIT 13, 56, 61
CoCo 13, 61
Code of Ethics (IIA) 14, 183
Codes of ethical conduct 14
Communications theory 123
Competency 14, 18
Compliance 183
    Objectives 57
Components of ERM 65
Computer-assisted audit techniques (CAATs) . . . 172
Conclusive evidence 116
Confidence level 138
Confidentiality 14, 17
Confirmation 165

Conflict of interest 33, 183
    Policy 16
Consulting services 183
Content, other 169
Continuing professional development 41
Control 183
    Activities 60
    Adequate 183
    Application 83
    Batch input 83
    Compensatory (mitigative) 83
    Complementary 83
    Concurrent 84
    Corrective 82
    Detective 82
    Directive 82
    Environment 58, 184
    Feedback 84
    Feedforward 84
    Financial 84
    Framework 55
        COSO 55
    Input 83
    Matrix 85
    Objectives for Information and Related
        Technology (COBIT) 13, 56, 61
    Online input 83
    Operating 84
    Output 84
    People-based 84
    Preventive 82
    Processes 184
    Processing 84
    System-based 84
Controls
    Accounting 103
    Budgeting 104
    Organization 102
    Personnel 103
    Policies 102
    Reporting 104
Cooperation 122
Corroborative evidence 116
COSO
    Components of internal control 58
    Framework 13
        Internal control 56
    Objectives 57
Cost-benefit analysis 148
Cross-referencing 169
Current ratio 161

Data
    Analysis 163
    Extraction 173
    Flow diagrams 89
    Gathering 113
        Techniques 121
Definition of Internal Auditing 10
Degree of persuasiveness 114, 117

Deposit slip	94
Difference estimation	145
Direct evidence	116
Discovery sampling	143
Distribution, normal	136
Documentary information	116
Dual reporting	31
Due professional care	37, 41
Effective listening	123
Electronic Syst. Ass. & Control (eSAC)	13, 56, 63
Embedded audit module	173
Engagement	184
Fraud procedures	73
Objectives	184
Opinion	184
Work program	184
Enterprise risk management (ERM)	65
Environment, control	184
eSAC	13, 56, 63
Estimation	
Difference	145
Mean-per-unit	145
Ratio	145
Ethics	
IIA Code of	183
Evidence	
Audit	116
Circumstantial	116
Conclusive	116
Corroborative	116
Direct	116
Legal	116
Exit interview	122
External	
Assessments	45
Confirmation	165
Information	116
-Internal information	115
Service providers (ESPs)	40, 184
Fact-gathering interview	122
FCPA	12
Feedback	82
Fishbone diagram	149
Flowcharting	
Horizontal	87
Program	88
Systems	87
Vertical	88
Flowcharts	86
Follow-up interview	122
Foreign Corrupt Practices Act of 1977	12
Fraud	184
Engagement procedures	73
Examples	70
Functional reporting	31
Generalized audit software (GAS)	172
Gleim, Irvin N.	iii
Governance	184
Gross profit margin	161

Guidance on Control	13, 56
Histogram	149
Horizontal flowcharting	87
Human relations problem	121
Impairment	35, 184
Implementation standards	10
Imposed control	101
Independence	30, 184
Independent	115
Indexing	169
Industry Comparison	162
Information	
Analytical	117
And communication	60
Documentary	116
External	116
-Internal	115
Internal	115
-External	115
Persuasiveness	115
Physical	116
Relevant	114
Reliable	114
Sources	115
Sufficient	114
Technology	
Controls	184
Governance	184
Testimonial	116
Useful	114, 115
Inquiries	165
Inspection	165
Institute of Internal Auditors (The IIA)	
Exam Syllabus, CIA exam	2, 187
Nondisclosure policy	2
Integrated test facility (ITF)	173
Integrity	14, 16
Internal	
Assessments	45
Audit	
Activity	185
Charter	19
Control	
Definition	56
Integrated Framework	13, 55
Questionnaires	120
-External information	115
Information	115
Processes	163
International Professional Practices Framework (IPPF)	9, 185
Interpretations	10
Interval (systematic) sampling	140
Interviewing	121
Exit	122
Fact-gathering	122
Follow-up	122
Memorandum	125
Preliminary	122
Scheduling	122
Telephone	125

Index

Inventory turnover ratio 161
Invoice 92
Ishikawa diagram 149

Job time tickets. 100

Knowledge. 37

Leading questions. 124
Legal evidence 116
Liquidity. 161
Listening 123
Lower control limit (LCL) 146

Management control approaches 101
Mandatory guidance 9
Mean. 136
    -Per-unit estimation. 145
Median 136
Mode. 136
Monetary-unit sampling (MUS) 146
Monitoring activities. 60
Must in Standards. 185

Net profit margin. 161
Nonconformance 44
Nonsampling risk 139
Normal distribution 136
Note taking 124

Objectivity 14, 16, 32, 185
Observation 125, 165
Operating profit margin 161
Operations objectives 57
Organization controls. 102
Outsourcing services. 116
Over-criticism 122
Overall opinion 185

P charts. 147
Packing slip 92
Parallel simulation. 172
Pareto diagram. 148
Payment voucher 98
Payroll register 100
Performance standards 10
Period-to-period comparison 162
Permanent files 169
Personnel controls. 103
Persuasiveness
    Degree of. 114
    Information. 115
Physical information 116
Policies, controls. 102
Population sampling 140
Populations 135

Precision. 138
Preliminary
    Interview 122
    Survey. 118, 121
Procedures 103
Process mapping 89, 118
Production processes 146
Proficiency. 37
Profitability. 161
Program flowcharts 88
Purchase
    Order 96
    Requisition. 96

Quality
    Assurance and Improvement Program (QAIP) . . 42
    Control, statistical 146
Questionnaires. 120
    Formal. 121
    Mail. 125

R charts. 147
Racketeer Influenced and Corrupt Organizations
    Act of 1970. 12
Random
    Sample 139
    Variations 147
Rating scale. 126
Ratio
    Accounts receivable turnover 161
    Analysis. 161
    Current 161
    Estimation 145
    Inventory turnover. 161
Recalculation 165
Relevance of information 114
Reliability of information. 114, 115
Remittance
    Advice. 92
    Listing 94
Reperformance. 165
Reporting
    Controls. 104
    Objectives 57
RICO. 12
Risk 185
    Acceptance 66
    Appetite. 185
    Assessment 59, 118
    Avoidance 66
    Exploitation 66
    Management 185
        Enterprise 65
        Processes 68
    Nonsampling 139
    Reduction (mitigation) 66
    Sampling. 139
    Sharing 66
    Transfer. 66
Root cause analysis 166

Sales order 92

Sample size 140
   Attribute sampling 141
   Classical variables sampling. 144
Sampling
   Acceptance 146
   Attribute. 141
   Block. 140
   Classical variables 144
   Discovery. 143
   Interval 140
   Judgmental 138
   Monetary-unit. 146
   Nonstatistical 138
   Objectives 140
   Population 140
   Risk 139
   Statistical. 139
   Stop-or-go 143
   Variables 143
Sarbanes-Oxley Act of 2002 (SOX) 13
Scanning, analytical procedure 165
Scope limitation 19
Segregation of duties 90
Self-
   Control 101
   Evaluation 121
Should in Standards 185
Significance 185
Soft controls. 64
Spreadsheet analysis 175
Standard
   Deviation. 137
   Error of the mean 138
Standards 185
   IIA. 10
Statistical
   Control charts. 146
   Plan 140
   Quality control 146
   Sampling. 140
Stop-or-go sampling 143
Stratification. 140
Strongly recommended guidance 10
Substantive procedures 165
Sufficiency of information 114
Summaries 169
Supervisors and employees 121
Syllabus, CIA exam. 2, 187
System mapping. 175
Systematic (interval) sampling 140
Systems flowcharts. 87

Technology-based Audit Techniques. 185
Telephone interviews. 125
Testimonial
   Evidence. 121
   Information. 116
Tests of controls. 164
Tolerable deviation rate 141
Tone at the top. 58, 66
Treadway Commission 13, 55
Trend analysis 161
Turnbull Report. 13, 56

Understanding 38
Upper control limit (UCL) 146
Usefulness of information. 115

Variables sampling 143
Vertical flowcharting 88

Work
   Program
      Engagement 184
Working papers
   Control 170
   Interviewing 125
   Overview 168
   Preparation 168
   Retention. 171

X-bar charts 147

> " I found in Gleim books a valuable support for preparing for the CIA exams: they are written in a very clear way, the method suggested for studying the content is very effective, and the information is organized in a rational way....Gleim material is an authoritative source for passing CIA exams at the first attempt and, even more important, is a reference for a "real life" auditor. "
>
> Alessandro Segalini, CISA, CIA, IIA 2014 Gold Medal Winner

> " I passed all CIA Exams on the first attempt within 6 months and I was pleasantly surprised to be notified by the IIA that I was the winner of the Kurt Riedener Bronze Medal Award...The Gleim CIA Review System enabled me to acquire the essential knowledge in a short time frame in a highly efficient and effective manner. "
>
> Drs. Mark de Jong, CIA, IIA 2014 Bronze Medal Winner

> " The Gleim CIA Review played an integral role in my passing of the CIA Exam part on the first try and earning the Silver Medalist Award... Gleim's study materials thoroughly covered each topic for every part of the exam, and reinforced those concepts with relevant multiple choice questions at the end of every study unit. Ironically, I also utilized Gleim materials 25 years ago when I passed all parts of the CPA Exam on the first try! Gleim materials have an excellent track record and are where I turn to for success in certifications. "
>
> Douglas S. Schmidt, CIA, CPA, IIA

> " I recently passed the CIA exam utilizing the Gleim Review System. I attribute my success to Gleim! I felt that the system provided me with a structured study plan and guidance throughout the process. My personal counselor was very knowledgeable and responsive. I would definitely recommend the Gleim system to anyone preparing for the CIA. "
>
> Ashley McWilliams, CIA

What our customers are saying